The Veritas Years.

A Narrative

By John Ruth.

"Imagine there's no Heaven,
It's easy if you try,
No Hell below us,
Above us only sky".

John Lennon (Imagine)

Copyright © 2017 John Ruth

Publisher: tredition, Hamburg, Germany

ISBN
Paperback: 978-3-7439-4124-3
Hardcover: 978-3-7439-4121-2
eBook: 978-3-7323-8985-8

Printed on demand in many countries

To Pi L
Enjoy the read!
Best Wishes To You Both
John R

Eternal thanks to Mum and Dad for all of their love
and best intentions.
To Brenda and Liam who shared so much of the
journey with me.
To all the Ponsbourne boarders who shared the
journey with us

You have all made this book possible.

Contents

Prologue

1954 was an uneventful year in the town of Letterkenny, County Donegal in the North West of Ireland. Even by world news values, nothing of any great note or news value actually happened in that post-war year in Ireland. It is therefore very difficult to associate great happenings with the year of my birth unless we look further afield to the wider world.

Some of the worldwide events that did happen in 1954 were of little relevance to our own quiet existence at that moment in time, but these events would certainly play a larger role in our later lives and influences, and would pave the way for our later journeys and experiences of life away from the Emerald Isle.

In the United States at that time, Hollywood actress and 'Sex Goddess' Marilyn Monroe was married to American baseball hero Joe DiMaggio. The very first nuclear-powered submarine was launched. Food rationing had just ended in post-war England, and Burger King opened its first outlet in Miami Florida. Elsewhere, North Vietnam was overrun by the South Vietnamese and the new Boeing 707 Jet airliner was making its maiden flight.

Of course, none of these events were to influence my life in any big way, and my innocent existence would certainly make no big contribution to world events either then or in the future. No famous people shared my birthday, and that was okay with me as I would never want anyone stealing my own little bit of thunder, if I was ever to possess some in the first place. The most boring day in history also occurred sometime in 1954, when newsmongers around the world struggled to find anything of interest to report. In short this was a pretty non-descript year for anyone to be born into.

Apart from all that, 1954 saw the birth of the Rock n Roll years with 'Bill Hailey and the Comets' releasing 'Rock around the Clock'. A young unknown singer named Elvis Presley was also starting to build a career for himself, and what was to follow became the 'stuff of legends'. This was an era of change, the war was behind us and the world was awakening to a new age of enlightenment. The baby boom was in its early years and I was to be a product of that. I was not destined to be famous or infamous. I was not going to be making a great impact of my own, or changing the world in any great way. I was however, about to embark on a life's adventure that would ensure a lust for knowledge, a suspicion of authority, and a mischievous irreverence that even to the present day, has occasionally surprised or shocked the people around me. Someone once said that "the boy is father of the man" and it has taken me most of my life to make sense of this revelation. Indeed I now have no doubt that the influences and experiences that we are exposed to in our very young days certainly do shape and colour our future experiences and make us into the people we become. The person that

12

I was to become was certainly not being shaped in my native Ireland, as any cultural development would take place across the Irish Sea in England. London would feature very large in my future, as would the rural back drop of Hertfordshire. England would give me a lot of opportunity and a lot of varied career paths, but most importantly, it would provide me with the ability, opportunity and stamina to change career directions almost as much as I changed my underwear.

We were living in a small housing estate called Mc Mahon Villas, but I don't believe that my birth heralded many celebrations on that cold January morning within our humble household. I arrived at a time when my mother and father were facing real personal and financial difficulties. These difficulties were compounded by a later pregnancy which produced a 'stillborn' child who my parents had named Brendan. Severe post-natal depression followed, and resulted in protracted hospitalisations for my mother. All of this was to take its toll on our family and, under advice from our family doctor, an old chap named Mc Ginley, we would soon be emigrating from our native shores in search of a brighter and, hopefully, happier future.

My father's hardware business had boomed during the war years; he, and his brother Patrick, had enjoyed great commercial success as they travelled the length and breadth of Ireland plying their trade. So successful was their business that they also traded with Northern Ireland and exchanged steel and iron with the British Government for allocations of aluminium which was fabricated into various household goods and exported abroad. Their bonded van would cross the border between the Republic of Ireland and Northern Ireland several times a month and the profits of their labour were reinvested in the business of Ruth Brothers. Unfortunately the post-war years saw the economy of Ireland stagnate and my father's business went slowly downhill to a point where it could not sustain itself any longer. This was exacerbated by a few inter-family disputes between the partners in the business which were never resolved.

Our family of five was in crisis and the only choice for survival was emigration to another country. My father had very little choice in the decision to emigrate and while he, at that time, described us as migrants, we would, today, be better described as 'economic migrants', the term now given to such things. The truth was that in the late 1950's we were just another group of Irish immigrants seeking, not necessarily fame, but certainly a little fortune in another country. It had always been a sad part of Irish existence that most of its young people would emigrate; in fact, it was said in 'jocular' circles that "the reason the grass was greener in Ireland, was because we were all abroad walking on someone else's".

Ireland's population had dwindled to less than four million, which had a massive influence on emigration, especially when you consider that prior to the famine of 1800's it had possessed a population of over six million. A nationwide potato blight wiped out most of the crop which was the staple diet of the Irish people at that time, and any of the crop that had survived the blight was sent by the British overseers back home to England. Inevitably, starvation, poverty and a few pyromaniac landlords drove the Irish population away from their native land, with many of them ending up in America. Many of these perished on the long sea journey across the unforgiving Atlantic Ocean, but those who survived, became the building block of, what is now, the most powerful country on the planet. The population of Ireland has never recovered to its previous numbers, even up to the present day, and one wonders how differently Ireland may have fared had it retained its larger population moving into the twentieth century.

John James Marion Ruth entered this world on the 26th of January in that year of 1954, there are no photographs of either my arrival or my christening, so I can't even lay claim to being a beautiful baby. My mother assures me that I was a beautiful baby, and that up until the age of three or four, I possessed a head of golden curls which all around me admired. For some obscure or unknown reason, my parents must not have possessed a camera at the time, although, I have pretty vivid memories of my father wielding a box brownie on various occasions since then. The same lack of photographs also applies to my brother, there is not one snap of either of us until the age of about five, we jokingly, claim to have been so ugly that my parents didn't want pictures of us around the house, and mum would put a string of sausages around our necks so, at least, the neighbourhood cats and dogs would come and play with us. My brother was quite a poorly child having been born with some kind of vitamin deficiency, and while he enjoyed a fair deal of bad health, he also nurtured a habit of sticking knitting needles into electrical sockets for reasons best known to himself. Needless to say even at that young age, I never made a habit of holding his hand while he was engaged in such activities.

The other strange thing that I can find to complain about in retrospect, is the fact that my chosen names were never used, and I inherited and answered to the name Seamus. This is not unusual for children born in Ireland – parents christen you with names derived from past relatives or grandparents, and then end up calling you something completely different. I have always wondered at this strange phenomenon which seemed to occur a lot on Erin's Isle, but it can be 'hellishly' difficult later on in life, when teachers, doctors and other officials require an explanation for the non-use of your given name. My names were going to cause me just a few minor problems in my future life for that very reason.

The addition of Marion was an even more unusual choice of name to give to a boy child, but it was given to me anyway. The explanation for this was that the Vatican under the leadership of Pope Pius the 12th allocated 1954 as a year devoted to the worship of the Virgin Mary. As the first child born to our Roman Catholic family in our town in 1954, it was thought appropriate that I should have the name Marion added to my christening names. This was always a cause of consternation to me, especially as I already possessed a female surname. I felt much better, when in later years, my father advised me that the other person that shared the name Marion with me was a famous Hollywood actor named John Wayne; The subject of my name was also to be taken up by a distant aunt of ours, named Essie, who was living in Phoenix Arizona at the time. She wrote an article in a Phoenix newspaper explaining the origins of her most recent nephew's chosen name, and we always joked in later years, that I was already enjoying my fifteen minutes of fame in the United States. In fact, this same aunt, was later sponsoring all of our family to go and live in the United States, and plans were already well advanced in this venture.

When Johnny Cash penned his famous song "A boy named Sue" he was blissfully unaware that the song applied equally to me and my brother, we became known as "two boys named Ruth". We were to receive plenty of 'stick' about our surname in years to come, and many a playground brawl would result in the possession of the name Ruth and its female connection. They say that 'whatever doesn't kill you, makes you stronger', and I think we have proved this theory to be quite correct over a few decades now. The nickname 'Ruthie' was quickly applied to me, and I have carried that 'tag' right up until the present day. It has always been a talking point wherever I have travelled or interacted with people, and it has also been the cause of just the odd derogatory remark, when less tactful people have impinged or remarked unkindly about my two feminine given names. My attitude on all of these occasions was 'bollocks' to them!

I know nothing much about the day I was born, except that the weather was cold and my Mum was very ill. We lived in our grey-rendered semi-detached house in the town of Letterkenny, county Donegal. The house had 3 large steps leading up to the front garden, and I recall some very tall conifer trees that were fun to both climb and hide in. The importance of the three large steps in the front garden became clear on my second Christmas on this earth when my Mother and Father purchased two second-hand tricycles for my brother and me and placed them under the Christmas tree. I recall the smell of fresh paint emanating from these two cycles, evidence of the loving care that my father had taken in their restoration. When we discovered them on Christmas morning, we were elated and excited beyond measure. My Mother had saved her money over the preceding weeks and months, and I have no doubt that her labours were well rewarded by the excitement of two small boys waking up to their presents on that joyous Christmas morning.

One of the big problems with using my first tricycle was those three big steps leading from the front garden on to the pavement below. As a mere toddler, they seemed like a massive hurdle in being able to reach the pavement, they might as well have been the edge of a cliff. I realised that the only way for me and my tricycle to reach the pavement was to 'tumble' it down the steps, and this was the 'modus operandi' that I employed on every occasion thereafter. Needless to say, my new bike didn't remain new for very long. Its shiny, bright paintwork would soon show the scars of several somersaults down the front steps and on just a few occasions I managed to accompany it on its way. I, nevertheless, spent many happy hours riding up and down the street at the front of our house on that special little tricycle, at least, that is, until it fell apart from all of the abuse.

As the fourth child of our family, I wasn't exactly a new experience in childbirth for my mother, but her illness (presumed to be post-natal depression) was about to take her into a downward spiral of bad health that lasted for many months. She was eventually admitted to a mental institution for the treatment of this, then, common condition. She described, much later to me, how part of the treatment for this depression was electric shock treatment. This procedure was extremely painful and unpleasant for her as an electrode was applied to her head, and a large dose of electric current was passed into the brain. Today it is hard to imagine such barbaric and drastic treatment being administered to someone suffering from depression, but back in the 1950's it was a common treatment for such illnesses. As a result of my Mother's illness, part of my early nurturing was taken up by a maid that my parents had employed, her name was Mabel. Mabel made no great impact in my life at the time, and the only reference to her presence in the household was a little rhyme that we would recite to her, it went something like this: 'Mabel, Mabel, set the table'.

It is thought my mother's illness may in some way have affected the bonding process between her and I, but I can see no difference in my interaction with my mother when compared to my other three siblings, although in later life,

I seemed to be the one that was always in trouble. My father claims that I was self-reared, that I only ever cried when I was hungry, and that he could sling a bottle in my direction and I would manoeuvre it on to the flat of my feet with my legs raised in the air, somewhat like a performing chimpanzee, and feed myself in this manner. Fortunately, I do not remember any of this time, and as my infancy has not been recorded in any other medium, I just have to accept the stories from other people around me at that time.

January, I believe, is not a good time of year to be born anyway, especially in this hemisphere where the weather is always freezing, and money is always a bit short. Birthdays are largely ignored because of their close proximity to Christmas, and people have an annoying habit of combining your Christmas and birthday presents into one. As a baby born in these winter times, you tend to spend the first few months of your life trussed up like an oven-ready turkey in order to keep warm. I have no vivid recollection of my own childhood at that early juncture, but I recall that my elder brother had, as a result of his previously-mentioned ilness, been required to receive regular injections into his hip. Thankfully I was not required to take the same treatment, as I have always had a healthy fear of needles. He on the other hand seemed to have needles permanently included in his daily routines.

At one stage during my mother's illness, my brother and I were sent to stay with an aunt, living not too far away on a farm in the little village of Glenties. We travelled there in a bread van, and the driver was a kind and funny individual whose mood was quickly changed when he found that on our arrival at Glenties, his two young charges had sucked the cream and icing off nearly every cake in his possession. We had also vandalised several loaves of bread, and anything else we could lay our hands on. I believe that money changed hands very rapidly upon our arrival, and the bread man was placated by my aunt Mamie who was not best pleased by her first experience of caring for two small boys. Life in Glenties was quite a lot of fun for both of us, as we raised havoc in every direction around the farmyard. Every morning I would pack up my little red suitcase and trundle down to the front gate of the farm, my Aunt would hurry after me enquiring where I thought I was going, "I'm off home to see me Ma" was the quick reply I would always give. Auntie Mamie would always talk me out of this with the offer of a treat, and for yet another day I was temporarily distracted from my purpose. The following morning would find me back down by the gate again, awaiting the arrival of the bread man. He never came. Perhaps he had remembered the little 'bastards' who had completely destroyed his stock on the journey from Letterkenny and decided that one experience of that kind was plenty for him.

We did eventually return home to Letterkenny, and all of the talk in our household at that time, was around our forthcoming emigration to the United States of America. Several visits to the American embassy in Dublin ensued, and, as previously mentioned, my father had been sponsored by his elder sister, Essie who was living in Arizona. We had all received medicals and inoculations for the trip, and our personal effects were being packed into tea chests for transportation across the Atlantic.

My early life in Donegal, was one of reasonable contentment and nothing of any great significance occurred during my early days on the planet. There were however, a couple of very serious incidents which were to threaten my existence in a very serious way. Both of these incidents occurred on the same beach known as Rathmullen. The first incident, as related by my mother was one which occurred while I was still crawling around on all fours. The whole family were spending a normal day at the beach, everyone was enjoying the warm weather, and a picnic was being spread out on the warm sand. They were all suddenly aware that I was missing from the family group, and the alarm was raised that a child was missing. No one had noticed my crawling away across the white sand and heading straight for the ocean. By the time the alarm was raised I was bobbing about in the waves about seventy yards from the shore and they could clearly see my golden curls as the current carried me gently out to sea in the general direction of America. Fortunately for me, my rescue was quickly and efficiently effected by a strong and very competent swimmer, who, after a great deal of effort to reach me, returned me safely to the beach.

On another occasion, and on the same beach, I was sleeping contentedly in the back seat of the car, and it was decided that I could be left there until I woke up.

Nowadays, they always warn people about leaving kids and dogs shut up in the car on very warm days, as the outcome is often very tragic. For some reason, I was left in the car for a lot longer than planned, and by the time anyone had noticed, I had become very sunburnt and certainly dehydrated; it was kind of touch and go, and I was very ill as a result. I suppose I could be forgiven for thinking that given both of these incidents, my family were not exactly careful in the care of their youngest child, or is that just slight 'paranoia' on my part? I certainly wasn't suffering from a lack of neglect, but maybe a little from a lack of attention.

It has taken a very long time to get around to sitting down and writing about my experiences as a young Irish immigrant to England. In fact 50 years have rushed by in a swirl of madness, mayhem and self-enlightenment, and these are probably the reasons that I had never thought to sit down and describe my life and times for others to share. I have just been too busy enjoying the things that I do, and making the mistakes that I have made along the way. I am fortunate that I am renowned for absolutely nothing, and this gives me the advantage of being judged by others merely for what they see and know about me. Fame, fortune and made-up reputations can easily distort the true image of a person.

Having spent, not a little of my life in the Newspaper and magazine industry, I am used to seeing my articles published. I have also watched as inconsiderate editors have spiked my writings and stories for their own 'fiendish' ends, or for the requirements of more space within a given publication. My ego, vanity and pride have all taken their fair share of big knocks during my varied careers, and I no longer bother to look back in either pride or anger at any of my accomplishments. I merely regard them as a disjointed group of jobs or careers that occurred during my search for my true forte or purpose. On further and deeper reflection, I realise that I am still seeking this particular grail. I hope I never find it, for I know that one has always got to have a goal to achieve, and the day I stop setting myself goals will be the day that I have finally tired of life.

I have never ever taken life very seriously, and this has earned me the sometimes undeserved reputation of being happy-go-lucky, self-indulgent and annoyingly outspoken. I can be highly-opinionated even on topics that I know very little about, and I am certainly no shrinking violet when it comes to a good argument or debate. Badges including 'stubborn', 'self-centred', 'chauvinistic', 'head strong' and 'slightly outrageous' have all been pinned to my lapel, and I willingly accept these labels without complaint, as I know that some, or most, of these analogies are, at times, perfectly true. I am often misunderstood in many of my motivations, because I always try to apply a nonchalant spin and happy-go-lucky tint to them, I would like to think however, that I also possess a sympathetic and understanding nature as well. These traits often manifest themselves in a more comical and light-hearted way. If, however, I feel that I am being impinged or undermined in any way, my ego and sense of outrage can sometimes result in a tirade of verbal abuse that given enough of it, would put the fear of God into anyone around me. I am not a nice person when such rare incidents occur. With stories and jokes alike, I have always tended to embellish, in order to make them more interesting to anyone who can be bothered to listen. In this rendering, and the fact that it is a written version of a true story, I am going to attempt to keep these embellishments to a minimum

I have written this account of my early years, to give an indication and snapshot of what life was like for, not only, a young Irish immigrant, but also, for a child experiencing the difficulties of settling into a new country and culture at the age of four or five. I want to share the experience of my becoming in later life the embodiment and product of the strict Catholic boarding school system as it existed in the late 1950's and early 1960's. Some of my unhappy or sad memories have been diminished and understated, many of them have been coloured by my ability to turn serious situations into laughter or comedy. I know that things were a lot worse than this because of the recollections of my elder sister and brother, who also experienced those same times and events in their own lives.

My elder brother and sister both look back in anger and disgust at the treatment we all received at the hands of what they are quite willing to describe as tyrants, bigots, and hypocrites. Our collective experiences of boarding school life, have always been tinged with an ability to colour the most serious situations with comical undertones, and to take the relentless 'piss' out of all of the players within them. I know that my brother carries anger and bitterness within him, that even to the present day fuels a rage that has not diminished with the passage of time. He feels that every achievement in his life was fuelled by a need to prove himself against the negative predictions that were made of his future abilities at the tender age of six or seven.

He has proved every one of their predictions wrong, by working extremely hard at achieving goals that they had unequivocally stated he never would. His achievement of these goals has given him the pleasure and ability to stick two fingers vertical at them, but, of course, many of them are no longer around to witness his climb to achievement. His own self-belief and past endeavours will have to provide the catharsis that he has searched for, for over half a century. In complete contrast to my brother's experiences, my elder Sister has literally forgotten most of what occurred to her during her boarding school years, perhaps because those times were so traumatic for her, that she has literally buried them somewhere in her deep sub-conscious. The mere fact that she has no memory of her time in either Ireland or later at boarding school, may also be an indication of times that she would prefer to forget.

I, for my part, take a different view of those days, perhaps because I was so much younger than my siblings. I do, however, share in the anger of my sister and brother, because I have seen the effect that those experiences have had on them both throughout their own lives. In many ways, their experiences are more valid than my own because I have managed to put a more light-hearted and positive spin on these happenings. Being the youngest of our family, I guess that I had more opportunity to adapt to the new situation that we all found ourselves in the late 1950's. My memories of the time have not left me with the great regrets experienced by my siblings, but they have certainly influenced my trust in authority and my interaction with certain kinds of people. My experiences have carried me on a totally different journey from my brother and sister and have not affected me in the same way. They, however, continue to live with a regret that may never go away, and I can only begin to imagine how hard that must be for both of them to live with. On behalf of my brother and sister I would like to shout a big 'Shame on you' to all of the people who contributed to any of the misery in their young lives.

This account does not intend to be judgmental, nor does it seek some big retribution from either the characters or places involved. It is merely a narrative of events and happenings, and the incidents that influenced my personal actions and opinions as a result. It is certainly fair to say that we were not unique in these experiences, although school children and teachers of the present day would probably shrink in horror at the mere thought of any of these incidents happening in the politically correct and more liberal institutions that now exist. The dictum in those not so far off times was "children should be seen and not heard" and it was this that drove much of the misery into some of the lives of children growing up at that time. Here is an account of my own personal experiences, seen through the eyes of the immigrant schoolboy. All of the places and incidents are actual, but many of the names have been changed to avoid individual embarrasment and for legal expediency. Enjoy the read.

Chapter 1
We arrive in England, goodbye U.S.A. It's a long, long way to Tipperary

In 1959 there was a very long, hot summer in England, and in July there was a heat wave in London. Flying ants were crawling out of every pavement and the capital and suburbs sweltered in a mini tropical micro-climate. In that year, the Americans had put 2 monkeys into space, Fidel Castro became president of Cuba, and the Russians had crash landed a rocket on to the dark side of the moon. My family were arriving in the London heat for the very first time. We had sailed by boat from Dublin to Heysham in Liverpool, and then followed a long, tedious and smoky train journey that found us standing outside Kings Cross Station waiting for my father to come and meet us. My father had emigrated some ten months earlier from County Donegal in order to arrange 'digs' and schools in readiness for the arrival of the rest of his family. I had just turned five years old at the time and had been educated to a small degree for about 15 months in a couple of Irish convent schools. I could count up to twenty in Gaelic Irish, and had learned a few polite phrases in that language. I had also learned a few too many expletives as well, and these would manifest themselves, mainly when I was annoyed. I was annoyed quite a lot in those early days.

There were a lot of new experiences for this five year old boy to take in. London was a 'shocking' place to experience, for someone who had never seen a tall building before. The skyline was obliterated by these grey monstrosities, and the noise and pollution of traffic echoed around the walls and windows of this massive metropolis. People didn't talk to each other like they had in Ireland, in fact, it seemed to me that they made a point of totally ignoring one another. On the tube trains, a whole carriage full of people would sit on top of each other in utter silence, save the rustle of their newspapers as they turned the pages in quiet reserve. This strange silence was almost deafening in an ironic kind of way, because it amplified the sound of the creaking train as it clacked across the joints in the railway lines. There was a mixture of strange odours permeating the whole railway carriage, hints of perfume mixed with perspiration and a strange 'carbony' odour which was generated by the electric current flowing from the live rail to the train itself.

One of the biggest shocks, that had me spellbound, was my first sight of a black person, which held my attention for a long, long time. I remember being entranced by this experience to the point of blurting out to my mum. 'Ma look at the Blackie'. I still recall the highly shocked look on my mother's face. I remember even more, the stinging pain, and feeling of shock as her large hand made contact with the back of my leg. I couldn't possibly have realised that I had inadvertently created a great deal of embarrassment to both the coloured gentleman in question and of course, my mother, but I was certainly aware that the back of my leg was beginning to sting from the afore-mentioned wallop. My mother explained to the man that we were newly arrived from Ireland and that the 'wains' had a lot of adapting to do. He replied, "Don't worry my dear, I am an immigrant myself, and I am also getting used to these strange faces in this very strange place." I suppose I could have been described as a 'mini racist' by today's standards. I was yet to find out that as well as the African and West Indian immigrants, the Irish were not exactly welcomed with open arms in the London of the 1950's either.

After what seemed hours of travelling on the tube train and walking for miles, we arrived at a house in Neasden, North london, in which my father had previously rented a room. I remember him telling my mother that the Irish were not really welcome around London and he would often see flats and rooms 'to let' that specifically excluded Blacks, Irish and pets. Signs would be placed in windows stating "Room to let, No Blacks, No Irish, No Dogs." Notwithstanding all of this, my father had found a good job in the glazing industry, and the local priest had found a good Catholic boarding school which would take his three children. The place that we had come to live was clearly far too small for our whole family, and the landlady, although Irish herself, was a bit of a tyrant to say the least. It's strange how some people treat their own country folk so badly, and this landlady certainly treated us badly. She was one of the most miserable people I have ever experienced meeting, and her interaction with both my parents was evidence of a situation that would not endear us to her in any possible way. We had to be very quiet at all times, and this was certainly not easy for three children that liked to let off steam occasionally. We were confined to just one bedroom between all five of us, and we had the use of one small living room until bedtime came around.

Within a few weeks, my mother had found another house to share in Neasden which was owned by a war widow named Mrs. Carless. Her son worked in the same hospital as my mother, and he thought it would be a nice idea for his mum to have some company after living alone for some considerable time. Mrs. Carless was a lovely elderly lady who had lost her husband in the First World War and then tragically, another son in the Second World War. She was very good to my parents and very kind to us, and she allowed us to play in her large garden and loved to sit and watch us. It was quite a struggle for me to tune into the new accents and the new places, but I guess, kids adapt very quickly, and within a few days I was settling in nicely to this strange new world. Mrs. Carless had a real hand grenade that had been hollowed out and disarmed by her son on one of his home leaves, and I loved to play with it at every opportunity. I had become so attached to this grenade that it would be in my small hand from dawn until dusk, and I was thrilled to bits when Mrs. Carless made a permanent gift of it to me.

Although London was a very odd place to us, we were growing accustomed to many of the strange things that we had discovered, like the giant two decked trolley buses that trundled up and down the main roads. The volume of traffic seemed relentless, and people scurried about always in a hurry, it was a far cry from our green and quiet past. The London underground was an adventure, in spite of its tendency to overcrowd, and I loved to travel around London on the tube. London buses were another brand new experience to me and I had never ever sat on the top of a double decker before. I was also fascinated that the trolley buses had these giant arms stretching upwards to the double overhead cables. Often these arms would become dislodged and the conductor would deploy a giant hooked stick with which to re-connect the offending pole to its electrical supply. All these new surroundings reminded me of how far I had come from the quiet and simple existence of the Irish countryside. I certainly missed our old home and the uncomplicated way of life that we had previously experienced, and I was also reminded of how much I had to learn in this strange new world.

My sister and brother soon got to know the areas around our house, and they would take me on long walks during the day. We always had a small bag of sandwiches with us and we would spend a lot of our time in a large park called Gladstone. This park had an outdoor swimming pool and a very a big hill that ran down to the railway lines. We would sit for hours watching long trains trundling up and down the lines with so many carriages that the front of the train had all but disappeared while the rest of it was still passing by. These trains were like huge snakes, and seemed never-ending as they passed by us on their journey to who knows where. All of us struggled to comprehend these new experiences and surroundings; it was certainly a far cry from our temporary accommodation in Thurles, Tipperary, where we had spent the best part of a year, while daddy was saving the money to bring us over to England.

Living in a town like Thurles had been a complete accident and diversion, as our original destination had been Phoenix, Arizona, where we had been sponsored by an aunt. We had been inoculated and visa-ed at the American embassy in Dublin just one short year earlier, and our furniture and personal effects were already sitting in a goods wagon in a Donegal siding awaiting shipment to the United States. The whole thing had been eventually cancelled as a result of a single half dollar that I had held in my small fist on the train journey back from Dublin. I was just three years old at the time. I recall that train journey so vividly, it was my first experience of a steam locomotive and I remember that before boarding for the journey home, my father had taken us to see the front of the locomotive with all its hissing and puffing as it sat ready for its journey. I remember the engine driver and his assistant winking at me as I enquired of my father "how come those men were so filthy?" On board, my mother shared a Toblerone with us, while my father dressed in his trademark brown twill overcoat was buried in his newspaper. The Irish countryside flew past us outside, as I made my way out of our compartment and along the train in search of some new excitement.

God only knows why my parents hadn't noticed that I had gone missing, I guess there was no risk of child-napping in those days in Ireland, and anyway I was on a train-what could possibly go wrong? There was this nice lady however, and I must have impressed her enough to entice her to part with a shiny new half dollar coin because I clutched it in my tiny fist as I made my way back to the compartment where my parents and two elder siblings were seated. The coin twinkled in my small hand, and there was no way that I was going to hand it up to anyone without an argument. My father had assumed that I had taken this half dollar from a tourist on the train and he went off in search of that person in order to return the money. That person happened to be an elderly American lady who had been touring Ireland in search of her ancestry, which every American pursues in their need to be Irish, or, at least, of Irish descent.

When she had confirmed that she had indeed given the money to this beautiful child, she invited him to sit with her for a while for a chat. Whatever adverse information she passed on to my father about the 'American Dream' must certainly have been compelling, because by the end of the train journey she had talked dad out of taking us all to the United States.

She had convinced him that he would be financially pushed to provide a good standard of living for his wife and three children, and as a newly arrived immigrant in the country, he would be hard-pressed to obtain a well-paid job. "Don't take these little angels to the States" she had said, "you will struggle financially from day one and always regret it." Dad listened carefully to all that the American lady was telling him, and so convincing and profound were her comments and opinions, that he experienced a kind of 'epiphany' that was to change his mind and alter the direction of our future lives forever. By the end of that train journey back to Donegal he had decided there and then to alter his plans about emigrating to the United States and that a new alternative would have to be found for the future security of the family. That was to be the end of our American adventure, and I have often wondered what kind of life we might have experienced, had I not accepted that big silver coin. My brother claims that we might have become a couple of California 'hippies' in the 'Summer of Love' but as our destination was Phoenix, Arizona, my imagination is hard-pressed to decipher how that would have come about. Suffice to say that fate moved us in a completely different direction.

My mother was heart-broken at the cancellation of our trip to America, all of the arrangements had been made, and she knew that as a qualified nurse, she would have no problem in securing a good post in one of the many modern hospitals in Arizona. She also knew that there was no turning back, and that our leaving Ireland was the only hope of our economic survival. She later told us that she had given my Father an ultimatum which he had no choice but to accept, If America was out of the question, then our only other alternative was to make a new life in England. They would find new schools for their children and they would both find jobs to support a complete new way of life. Ireland was certainly out of the equation and so now was America.

No matter, the decision was made and my father reluctantly agreed to take us to England, but not before we had travelled to Thurles in Tipperary on route for the 'Big Smoke'. He had decided to go to England ahead of the rest of the family in order to save some money and, more importantly, sort out a home for us all to live in. Within a few weeks we had left Donegal forever and we were now living with my Uncle Dick, in a town called Thurles in County Tipperary. Uncle Dick shared a beautiful house with my three cousins Jim, Fintan and Margaret Ruth. Uncle Dick's wife had been institutionalised with a nervous disorder quite a few years earlier and he had been left to bring up this young family by himself. As a welder by trade, uncle Dick was in a steady job which in the Ireland of the 1950's was a rare thing indeed, and so in December 1957 we settled in Thurles. As a three year old in these new surroundings, I was fascinated by my elder cousins. Their accents were so different from our own northern Irish ones, and I had great difficulty in understanding what they said.

My cousins were a lot older than me, with the exception of the youngest child, Margaret, who was a year younger. The two boys, Finton and Jim, were probably about nine and ten respectively and my first sight of them presented two independent lads about to attend their local scout meeting. They were dressed in fantastic green and beige uniforms with impressive orange neck scarves held in place by the famous woggle of scouting troops. Impressive dagger looking knives were straddled to their belts, and their green woollen socks were held up with tasselled garters of yellow silk, I was so impressed with these smart clothes that at any opportunity in the future, I could be spotted running round the house in a mixture of scout attire and any other toys or accessories that could be pilfered from my long-suffering cousins. I vividly remember a row of plastic indians that spun on a frame when you hit them with an arrow from a plastic bow, and on the top of one of my Uncle Dick's cabinets was a beautiful hand-built Spanish galleon that he had made himself. This galleon had beautiful material sails and rigging, and was also wired inside with tiny lights that twinkled on every deck of the boat.

Cousin Margaret was a very quiet girl, always lost in deep thoughts and saying very little. Despite this, she was a real 'tomboy' and could mix it with both of her elder brothers without any difficulty. A mere 'runt' like me was no threat to this independent and headstrong individual, and I felt the full force of her short temper on many occasions. She was also very generous, and always shared her sweets and belongings with her visiting cousins without complaint.

Although I was just three years old, I had already been in kindergarten school in Donegal and it was no shock or surprise that I had been duly entered into the local Presentation convent school along with my brother and sister and, of course, my three cousins. The school was situated about half a mile from uncle Dick's house and the journey to school was completed every morning by a cross-bar ride on our cousin's bikes. Needless to say there was the usual falling offs and scuffed knees, but I loved the excitement of weaving through the Thurles traffic (such as it was) on our journey to school. My cousins were like super heroes to us, as they not only provided our main entertainment, but were also very protective of their young charges. We soon became as street-wise as them, and my mother claims that on my return home from school one day I launched into a tirade of obscenities that shocked both her and my uncle Dick. Words like "fecking gobshite" and "fecking eedjit" were just a small portion of the new vocabulary that I had mastered in those early days, and I was certainly whacked about the legs for every utterance that may have been heard by my mother.

It was at this time that I caught sight of my first real nun, and the ones at the presentation convent were as tyrannical as nuns could possibly be. I learned very quickly to avoid as much as possible these strange looking women in their even stranger attire, but I was lucky in that my class teacher was a secular young woman. I recall my elder sister, dropping our packed lunches one morning in the corridor on the way to the classrooms. Milk cascaded out of the small red case that housed our lunches, and spread out across the highly-polished floor of the convent. Before we knew it, my sister was being berated by one of the incumbent nuns, and my last vision of her was wielding an enormous mop. I doubt if we had any lunch that day.

At about this time I discovered the F. W. Woolworths store in the centre of Thurles, and on our way home from school we would regularly walk into the store to look at the toys displayed there. Being totally unaware of money values and the rules of retailing or buying and selling, I would cheekily put my small fist into a pile of sweets and walk away with my ill-gotten gains. Strangely I was never spotted by any of the staff, and so I became a regular visitor to the store on most afternoons.

Our next door neighbours were a kindly family who welcomed us into their home without hesitation, they kept a large quantity of hens and ducks in their back garden, and I was immediately attracted by the brightly coloured feathers and the noise these birds made when one chased them. One of the larger ducks had no objection to my joining him in his roosting box which resembled a small dog kennel. I would sit in there for hours without any protests from the resident, although, on one occasion when I fell asleep in there, a lot of panic was going on around the streets of Thurles when a small boy was reported missing. That duck filled up a lot of my time while living at uncle Dick's house, and the duck and hen house became my permanent hang-out after school. Sadly, we were soon on the move to new 'digs' near the town centre, and that put paid to my daily visit to the neighbours ducks and hens.

Our new habitat was a deserted betting shop with a small flat above it. I remember an old commode on spoked wheels was parked in one of the main bedrooms, and though it stank of ancient pee and defecations it was certainly a fun thing to get pushed around on. I spent a lot of time either pushing or being pushed up and down the corridor by my long-suffering brother. We also spent a lot of time kicking the 'crap' out of one another as there was just 18 months difference in our ages, and at the now ripe young age of four years old, I was already beginning to assert my infantile prejudices, opinions and temper at anything that seemed to be bothering me. This situation was further aggravated by the lack of our cousins who would normally intervene to stop the pair of us fighting. Our in-fighting carried us through a lot of our lives and even into our teenage years, probably fuelled by our closeness in age. The rows that ensued would get quite physical at times, and we would kick the 'crap' out of each other for the simplest of reasons. Despite all of this, we were also very close and tight knit, and God help anyone who upset either one of us, as they would have the other sibling to contend with.

Right next door to our new home was a servicing and repair garage, and the smells emanating from this establishment were a completely new experience for my nasal passages. Petrol, engine oil, thinners and gear oil all have their own unique smelling signature and they easily permeated into our new dwelling place. They were also carried in on our clothes, shoes hands and faces as a result of our constant excursions into this new motor trade world. The mechanics and fitters were a very friendly bunch, and we were often treated to gifts of sweets and soft drinks. I also acquired a nice few new swear words to add to my limited vocabulary from the same fitters and mechanics. I carried these profanities proudly home to see just how offensive both my peers and mother would consider them – they were all pretty disgusted and I found myself on the receiving end of a good few slaps.

Strangely though, that little experience of being around cars and the smell of gear oil, petrol and diesel fumes was to return to me many years later when I took up a future job in the motor trade. It also instilled in me a love for all things mechanical, and while I was only a little lad at the time, I had already watched with interest the mechanics pulling gearboxes and engines out of cars for repair. I remember seeing the inside of gearboxes and engines, and being completely fascinated by the pistons, con rods, gears and sliders which made up these intensely complicated pieces of engineering. All of my waking hours outside of school would find me in that greasy environment, and my family always knew where to come looking whenever I was on the missing list. The mechanics looked kindly on my presence, and would regularly share their lunchbox sandwiches, as I messed about with their spanners and wrenches pretending to fix the cars with them. Of course, being in a close proximity to all of these hard working mechanics. I continued to learn an incredible amount of swear words and bad language. My mother would often be treated to a tirade of expletives that I had picked up in that garage environment and some of these took me a long time to shake off. They were, however, always remembered.

One of the mechanics taught me a rhyme which I have memorised to this day: "Yum, Yum, Pig's Bum, mixed up with chewing gum, when it's nice take a slice- Yum Yum Pig's Bum" This rhyme, together with the bad language, earned me many a good 'clout' and an occasional afternoon in the bedroom. Even I had begun to realise, at that young age that my mother was going to have a real problem cleaning up my vocabulary. Years later she was still having the same problem, and she said that of all my siblings, I was the most vocal and contrary one, always willing to display my defiance regardless of the consequences. Ironic, then, to realise that it would be a bunch of 'tyrannical' nuns that eventually and temporarily, mended my ways and more than cleaned my clock and mouth for me. My future experiences would distance me inexorably from that lively and fascinating existence that filled up every waking moment of my childhood.

My next seven years of existence were to remove me permanently from the comparative peace and tranquillity of rural Ireland, and drag me kicking and squealing into the incessant hustle and bustle of the London suburbs, and the strict and oppressive atmosphere of an English Roman Catholic boarding school in rural Hertfordshire. The scene was set for me and my siblings to begin a completely new life across the Irish Sea.

Chapter 2
Ponsbourne Park. The early days and a little bit of Tudor and modern history.

Nestling in the wooded, Hertfordshire countryside near a small village called Newgate Street. is the impressive 19th Century country mansion house and grounds of Ponsbourne Park. Since just before the Second World War and well into the late 1960's it was home to an order of Sisters who created St Dominic's Priory Preparatory School and convent. In more recent times, it has changed hands a few times and become a management training centre replete with golf course and other outdoor sport activities. It is currently a wedding and bistro hotel venue operated by a large international hotel group

Ponsbourne Park previously occupied hundreds of acres of beautiful forest and parkland and this large estate was purchased by the south African founded Dominican Sisters in the early 1930's. In September 1959 it would become home to myself and both my elder brother and sister. My own tenure there would last for some seven years, and little did I know then, that it would become one of the most influential factors for nearly all of my future life. During our time at Ponsbourne Park, we learned very little of its previous history, and its story was, sadly, never imparted to us within the school curriculum. I suspect that very little research was carried out at that time, because my own later discoveries about the estate would certainly have made a big impact, had they been known to the teaching sisters who were responsible for our primary education up to age twelve. There was of course no world wide web at that time, and any historical research involved hour upon hour of painstaking and laborious manual searching in various libraries and public institutions.

Had we been aware of the heritage of this place, we may well have taken more time to research its history. The Ponsbourne Estates had a big connection with the reigns of kings Henry V11, Henry V111 and queen Elizabeth 1 of England, through their connection to a family named Fortescue. I have no doubt, that such knowledge may have endeared us a little more to the school and it's impressive surroundings. It would certainly have made our history lessons more informative, and my later love of the Tudor story may well have been enhanced by that knowledge. I can only suppose that the Dominican sisters of St Dominics's Priory would not necessarily have embraced many of the connections of Ponsbourne Park to the Tudors. After all, Henry V111 and his daughter Elizabeth 1 were not exactly endeared to anyone who may have supported the traditional Roman Catholic creed that these monarchs worked so hard to destroy. Nonetheless, it was a very big omission on the part of our teachers and carers, and I feel they missed a great opportunity to increase the 'kudos' of the school and its surrounding countryside.

It was only in researching its previous history that I discovered that during the 14th, 15th and 16th centuries the Ponsbourne Park Estates were the property of several generations of the prominent English Fortescue family. Sir John Fortescue who owned the Ponsbourne Estates was a great influence in the early court of Henry V111. He was descended from Richard Fortescue who in the reign of Henry V11 was the Lord Chief Justice of the Common Pleas in Ireland.

Sir John Fortescue was also the Lord Chief Justice of England and Wales during the reign of Henry V111. To say that the Fortescue family were influential would be a great understatement; In fact, they were one of several very influential families outside of the monarchy itself that were to influence the Tudor courts in no small way.

Unfortunately, Sir John's son, Adrian, would gain fame and infamy at the court of Henry V111. Adrian was first cousin to the father of Anne Boleyn, and a great personal friend of the king. Adrian was previously a personal guard to Catherine of Aragon the king's first wife. After Henry's controversial marriage to Anne Boleyn, Adrian was asked to sign the Act of Succession drawn up by the king and Thomas Cromwell, a failure to sign this had resulted in the death of Sir Thomas More, and several others. Now Adrian Fortescue found himself in the same situation as these prominent courtiers and also refused to take the oath.

Although not vocal, Adrian opposed the king's marriage to his second cousin Anne Boleyn, as well as Henry's breaking with the Church of Rome. He also disagreed with the dissolution of the monasteries, and in July 1539, after a long period of imprisonment, he was beheaded at the Tower of London for treason against the crown. It was alleged that he had dissented against the king's personal, fiscal and church policies, and while never sitting trial for his crime he was, like so many other dissidents of the time, convicted of High Treason.

Prior to all of this Sir Adrian Fortescue, in the service of Henry V111, had been created a Knight of the Order of St John in 1532, and as early as 1503 he was a Knight of the Bath. He also participated in England's war against France in 1513 and again in 1523. All of this service provided him with wealth, position and influence in the English court of the Tudors.

During his soldiering career Adrian became a Dominican Tertiary or follower of the Dominican teachings and he, as a widower, married Anne Rede the young widow of Sir Giles Greville. Now Sir Giles Greville was previously comptroller of Princess Mary's household and also Chamberlain. The connections to Henry V111's court and, indeed, all of the Tudors of the time illustrates that Sir Adrian Fortescue was indeed a 'biggish' influence in those troubled times in English history. He clearly had the ear of the king, and his influence at court was certainly well respected. He eventually became a gentleman of the king's Privy Chamber and was summoned to the king's personal service on many more occasions.

After his execution in 1539, Adrian Fortescue along with several other members of Henry's court was created one of the English Martyrs by the papacy. He was later beatified by Pope Leo X111 in 1895. His widow Anne went on to serve in the court of Elizabeth 1, having found favour with the new queen. She, in spite of her husband's treason to Elizabeth's father, was later returned some of the property at Ponsbourne.

I try to imagine what Adrian Fortescue would have thought, as a Dominican Tertiary, a member of Henry VIII's court and a martyr of England and Wales, that some 400 years later his family seat and home would become Roman Catholic once again with a thriving community of Dominican nuns occupying that same piece of the Hertfordshire countryside which he called 'home'.

The Roman Catholic connection with Ponsbourne Park had come full circle. It seems a strange twist of fate that the Dominican Sisters seemed to know nothing of the history of the Fortescues. The Fortescues with their many connections to the Tudor monarchy of England prior to and during the 'Reformation' years, were never mentioned during all of our time at the school in Newgate Street.

In more recent times, Ponsbourne Park was owned by the Carlisle family. The most recent resident was Sir Hildred Carlisle, a politician and businessman. Sir Hildred was educated at St Albans school, and his brother Wilson was the founder of the 'Church Army' a Church of England organisation, similar in many ways to the Salvation Army. Sir Hildred was created Lieutenant of Ponsbourne Park, during his Parliamentary years and resided at the 1875 built mansion until his death in 1942.

This then, was the same Ponsbourne Park which in 1959 would become home to my sister Brenda, my brother Liam and myself, and this was also the place that would influence my life's future direction and perspectives forever. The large black and white sign at the end of the nearly one mile driveway at Ponsbourne Park read as follows: St Dominic's Priory, Ponsbourne Park, Day and Boarding School for boys and girls. Telephone: Cuffley 3142. The only other information in its address proclaimed it to be near Hertford, Herts, and the school emblem bore the Latin legend 'VERITAS' which simply translated from Latin into English is 'Truth'. The main entrance to Ponsbourne Park was framed by two amazing granite pillars with a large pair of stone pyramids sitting on top of them, and two large wrought iron gates protected the privacy of the estate entrance.

The drive from the main gate took us along a potholed shingle roadway surrounded by open farmland on either side, and the main house of Ponsbourne Park could be seen for more than a mile in the distance. It shimmered sandy white in the bright September sunlight just like the Taj Mahal, and from that distance; one could see that the surrounding forests and hills covered a vast acreage of the Hertfordshire countryside. Two hundred acres to be precise. A large green, glazed dome could be seen rising from the grey leaded rooftops to the western side of the house, and the creamy white brickwork gave the whole place a magical and surreal appearance. Even at a mile away, the house dominated the hillside on which it was built, and a series of gentle grassed valleys swept down from its long facade. A sweeping multitude of light grey granite steps accentuated by curved landings, gave the building a regal appearance emphasising its opulence and grandeur.

Even today, so many, many years later, in its role of country hotel, the building has retained many of its former features endorsing the value of the listed buildings act. Unfortunately, most references to the school itself have long been removed, and many of the outbuildings have been demolished, leaving just the mansion itself and a few later additions which serve as conference meeting rooms and staff accommodation.

The main porticoed entrance to this imposing mansion house was a throwback to a bygone age where carriages would sweep in under its pillared archway to deliver passengers right up to the large double front doors, and preserve them from the elements. The façade of this archway was decorated in Roman laurel crowns interspersed with leafy chains of vine leaves and laurel wreaths and beautifully carved cherubs in each corner. Along the gravelled driveway, stone posts in the shape of giant mushrooms were chained one to another in neat rows. These shone brilliant white in the afternoon sunshine and added an element of order and division to the surrounding lawns. These elements left a lasting impression on my five year old mind and even at that small age, I realised that something very different was happening to both mine, and my siblings lives. A large bronze bell hung above the main portico on a facing wall, and even as we arrived it was tolling the call to the Angeles. I was soon to discover that this bell controlled the complete timetable and lives of the school and the convent housed within these beautiful architectural surroundings. The nuns who served as teachers, house keepers and matrons to the over 100 boarding and 70 day children in their care were fastidiously obedient to this bell as it tolled away the hours, days, months and years of theirs and our existence

In other much more recent 20th century history, a young pilot officer of the Royal Flying Corp was flying his twin-winged Tiger Moth aircraft above the local town of Cuffley in 1916. As he soared into the clear blue sky, on what was a routine reconnaissance mission, he encountered a German Zeppelin heading straight toward him armed with incendiary bombs and heavy guns. This zealous young pilot was Group Captain Leefe-Robinson and his action against that threatening Zeppelin was to earn him the first ever Victoria Cross for action above the British mainland.

He immediately confronted the giant Zeppelin with an automatic gun fixed to the side of his tiny aircraft. His shots seemed to have little effect on the German 'blimp' and as he was heading for his Essex home having run out of ammunition, the Zeppelin suddenly exploded in a mass of flame. This explosion was witnessed by people from villages all around Ponsbourne Park, and was recorded in several local and national newspaper publications at the time. Leefe Robinson's flying career was eventful to say the least, He was reputedly shot down by the infamous

Red Baron (Baron Manfred von Richtoven) and ended up in prisoner of war camps in Germany where he attempted escape on two occasions. His list of achievements during his short career in the Royal Flying Corps were legendary, but sadly, he died prematurely after contracting Spanish flu while on leave visiting his sister. He is buried on the Uxbridge Road in Stanmore, Middlesex, in a small cemetery right opposite a large public house which now bears his name. The flu which took his life, was to kill more people than the total amount of soldiers killed on all sides during the Great War. How ironic that someone so full of valour and action should fall victim to such a simple illness.

As an inspiring building in a beautiful environment, Ponsbourne Park House had definitely set the bench-mark for looks. One could be forgiven for thinking that we had landed on our feet, especially when compared to the post war inner city areas that had become bomb-sites and slums for many of the inhabitants of London. Rationing had only just finished and money was not in good supply. Many of the essential services were being run and staffed by immigrants. When compared to the Neasden suburb where we had spent our last 6 weeks after leaving Ireland, this place was almost a 'Valhalla' in comparison. I have no doubt that our parents were absolutely delighted that in spite of expensive fees to be found, their children were now in a safe, stable and idyllic location. The reality for us as children and siblings was slightly further away from that of our parents. We were soon to learn the bizarre practices of a strictly segregated and often cruel boarding school life, a life that was to colour and influence all of our future times, even in to adulthood. The journey into a fully disciplined, cruel and fascinating reality was about to begin for all of us.

Ponsbourne Park was essentially a beautiful mansion house converted into a convent school. Its many outhouses and other properties were to provide accommodation to an infant, junior and senior section for both the boys and girls who boarded there. The mansion was built in the 1870's and all connections with the neighbouring Fortescue property had been severed with the demolition of an original Tudor house which, I believe, stood in what is now the school football field. This later and much 'grander' mansion exuded opulence in both its exterior and interior appointments. It still retained many of its original features including hand-carved balustrades, marble floors, Adam fireplaces and an impressive domed observatory which now housed the school chapel.

The convent building itself comprised the dormitory accommodation for the girl boarders and the individual cells or bedrooms for the twenty odd nuns that staffed the school in various capacities. Adjacent to the girl's dormitories were the large kitchens and nun's dining rooms as well as the two segregated dining rooms for the girls and boys. The school possessed some one hundred fee-paying boarders and about seventy day pupils who travelled in from the surrounding villages and towns every day. The day to day experiences of these children would vary vastly according to whether they were attending on a daily basis and returning to their homes each evening, or, if like us, they would be permanently domiciled in the school buildings, away from parents and homes, as permanent boarders.

The boys section of the school consisted of two large buildings situated along a densly- wooded driveway which climbed an incline about 400 yards away from the main convent building. This area also housed the main school playground, tennis courts and a vast walled garden and orchards with several large greenhouses producing much of the fruit and vegetable staple used in the school kitchens. There is no doubt in my mind that these gardens had probably existed right back to Tudor times, and were providing the same fruit and vegetables after all of those many years.

The first of the boys' accommodation buildings was a two-storey converted stable block built around a substantial cobbled courtyard. Its three cornered exterior housed a large glazed veranda supported by wooden pillars and this was where the classrooms were situated. This building also housed both the juniors and seniors section of the school. The whole thing was dominated by a substantial four sided clock tower which rang out every quarter of an hour and boasted a full Westminster chime at the top of the hour. This clock was to figure very highly in the lives of the boy boarders throughout their complete existence at St Dominic's Priory.

Behind this courtyard was the aforementioned substantial walled garden that would provide future adventures and after-dark expeditions. The existence of a massive orchard with a vast variety of fruit trees, was a constant temptation for 'scrumping' by any boy brave enough to wander in. There were also bee-hives and several greenhouses all producing vegetables, tomatoes and every kind of berry imaginable. Pupils were encouraged to participate in the useful production of these vast gardens by helping with fruit-picking and other tasks during the seasonal calendar.

The other accommodation building was a three storey white cottage which housed the infants up to the age of six years old. Those of us who started our school life in the cottage were given the tag 'cottagers' and became largely fair game for any bullies occupying the juniors building and classrooms. 'Cottagers' would run the gauntlet of taunts and jibes from their elder peers in the juniors section, but equally, the juniors would also be running their own personal gauntlet from their bullying peers occupying the seniors building. As well as all of this there was another bigger threat to every one of the pupils in the guise of the strict Dominican nuns, some of these were to prove to be the cruellest and most sadistic tyrants that ever walked God's earth, while a few others of them were among the kindest and most 'saintly' and caring individuals one could meet.

Here was a school system that ran like clockwork and your contribution to its efficiency would be mapped out over the coming years by a strict disciplinary code that drove the complete curriculum both within its walls, and even outside of them. There was no hiding place for shirkers, who would be discovered very quickly and straightened out in the strictest possible terms. You would become an essential cog in the running of this vast machine, and the name of the game was to quickly learn the pecking-order and where you fitted within it.

Everyone was fair game in this strange combination of strict discipline and enforced law and order, and so it became the survival of the fittest whether the threats were coming from either your peers, your elders or indeed, the nuns who controlled the complete day to day running of the school. There were also some teacher nuns who had their own peculiar and sadistic methods of 'cowing' the children in their care. A pecking order was soon established in this regard, and we all learned very quickly about ducking out of the way of 'would be' predators, bullies and nasty nuns. At the age of five, I was already aware that this place was not going to be an easy one to stay out of trouble in, and I quickly found out that cruelty came from several directions, and in the guise of both adults and kids alike.

My first day at Ponsbourne Park is still a vivid memory, because on that day I was to learn how cruel some people could be. Worse than that, it would introduce me to the real feeling of abject loneliness which I had never before experienced. It would be indelibly imprinted in my mind for many years to come, and remind me that good and evil can sometimes share the same close spaces.

My mum and dad had delivered all three of us to Ponsbourne Park on a beautiful sunny September day in 1959. I recall the bustle of the school playground and the games of rounders, cricket and football that were going on as we made our way to meet the nuns in whose care we would be placed for the next several years. I looked around me and saw what appeared to be several happy children. These kids seemed to be enjoying life to the full and some of the younger ones immediately befriended myself and my elder brother and sister. We happily ran off into the playground with them and were soon enjoying games of soccer and cricket with our new peers. On the face of it, this looked like a nice school, but I was totally unaware that this was a school unlike any other that I could have imagined. This was a school that I would not be going home from on a daily basis. That concept was as foreign to me as these kids that I was currently running around with. My Irish accent was a real barrier in making myself understood to both children and teachers alike. I had no idea that on this day in 1959 I had been virtually and physically removed from the security of my parents and placed in the care of these strange women dressed in black and white robes that concealed every single hint of their femininity.

All nuns are named after the Virgin Mary and so receive the middle name 'Mary' as part of their title; at the time of their entry into the sisterhood, they become effectively married to Christ in the role of handmaiden. They dress in a long black and white habit called a 'scapular with a black starched veil held in place by a 'coif' or 'wimple', which hides every hint of hair. On their left hand they wear a silver ring, while around their waist, supported by a plain leather belt a large rosary is hung. They also take on the name of a saint which is given to them when they are accepted in to the order. Some nuns and priests self-flagellate with the aid of cotton whips or hair shirts. This practice has mainly died out since the 1960's and was used to focus the mind on spirituality.

Observing a group of nuns in procession is rather like watching a group of giant penguins walking two by two from the Ark, although unlike the cuddly appearance of the penguin, the average nun appears a lot more sinister in both looks and actions. They bustle around with both of their arms folded under their garments giving them an almost ghostly appearance. I was to have had the shit frightened out of me on several future occasions when unexpectedly encountering a lone nun on a dark corridor. They float along as if on invisible wheels, silently and robot-like. They appear out of nowhere in a sinister combination of silence and stealth, and will whack the 'crap' out of you if you deign to put a foot wrong.

Sister Mary Agneta was the school Bursar and she was responsible for collecting the school fees and keeping the general accounts for the convent. On the whole, she was a kindly nun, who, apart from her accountancy duties was also a teacher in the school. Sister Agneta was the very first nun that I had ever met close up, and on first appearances and given my five year old perspective on life, I felt that maybe these nuns were not too bad, especially if they were all like this one. The reality was much further from my original perception and was about to be a very big shock to myself and my brother and sister. Sister Agneta assured my parents that we were all in very good hands, and my parents felt happy that we had been placed in the care of nuns who shared our Irish heritage, and would therefore provide a lot of care and protection to all of us.

I was unaware for several hours, that my parents had left the school, so involved was I in the games and laughter of the playground. The nuns had advised my parents to leave us playing rather than subject the family to what would definitely be a 'tearful' and 'traumatic' goodbye. My Dad described much later his utter devastation on the journey home to north London, and we were to find out a few hours later that the same devastation would be our own experience for many days to come. The discovery that my parents were gone was such a big shock to my system that I literally blew a fuse, I was totally inconsolable, and so bad was my grief that I was to receive my first massive whack before this, my first day, was even over.

The initial shock of missing my parents was one that would last for several days, and it was always the norm for boarders to cry themselves to sleep each night at the realisation that there would be no contact with their parents for a very long time. My devastation was compounded by the added knowledge that both my brother and sister were also segregated from me, by living in different parts of the school. It was often a real challenge to get access to them during the busy school week, but I managed to see my sister at a distance as she played with her peers in a separate playground reserved just for the girls. If you were spotted by a nun even talking to a girl, you would be in big, big trouble. I received many a slap around the side of the face for trying to speak to my sister, and as time went by, we grew accustomed to just distant waves and occasional smiles as we passed like ships in the night on our way to our individual destinations within the school.

The separation from my parents was definitely one big thing that had to be taken on board, but the separation from my brother and sister was an even bigger blow to my young mind, and I was now cast adrift like a stranger in this totally hostile environment;

Here I was just five years old with no real knowledge of the English culture being led away and separated from my siblings in a world as alien to me as it could possibly be.

Access to my brother was to get little easier as the weeks passed by because we shared the same playground at lunch, milk and tea breaks, but we still occupied separate buildings and dormitories during the school week. That separation was hard enough to endure, but I was fortunate that Liam would keep a close eye on me during the playtime periods, and any 'bullying' or 'threats' against me were 'vigorously assuaged' by my elder brother. On one early occasion, I was taking a good kicking from one of the several bullies that occupied our spaces, when out of the blue a flying pair of feet made contact with the guy's upper torso, and my brother had removed another threat to my person in gallant style.

We became close knit and watched out for each other in every aspect of school life, we never fought between each other at school, preferring to kill each other on the school holidays when it wasn't him and me against the world. So close were we at that time that the nuns kept a very sharp eye on our activities, always hoping to catch us out in one manner or another. They secretly christened us 'the sly Ruths', as we managed to deal our way in and out of trouble with a tenacity and single-mindedness that we had built up very quickly. We devised a policy of never sharing any of our activities with anyone likely to be a threat to our purposes, and never sharing a secret with anyone but ourselves. It was literally me and him against the rest of the boarding school system, and as for any contact with our sister, we may as well have been on a different planet so segregated were the girls from the boys at that time.

My sister's own experiences of that time were as difficult and traumatic as our own, and she had her own dragons to fight on her journey through school. My brother and I became very self-sufficient, exchanging knowledge and experiences with one another and never confiding or relying on anyone but ourselves. Any access to our parents was very limited, being constrained by both the geographical distance and the limitations on personal visits. Parental visits were very sparse and these were allowed fortnightly on Sundays only. It wasn't always possible for our parents to visit on every available visiting Sunday, especially if my mother's nursing duties coincided with these. There were also serious financial constraints that would sometimes stop them from being able to visit at certain times. Although these visitations occurred fortnightly on Sundays, there was never any guarantee that they would be able to attend.

Those that could make the journey would arrive after lunch from 2.00pm until 6.00pm. If your parents were unable to make the journey, the kids without visitors would be rounded up and sent to the football pitch where two football coaches would keep you busy for the next four hours. All of the boarders receiving visitors, would be dressed in their Sunday best and sit in the main playground awaiting the arrival of their parents. Most parents at that time did not possess a car, and so they would make their way to Goff's Oak station in Hertfordshire where a school bus was laid on to take them on to the school itself. The kids would all sit excitedly in the playground awaiting the arrival of their parents, and as they spotted them walking up the long school driveway they would run off to meet them. Some, of course, would be disappointed when parents failed to show up, and many kids did not have visitations for months on end, especially if their parents were working abroad, or could not afford the fares to come and visit.

We had a few moments like that, as my parents were both working mega-hours to keep up with rents and school fees, but in the main, we always managed to see either one or both of them every fortnight. Their journey from North West London would take them at least two hours each way, bearing in mind that public transport in those days was very limited, especially in rural areas. We wrote letters to our parents every Saturday morning, and these would be read by the nuns before being placed in the envelopes for posting. If your letter contained anything detrimental to the school, or comments which the nuns did not approve of, you were required to write the whole thing again. All incoming mail was treated in the same manner, and this was my first experience of real censorship at work, although the term had no real meaning to me at the time.

Visiting Sundays were a time of great excitement for everybody, knowing that you would be seeing your parents for the first time in weeks. It was also a time when one realised how poor or wealthy the parents of your peers might be. Cars arriving in the school driveway varied from Rolls Bentleys right down to modest little Austin A30's which even at the cheaper end of the car buying spectrum was still quite a privilege. Just owning a family car was a very big thing in those days. Most of our parents arrived on public transport, and were then coached to the school in a small fleet of buses and coaches for the princely price of Half-a-crown. One of my friends lived in Dimchurch in Kent, and his parents would roll up on a motorcycle and sidecar, dressed in long leather coats and wearing flying helmets and goggles, they looked like they had just stepped out of a war movie about the battle of Britain.

Chapter 3
Aloysius introduces herself. Where are my mother and father? A little touch of kindness. Let the lessons begin.

The slaps came from out of the blue and swept me off my feet like a 'tsunami' hitting my whole body. A terrible stinging sensation spread across the whole left hand side of my face, and created a ringing in my ear that was to last for well over an hour. Now I was no stranger to the odd slap, as I had experienced quite a few from my Mother on various occasions, but these were a slaps on a completely different level. These slaps were fuelled by pure venom, and administered by a person who knew exactly where to hit in order to deliver the most pain. As I struggled to my feet another whack caught me on the back of the leg and literally swept my feet out from underneath me, I was now sprawling on the floor in a state of shock, pain and confusion. This was to be my introduction to the infamous Sister Aloysius, a nun who literally put the fear of God into every kid that encountered her. Just minutes earlier I had been enjoying a game of rounders with several other little lads that would become my friends and future peers. The sound of a shrill whistle had brought all of the playground activities to a complete standstill, but being the new boy and not being aware of the meaning of this whistle, I had fallen foul of the mistake of continuing to play after the whistle had blown.

Aloysius appeared to be built like a man, and she certainly possessed a strength more associated with that gender. Her aggressive, fat face sheltered behind a thick pair of round heavy rimmed glasses which increased the size of her eyes, and added an element of menace to her contorted features. Her crisp white habit was accentuated by a black bibbed full length apron, which billowed as she walked. She never actually talked, it was more a bellow that 'cowed' every kid she came into contact with. The next large whack that had caught me on the back of the leg had been administered by a large black strap which she had girded around her waist like a dagger. One slap from this was the most excruciating pain one could ever experience, and she always aimed them high on the leg just below the buttock. This was her way of dealing with the distress I was feeling at the sudden loss of both my parents and my siblings, and this was also our first introduction to one another as antagonist and victim. Here was the first indication of what life held in store for my brother, my sister and myself. Here was a person that I had never met before whacking the 'bejaysus' out of me for no good reason that was apparent at that time. This must be some kind of living nightmare that I might wake up from at any moment, but no, this was the real thing, and for the first time in many, I cried for my mother and father who were strangely missing. Where had they gone?

The shock of this first meeting was never ever going to leave me, especially as I had been in the school for a mere couple of hours. 'Get into line you little imp' she hollered, and as I struggled to get up off the ground she dragged my left ear up to her waist level and shoved me into line among the other cowering kids who were lining up to report to their various dormitories. I didn't have a clue what to do, I guess I must have been in a huge state of shock at this unexpected assault. I was sobbing uncontrollably at this stage and could hardly see to walk, fortunately for me, an elder kid grabbed hold of me, pushed me into line, and ushered me along, sometimes dragging me like a rag doll, until we reached the comparative safety of the big white Cottage building.

I remember getting into a real panic, when I realised that not only had my mother and father disappeared, but, strangely, my brother and sister were also nowhere to be seen. We had all been segregated without warning, my sister having been transferred down to the main convent building which housed not only the nuns, but all of the boarder girls as well. At the same time, my brother Liam was put into the junior section of the school which was also a completely separate part of the living accommodation in which we all now found ourselves. There is no doubt that I would have thrown a massive 'wobbly' when I had found that my mother and father and brother and sister were nowhere in sight, but this assault from Aloysius had seemed almost relentless and as the blows rained down on me from every direction, I got the distinct impression this hateful woman was almost trying to kill me, and loving every bloody minute of it. That night as I gathered my five year old thoughts about me, a lad named John Mallory, the same lad who had pulled me in to line after the onslaught, befriended me in the Infants' dormitory and explained that Aloysius was feared by everyone who came into contact with her. She had been given the nickname of Annie Oakley, which didn't mean much to me at the time, but in later years I discovered that Annie Oakley was a 'loud-mouthed' famous wild western 'sharp shooter' who became famous for her cowgirl roles in the Buffalo Bill wild west shows that toured the world in the twenties and thirties.

My sister, brother and myself were all to experience a very lonely and sleepless first night away from our parents, but my utter devastation knew no bounds as I sobbed continually at my plight. That first encounter of real violence from a nun is one that I would never ever forget. Sister Aloysius had set the benchmark for cruelty in that landmark moment, and it was to be the first of many such encounters. I was, however, to later discover, that there were also some very caring sisters among the many at Ponsbourne Park. For the moment however, the name of the game was to try to minimize my exposure to both Aloysius and any of the punishments that she meted out so ferociously both now and in the future. These were quite profound thoughts to be experiencing just one day into my boarding school life. My mother and father were gone, choosing to leave quietly while we were still at play. My father later described the event as 'heart-breaking', and he would spend many future weeks of anguish and sadness at our sudden absence.

In complete contrast to the cruelty and strictness of Aloysius, there were two kindly Sisters known as Ambrose and Oliver who cared for the 'cottagers' or infants, and it was Sister Ambrose who comforted me on that first night away from my parents. Sister Ambrose possessed a very kindly and sympathetic face. She had vivid blue eyes and very soft skin which smelled faintly of scented soap. She possessed a very soft spoken Irish accent and a beautiful singing voice which all of the kids in her care loved, especially at bedtime when she would sing soft lullabies to all of them. Ambrose had been told by the other kids of my encounter with the 'tyrannical' Sister Aloysius and apparently gleaned that I had stepped out of line in the playground as the kids assembled to report to their various buildings and dormitories. In a very kind attempt to comfort me, not only for the searing pain that had been inflicted, but also, the devastation I had felt when I realised that my parents had gone, Sister Ambrose presented me with a small black, woolly monkey with rubber hands and feet and a cute rubber face which sort of smiled as you looked at it. Sister Ambrose told me that she had spoken to my mother at home, and that she had said that I was to be a good boy and settle down nicely for bed.

I remember wondering how she could possibly have managed to speak to my mum, as I knew we did not possess a phone at the time. I did however take comfort from her words though, and knew, even as a mere infant, that this lady was trying very hard to help to right a wrong which even in her own eyes was very unacceptable behaviour. Ambrose prepared me a drink of sweet hot malted milk and sat by my bedside humming tunes until I eventually fell off to sleep. I was accompanied by the newly christened monkey who we had both agreed would be called Mickey. I little knew at the time, that Mickey the monkey would soon become the object of all of my affections for quite a large period of my future life at Ponsbourne Park. Ambrose had also positioned my bed next to young John Mallory who promised to take me under his wing and show me the ropes of boarding school life. Tiredness had eventually overtaken my grief for the present, and Ambrose stayed by my bedside for a long time on this my first night in these strange new surroundings.

The following morning she helped me with my washing and dressing, and even allocated a slightly older lad to keep an eye out for me and take me through the new routines that would govern my future here in the cottage. Breakfast consisted of a mixture of porridge mixed with cornflakes, and I soon acquired a taste for this strange concoction. 'Cottagers' did not attend the main refectories with the junior and senior boys until their second year in the school, and this gave us, at least, a kind of security and feeling of well-being that could never exist outside the walls of this big white building.

I knew almost instinctively that Sister Ambrose would be a great influence in my early days at Ponsbourne. I knew that I could confide in her without fear of retribution. I also knew that Aloysius would be a protagonist who, given the opportunity, would make my life a misery at every opportunity. In retrospect these were probably big realisations for any kid to shoulder at his time of life, knowing who to trust and who to avoid. Even among my peers, there were sure to be a few enemies, especially among the anti-Irish contingent, who even in these very early days, would make your life a misery with insults and physical attacks. My Irish accent would be a big factor in attracting some of the prejudices that were certain to come my way.

Falling in to new routines can sometimes be quite difficult for anybody, but for this five year old who had never ever heard of a timetable, the strict list of boarding school rules and activities would prove to be a rude shock to my system. I realised very early on in my academic life, that if I was going to survive the daily challenges in this 'hellishly' strict environment, I would need to acquire a set of new skills and a cunning to counteract the daily threat of violence from some of our carers and pupils alike. I soon learned from my new 'mentor' John Mallory that Sister Aloysius had acquired the nickname 'Annie Oakley' as a direct result of her 'mannish' traits, and strangely, she was the only nun in the whole of the school who had actually been given one. This, I suppose, spoke volumes about her character, and made some of the other strict nuns appear like 'fairy godmothers' in comparison to her level of cruelty. "Annie Oakley on the warpath" was the regular warning shouted to all of the kids who were likely to encounter Aloysius in her travels. We ran like hell to avoid any contact with her, knowing that just a brief encounter, no matter how innocuous, would certainly end up with at least a tirade of frightening abuse ringing in your ears, and maybe a bloody good 'strapping' for no good reason. It was impossible to stay out of trouble with this sadistic nun, and she seemed to appear out of nowhere, especially when you least needed or expected her to. I was unfortunate enough to have her as my first form mistress for class 1 and so I was aware very early on in my scholastic journey that my avoidance of her was going to be virtually impossible for that first year. Without any basic reading or writing skills to speak of, I knew that I was completely at her mercy in the classroom, but more worrying than that was the fact that she filled up almost every aspect of our school life both in the dormitories and in the refectories. It was just impossible to avoid this tyrant and her 'trusty strap' no matter how much one tried.

The strap was a lethal weapon, wielded with accuracy and efficiency, it looked like a thick stick of black liquorice about the size of a shoe sole. One smack of it in the palm of the hand would render the recipient numb for about an hour afterwards, but the initial blow was unbelievably painful. Aloysius had a clever way of administering it on the side of the buttock, well above the trouser line and in that part of the anatomy which was the most painful. The searing pain would travel down the upper part of the leg and right into the bum cheek. If you received more than two of these, you would not be sitting down for a few hours. Many of us received six at a time, and to us, that was like a mortal wound and would require a good sit in a cold bath or sink to take away the pain. Of course the resulting bruising and redness would last for quite a few days, but these wounds were never visible because they were covered by trousers.

The boarders at Ponsbourne Park were strapped regularly for not just most serious misdemeanours, but for minor infringements as well. Strangely enough, the day pupils were rarely given this punishment. I guess that if any parent of a day child saw the kind of bruising that the strap inflicted, they would be 'up in arms' about it and certainly protesting to the school about heavy handedness. The boarders did not have that choice, and as our parents were never there to either witness or be told about such beatings, they could be inflicted with impunity and regularity without fear of discovery. The girl boarders were never strapped as far as I am aware although they could be fairly chastised with a good slap on the back of the head, the back of the hand or the back of the legs. My sister described a tyrant music teacher who would stab her pupils on the back of the fingers with a sharp pencil or the side of a ruler if their piano practice wasn't up to scratch.

Another weapon in the Aloysius armoury was the green cricket stump, this piece of equipment was used as a blackboard pointer to teach us our ABC's and point at various posters and pictures around the classroom walls, it was also very effective as a cane and if you ever received a whack on either the hand or the backside with it, the resulting welt would produce a very black bruise indeed. Boys would regularly display their war wounds in the dormitory at night and you were hailed as a kind of hero if your bruises from either the strap or the stump were blacker than the next man's. On serious beatings, the victim would immediately make for the boys toilets where their peers would have the cold tap running into the sink so that one could immerse one's hands or bum into the cold water, I was never convinced that this made any improvement to the pain, in fact, in some cases it felt even more painful especially in winter when the water was barely above freezing. It was, however, a tradition and so we all went along with this. As one got older and more mature it was customary to receive your punishment but to avoid crying as much as possible, this made you an even bigger hero in the eyes of your peers and co-recipients. I soon learned to suppress my tears, not because I didn't want to cry, but more as an act of defiance and a great big 'fuck you' to the person handing out the punishment.

A general warning of impending punishment normally started with the legend "hey Ruthie you're in for it, I'll go and run the tap for you" or "hey Ruthie, Annie Oakley's on the warpath and she's looking for you." Any of these words filled us with dread and one knew that it would only be a matter of time before Aloysius captured you. The nickname Annie Oakley was certainly very appropriate, and although I had never seen any of the movies or shows featuring this masculine cowgirl, I was assured that Aloysius possessed all of those traits. I pictured her with a rope lassoo and six-shooter raising hell all around her.

There was no hiding place from Aloysius, because she always knew by the school timetable exactly where to find you at any time of the day. It could be in your classroom, in the chapel, in the dormitory or in the refectory. The playground was probably the best hiding place as there were always a lot of people there, and it was always easier for us to spot a nun than the other way round. inevitably you would be captured and the consequential punishment would depend solely on the nature of the crime and the focus of the nun administering it. Aloysius took no prisoners, her punishments were always serious and she dispatched them with efficiency and gusto. Her sole purpose in life, appeared to be the infliction of pain and fear. One blow of her whistle was enough to strike the fear of God into any kid, and that whistle appeared to be never out of her mouth. Here was a seriously 'scary' person by anyone's standards and she unfortunately figured in my life just too much for comfort in those early months and years at Ponsbourne Park.

My reading and writing skills were Aloysius's immediate priority, and every morning after breakfast and before class time at nine o clock I had to report to her classroom and practise reading my Janet and John book. I always dreaded the moment when she would turn up to test my knowledge of the words as I knew that a certain amount of physical pain would accompany the lack of knowledge that I displayed in those early days of learning. I had learned to count in Irish, but I had absolutely no reading skills whatsoever. I was also a slow starter at writing and arithmetic, all of which had me running Aloysius's gauntlet of cruelty. Left handed writers were frowned upon and so my left hand was tied behind my back whenever there were writing lessons. One had no choice but to learn how to write with the right hand, but this method of teaching would certainly come up for criticism in today's schools. To say I learned quickly would be an understatement, I quickly sought help from the wonderful Sister Ambrose who would patiently spend time with me after lights out and bring me up to speed on all of my subjects. I became adept at using both hands for various activities, and this resulted in my writing, and eating with the right hand, while all other activities including football, tennis, cricket, rounders and volleyball were all carried out with either my left hand or left foot.

If you were a 'dunce' in any of the subjects in Aloysius' lessons, her punishment was normally a slap around the ear, and then you were put in a group to watch programmes called the Wooden Tops or Andy Pandy on the television. I quite enjoyed watching the Wooden Tops and I didn't give a damn that it was regarded as both a punishment and, supposedly, an embarrassment for those who were selected to watch it. I also enjoyed watching Muffin the Mule, Noddy and Big Ears, Tales of the river bank and my favourite Bill and Ben the Flowerpot Men. Needless to say I was a 'prolific' dunce in those early days of my schooling. It was one of my few enjoyments at the time and so I even feigned being the 'dunce' quite often.

Aloysius, in her so called 'fun moments', often played a weird game of chase with the boys which comprised the strangest rules imaginable. The boys would stand in a large group around her and chant the following legend. "Sister Aloysius is no good, chop her up for fire wood, when she's dead take her head, and turn it into ginger bread". At the conclusion of this rhyme she would blow her whistle and all the boys would run off in different directions around the large playground. Aloysius would begin chasing them down with a basket full of balls which she fired at them with gusto. The basket held about 50 balls of varying hardness, and Aloysius could run like the wind. If you were hit by a ball you had to retire and sit on a bench at the top of the playground. Now this probably sounds like a lot of fun, and maybe it was to some of the boys, but my first experience was one of immense pain as I received a stinging , high speed tennis ball right on the side of my face which sent me sprawling to the ground in a heap- I didn't like this game;

The game concluded when all of the participants were sat on the bench, the very last man standing received a prize of either a bar of Caramac chocolate or, if he was really lucky, a bar of peanut brittle. The strange thing about this game was that it was always played just before bedtime and only with the boarders. This didn't strike us as very strange at the time, but in retrospect it does come over as a very weird activity indeed. It was certainly very physical, and Aloysius didn't care where the balls ended up hitting you; There is no doubt that there were lots of tears, especially if a ball hit you anywhere tender, and they often did. I guess she never played this game with the day pupils for fear of criticism or misinterpretation from their parents.

I got pretty good at the game, not because I liked playing it, (which I really didn't) but because I was sick to death of nursing another whopping bruise courtesy of a tennis ball impact on the side of the face, the groin, the bum, or on any other part of my anatomy that she chose to aim for at the time. I had learned very early on that Aloysius had a peripheral vision problem, and that coupled with the fact that her habit and veil restricted most of any sideways vision she might otherwise have possessed, I always managed to blindside her and so often received the welcome prize of peanut brittle or Caramac. I always felt however that she resented my ever winning, which made the prize even more pleasant and acceptable to me.

Another favourite pastime of Aloysius was looking after and breeding budgerigars and canaries. These birds were housed underneath the glass veranda that spanned the outside of the school classrooms and the upper dormitories. Cage after cage held several different species, some of them were capable of talking, and Aloysius encouraged the children to speak to them as much as possible. If you were very privileged you would be given the task of topping up their water fountains and re-filling their seed trays. Others were allowed to change the bedding trays at the base of each cage and replace them on a regular basis with new gritted paper ones.

I never got involved with the caring for the birds, and I always felt sorry for those caged little creatures who must have looked out at a big wide world where other wild birds could fly freely. It was somewhat of a paradox that Aloysius could shower these creatures with love and attention, while treating some of the kids in her care with utter contempt and cruelty. This really was a strange mixed up place in which we existed. On one occasion, a parent donated a large Macaw parrot and cage, and he was placed away from the other cages in a little corner spot of his own. For hours we would stand in front of the parrot's cage trying to teach it how to talk. Phrases like 'pretty Polly, and pretty bird were the main narratives delivered to its seemingly deaf ears, but a few of us were also keen to teach the bird a few expletives just to add to the excitement.

It became very adept at repeating 'fuck you' as it was constantly bombarded by the phrase at every waking moment. One morning Aloysius came down from the dormitories to find that the parrot's cage door was opened and the bird had flown off. For days afterwards she had almost the whole school searching the grounds and scanning treetops for any sign of the missing parrot, but, of course, it never was found, and I was quite pleased that at least one of these beautiful creatures had found its freedom. Aloysius was convinced that one of us had set the bird free, until it was pointed out to her that the catch on the cage door was far too weak and inadequate to effectively contain such a large bird. Prior to that I had premonitions of Aloysius coercing someone into admitting that they had set the bird free, in order to just blame anyone. I was delighted for that beautiful parrot, until I found out that it would have difficulty surviving in the wild countryside of England and its harsh climate.

Chapter 4
Rude Awakenings. Ignorance is bliss.   A left-handed Devil and dirty socks and underwear.

Those early days at Ponsbourne Park are still as vivid to me today as my most recent memories. They have left an indelible impression on my whole psyche and have coloured and influenced my actions ever since. Whenever I feel that things are getting too difficult to handle or cope with, I think back to the sense of resentment, helplessness and misery that I sometimes experienced back then. It felt like the whole world had somehow abandoned us to our own devices. Whenever we felt threatened or impinged, we always found a way to cope with and overcome those challenges. I realise even nowadays that nothing could ever be that difficult again, and I thank providence for it.

My first days and weeks were a flurry of getting used to new rules, a new environment, and almost a new language. The school was run on an almost military routine, and timetables had to be strictly adhered to. God help you if you were found anywhere that you were not supposed to be. The term used for this was 'slacking off' and I found out very quickly the serious consequences for being caught either 'out of bounds' or 'slacking off'. Playground games, were also very strange to me, especially as the only game I had attempted to play prior to my arriving at Ponsbourne was Irish Hurling. Even at five years old I had become quite adept at whacking a ball with a hurling stick. Games like rounders, cricket, hockey or tennis were complete strangers to me, but I was not fazed by them because they all required whacking a ball with a stick of some sort.

During my previous short schooling in Ireland I was taught everything I knew through the medium of Irish. If someone asked me to count I would do so very efficiently in the following manner: "a haon, a do, a tri, a ceathir, a cuig, a se, a seacht, a hocht, a naoi, a deich" and that was the Irish from one to ten. I also had a limited Irish vocabulary and knew quite a few phrases that were used on a day to day basis. Although I also spoke and understood English very well, I did, of course, possess a fair amount of Irish swear words which were often employed whenever I was frustrated with any bad situations or annoying peers. Words like. "Fecking eedjit, big bollix, and Fecking hooer, were all expletives that regularly flowed off my tongue. Most people on the receiving end of any of these tirades didn't really understand their meaning, and because of this I rarely got reported for swearing which was a major and capital offence at St Dominic's Priory. Of course, I soon picked up a few of the naughty English swear words as well these were an absolute must if you wanted to pursue arguments or fights in the playground.

My biggest problem, and the cause of most of my trouble, was that I could not communicate very well on a day to day basis. Most of the other kids did not understand my

Irish accent, and I also had difficulty in understanding some of the vocabulary and slang words used by them. There was a mutual misunderstanding within the school population, created by the diversity of their nationalities and the variation of the languages they spoke. The pupils came from Ireland, France. Italy, Spain, the Middle East and even Africa and the varying wealth of their families was as diverse as the languages they spoke. It didn't really matter what beliefs you held or what language you spoke because the nuns at Ponsbourne Park would 'knock' you into their very own kind of shape within a very short time. Any ideas that your own culture would survive inside this environment were soon put aside, as the Catholic school regime re-shaped and moulded you into something very removed from what you were. One thing was certain though, there were more rules and regulations governing our school life than anyone could ever have imagined, and I was going to fall 'foul' of quite a few of them during my early learning stages.

In class one Aloysius realised that, apart from a few scrawled numbers and a complete lack of alphabet, I would have difficulty in keeping up with the normal Anglo-Saxon kids in my class. My broad Irish accent was very distinct, and was little understood by any of my peers, and even less by my teachers. She decided to remedy this situation by doubling up on my lessons in the mornings before class began, and again in the evenings while all of the other kids were either at 'prep' or in their dormitories. She hollered, screamed and scowled at me through the first four books of Janet and John and I got so many whackings and wallops, that I was becoming absolutely terrified of reading. With my left hand tied behind my back for writing, I soon learned to make good use of the right one. My ears were ringing after every lesson, not just from all of her shouting, but more so from the frequent slaps that were rained down on me. I was beginning to learn the meaning of hate and all of this emotion was reserved for this wickedest of women. Thankfully there were the kind ones like Sister Ambrose to restore the balance, and provide a little care in this bizarre environment.

This whole episode was a baptism of fire for me, but it taught me very early on how cruel Aloysius could be. I realised that the quicker I mastered the reading and writing, the quicker I could escape this awful nun. I was also given extra 'elocution' lessons by a kindly lady who travelled in from Cockfosters every week. She coached me in pronunciation, diction and deportment and also helped a lot with my reading. I knew that she was aware of the cruelty that some of us were experiencing at the hands of Aloysius, I suppose she could either see or sense the fear that we exuded, her kindness was a brief but welcome respite from the daily routine that we experienced. I did however feel a complete idiot as I marched around her class with a pile of books on my head reciting the 'Grand old duke of York' in my finest Oxford accent.

The T.V. punishment for those kids who did not make the grade at reading or writing in Aloysius' class would always be segregation from the rest of your peers. So fond was I getting of this punishment, that I continued to pretend not to know the answers to simple questions in order to join the dunces in the T.V room. It was a great relief and escape from the slaps and whacks that we endured as a normal part of our education. It didn't worry me in the slightest that one could earn the reputation of being a dunce. There were far worse insults and threats lurking in every location around the school.

Any one of my peers or classmates, who even hinted that I was a dunce, however, would receive the sharp end of my foul tongue and even the odd smack in the gob. It took a long time for me to adjust to this strange and strict educating process, but I applied myself to the task in spite of Aloysius' cruelty. I was also very lucky that I could confide in Sister Ambrose who seemed almost proud of my progress in this harsh environment. She did her best to counterbalance the cruelty of Aloysius and made a lot of the hardships almost tolerable.

By the end of my second term at Ponsbourne Park, I was to become an above average reader, and I thought that life might get just a little bit easier in this strange place. How little did I realise at that time, that there would be much more misery to follow, and that most of it would emanate from the dreaded Aloysius.

Writing still presented a lot difficulties for me, not because it was difficult, which it was, but more so, because my left-handedness continued to dominate in spite of the tying-up. I was a left hander. I have no idea why being a left-hander was such a problem, but it certainly was, and myself and one other little lad named Thomas Paull became the two culprits in my class who needed to shake off this 'devilish' practice. Having Thomas as a fellow 'leper' made me realise that I wasn't the only one who was different, and we both drew strength from this knowledge.

Now the rules for writing at Ponsbourne Park were very much defined and very strictly adhered to. From year one to year three all writing was completed in pencil, there was no deviation from this rule at any time. From year four to year six joined up writing was introduced, but this was only to be carried out by fountain pen. Although 'biros' and ball-point pens were in quite popular use by this time, they were completely banned by the school, and all pupils were required to provide a premium fountain pen for the commencement of their fourth year. These fountain pens were even stipulated by brand, Parker and Platignum being the more acceptable choices. Pupils were also expected to learn 'calligraphy' as part of the written curriculum, and a strict use of italic writing was enforced at all times.

Italic writing would be an added challenge to my left-handedness, and I was beginning to be almost grateful that I had eventually learned to write with my right hand. I had also learned to eat right-handed using my knife fork and spoon in the appropriate hand.

Thankfully, this right-handed rule was not enforced on the football field or in any other racket games, so my competence at sport was not affected. The whole episode however, has had the strangest effect on the usage of my hands up to the present day. I continue to write with the right hand together with many other tasks, but I still employ my left hand for using tools when I'm working. I also kick football with my left leg and most strenuous operations are still carried out with my left hand, it is also my strongest hand and has, over the years, made me ambidextrous. I learned many years later from medical friends that changing a child's hands or legs usage can be very damaging to youngsters. They can develop, ticks, stutters and other speech impediments as a result of the switching of a person's limb bias. I must admit I was lucky to avoid any problems of that kind. I did, however, used to keep my left hand behind my back for a couple of years after mastering handwriting, because I had become accustomed to it being there. Other kids would laugh whenever I was essay writing or writing letters home, because my left hand would always be tucked behind my back and I would poke my tongue out when concentrating. This was also the case while playing football or running in the playground, I just found it more comfortable that way.

The big advantage of mastering the ability to write properly, and then excel at competition and grammar, was that it allowed me to offer my writing services to other kids and peers that were perhaps not so adept at it. The school required every kid to write to their parents once a fortnight, normally on a Saturday morning. Such a task was time consuming and boring, as the format of the letter was already dictated by the school. I earned many a bar of chocolate or other tasty morsel of tuck, by agreeing to write letters for lads that were either too lazy to write, or just did not possess the desired skills for such a task. A typical letter home read as follows:

St Dominic's Priory,
Ponsbourne Park,
Nr. Hertford, Herts.
9th February 1962.

Dear Mummy and Daddy,

I hope you are very well and happy. I am also very well. Thank you very much for the fruit cake that you sent for my birthday, it was delicious and I shared it out with a few of my friends.

Could you please send me five shillings for a school trip to see the film King of Kings which is playing at Hatfield in two weeks' time.

I am working very hard at school, and I am about to go into class 2 where we will begin to learn joined-up and Italic writing with pencils

Sister Angelica said that I would soon require a Platignum or Parker nibbed fountain pen for next term, as well as 1 bottle of Quink ink in black, and another bottle in blue.

I am very happy too and look forward to seeing you in the summer holiday.

That is all my news for now.

Your loving son.

Seamus xxx

These letters followed various formats, and were fully scrutinised by the class teachers before they were allowed to be put into your stamped, addressed envelope and sealed. Censorship ensured that no letter ever left the school with adverse comments from any of the children. All incoming letters were also opened and read by the school before being passed out to any pupil. The stamps were normally removed from all of the incoming post, as the nuns raised charity money by re-selling these. Many pupils tried to get letters out of the school by other means; one of the easy ways was to ask a day pupil to take it for you. This method was closed down by fear of capture, which would ensure that the pupils concerned would receive a good strapping. Very few people dared to break this rule for fear of the consequences. As well as the above, the day pupils could not be relied on to keep a secret and were the cause of many a boarder getting into serious trouble for the slightest misdemeanour.

Most mornings and evening would involve religious services as part of the school regime. On alternating mornings the boarders would attend mass at 7.00 a.m. and most evenings were devoted to either benediction or the reciting of the rosary. It was inevitable that a convent school would require its pupils to attend all of their religious ceremonies, but when it came to religion at Ponsbourne Park, it seemed we were always on our knees in the chapel for one reason or another. It didn't matter which religious background or persuasion you happened to come from, there was no getting away from the strict religious regime that epitomised St Dominic's Priory. We marched everywhere in military style, and the three lines of pupils making up church parade dressed in the colours of the three main school houses. The house colours were displayed on the school ties, Patrick's in green, Andrew's in blue and George's in red. Day pupils would wear the black and white tie that we boarders wore on Sundays, and their house was Dominic's. We would compete with each other to be the best marchers and the best in line. The grand old Duke of York would have been extremely impressed with the various marches that we learned at the time.

Each house had a Captain and vice-captain, and they would run up and down the rows of boys shouting and pushing them into position, checking that all ties and caps were straight. The house captains were selected by the nuns according to their academic and disciplinary skills, and these boys wielded a lot of power in every aspect of school life. Caps had to be 'doffed' if passing a teacher or any other nun and priest you might encounter. On occasions when hats were not worn, you were required to salute and greet them with an orderly 'good morning Sister', 'good afternoon Sister' or 'good evening Sister'. Marching was the order of the day and we marched to and from our classrooms, to and from our meals and to and from church services. Even the odd outings to the local villages would be preceded by a near mile march to the main gates of the school. Marching to chapel was of major importance to the house captains, because they were aware that everyone would be under scrutiny from all of the nuns assembled for religious ceremonies. If you were unfortunate enough as a house Captain to be chastised for the inadequacies in your ranks, there would be hell to pay for everyone right down to the youngest of us. My backside was kicked several times for bad appearance and marching out of time or line, and I soon learned that compliance was the least form of resistance in this regard. Anyone found with their hands in their pockets were immediately reprimanded by both the house captains and the nuns alike. This was a particularly difficult rule to observe for small boys, especially in the cold winter months.

The school chapel itself was a converted observatory complete with an impressive domed glass roof that, at one time, revolved to follow the movement of stars and planets in the night sky. An impressive rockery covered one complete wall from floor to ceiling, and from this rockery an invisible waterfall fed a very impressive and well-stocked fish pond at its base. The rockery also contained some of the most beautiful flowers and plants I had ever seen, and these gave off a multitude of wonderful smells that seemed to fill the whole chapel area. These smells combined with the odour of burning incense and candle wax to provide a range of essences that one can never forget. Built into the rockery was a depiction of the Virgin Mary appearing to St. Bernadette, the whole rockery was a masterpiece of design and impressed the many visitors that frequented the chapel.

Beneath the expansive glass dome was a beautiful frescoed coving depicting the laurel wreaths and vine leaves of ancient Greece. The floor was fashioned from a very fine multi-coloured marble mosaic featuring the 'legend of Bacchus' and this had been enhanced with the school motto 'VERITAS' together with the emblem of the Dominican order. Clever use had been made of all of the space within the chapel, and eighty or ninety kneeler chairs faced sideways on to an impressive altar housed within the adjacent nun's chapel. Chapel was one of the rare opportunities for the boys to see the girls, because apart from time spent in the classroom, all other mixing of the sexes was non-existent. If you were caught looking at a girl in church you would be dragged out of line after church service and given a good strapping for having immoral thoughts. On such occasions, I always contested that I was looking out for my sister, but that made absolutely no difference to the outcome.

All boys were required to train as altar servers from the age of seven upwards. A vast array of cassocks and white tops known as 'surplices' were housed in the chapel for that purpose. Any mistakes or messing about as an altar-server were severely dealt with, and if reprimanded, would be regarded as one of the biggest crimes one could commit. My favourite role as an altar server was the carrying of the 'thurifer' which was the large brass chained container used to house the incense burner. This complicated piece of equipment was a hard thing to handle and operate, but we had a lot of fun over-incensing the thing and then gassing our peers out of existence with clouds and clouds of heavily scented smoke. One of the major misdemeanours regarding the swinging of the 'thurifer' was visited on me on about the third occasion that I had ever carried it. I inadvertently swung a block of burning charcoal out of the small container onto the beautiful green carpet that covered the altar area. So shocked was I by this incident, that I foolishly lifted the burning charcoal with my bare fingers giving myself severe burns that had to be treated in the infirmary. Needless to say this incident was reported to Aloysius by all of the other nuns in church that evening, and I received a smack around the head and ears for my carelessness. No mention was made of my severely burned fingers and apart from a lot of sympathy from Sister Albertina in the infirmary, I was pleased not to have been 'strapped' for the burnt carpet.

Another big crime in the daily life at Ponsbourne Park was bed-wetting. There is little doubt that most kids at one time or another will have wet their bed, and nowadays it is not so frowned upon. In my school days bed-wetting was little tolerated, and while you may have been excused an odd incident, God help you if it ever became a regular occurrence. If you managed to enter the seniors dormitories which occurred at about the age of eight or nine, your life would become abjectly miserable if you were a persistent bed-wetter. Sister Aloysius had another novel way of dealing with persistent bed-wetting. She would move the individuals and their beds to an area of the building which housed the school clock.

Now the school clock dominated the dormitory block. The block had originally been riding stables for the nobility that inhabited Ponsbourne Park in its previous existence as a country mansion. This clock had four enormous faces built into its tower above the rooftops of the dormitories. It also had a massive weather vane in the guise of a cock crowing, and it caught the wind from every direction. The main mechanics and workings for this clock were housed in an enormous cupboard between two of the connecting dormitories. If you were an unfortunate bed-wetter this was where they would park you and your bed. It was almost impossible to get any kind of decent sleep there, as the constant clanking and ticking of the clock would keep you awake. Imagine the horror for anyone, when every fifteen minutes this giant clock would crank into life in order to deliver a Westminster chime. This became worse on the full hours because not only, did they crank out the full tune, but they also struck the hour in a repetitive and booming ringing of bells. Fortunately for the bed-wetters in the junior dormitory the workings of the clock were housed in a space adjacent to the senior dormitory, but that didn't stop old Sister Albertina waking them up on a regular basis to go to the toilet. The bed-wetters in the seniors' dorms fared less well, but I will describe their experiences a little later on.

Nothing could sleep in this environment, and yet a few poor unfortunates would still manage to wet their beds every night, and face the consequences for this misdemeanour in the most public and embarrassing way. After a horrible 'dressing down' in front of their friends and peers, these kids would be made to wash their own sheets in the dormitory sinks, and then hang them in the boiler room every day. They would then have to run the gauntlet of ridicule as everyone knew who the latest and most prolific bed-wetters were, because they would be spotted carrying their dirty laundry to and from the boiler room. Persistent bed-wetters were also punished with the strap, and they could be easily identified as they always smelled of stale urine if you happened to sit or stand near them. I used to feel very sorry for these lads and often helped a few of them wake up in order to avoid the bed-wetting or laundry trips.

On the subject of laundry, there were two very novel and amusing activities that happened once a week in the juniors' section of Ponsbourne Park. One was called 'the 'stamping of the socks.' The other one was aptly nicknamed the 'Kacks Inspection'. These two activities were spearheaded by little Sister Albertina, and would promote either fear or pleasure in equal measures. Sister

Albertina was in charge of the junior's dormitory, and she had about 35 children under her care. On the whole she was quite a kindly, older nun with a gruff Irish accent and a very friendly smile. She had a large hooked nose that always had two or three hairs sprouting out of the top of it, and a profusion of grey hairs growing out of her nostrils and leaking out from behind her white and black starched veil. She smelled constantly of either soap bleach or disinfectant and seemed very old to us at the time. I suspect however, that she was probably only in her early sixties. I liked Albertina a lot because although she was always strict, she was also very even-handed in her dealings with her charges. She cared a lot for the boys in her care, and the boys all regarded her as not a bad 'old stick'. I managed to manipulate her a lot by complimenting her at various times on her energy and kindness and occasionally hoodwinking her into believing I was feeling poorly. This normally triggered her maternal instincts albeit rare ones, and earned one a day or two in the infirmary which was like a hotel in comparison to the normal draughty and cold dormitories that we inhabited. The slightest hint of a virus in the population would trigger an immediate transfer to the infirmary for the offending 'sickie', and for a few days, at least, you would enjoy some welcome respite from the strict daily routine. Sister Albertina would provide you with the best care and attention going, and the daily meals would be prepared to your own personal choices within reason;

She did however, also enjoy spasmodic bouts of temper which would occasionally result in her using the back of a hairbrush as a punishment for any misdemeanours. One of her weekly routines was inspecting the boys' underwear. This occurred every Saturday night without fail, and before issuing the boys with a replacement set of 'undies', Albertina would carry out her inspection of every individual boy's worn ones. I always thought that this was a weird and perverse activity at the time, but given the benefit of hindsight, I suppose these inspections were carried out to encourage better personal hygiene and a more efficient use of the stiff and crispy paper that passed for toilet roll in those days.

God help you if there were any skid marks in your underpants at the end of the week, she would whack you with either the back of the brush across the back of the knuckles or in the palm of the hand depending on what fancy took her at the time. All of the boys would line up in the dormitory with their underwear ready to be put in the big laundry basket, if your pants were soiled, you were really for it, and you would get either the hairbrush, or a stinging big slap across the bare back which would leave a neat red imprint of her hand for about two hours. There were always lots of red handprints on various backs, and those of us who managed to avoid them would smile smugly as another victim passed you in the dormitory. I learned to wear my underpants inside out for most of the week, so that they would pass the Saturday inspection. On most Friday evenings after prep, there would always be a string of lads washing the skid marks out of their pants in the boy's toilets, and hanging them surreptitiously in various hidden locations around the dormitories in readiness for the Saturday night inspections. Various crude comments like 'more skid marks than the M1' or 'more streaks of piss than a public house', were all legends that would be voiced from time to time between the boys in their banter.

Sister Albertina also worked in the large school laundry during the day, and was responsible for the smooth running of all the laundry operations. This was probably why she was so obsessed with clean underwear, and why she was responsible for the cleaning of the boys' socks on a separate basis.

Now all of the boys knew that if you were chosen to 'stamp' the socks, you would be well rewarded with sweets, chocolates or cakes on the completion of the task. Basically, it involved two big baths full of stinky dirty socks which required washing. Sister Albertina would fill the baths with hot water, and then add about 300 pairs of boy's dirty socks. To these socks she would add a couple of handfuls of Sunlight soap flakes, then 3 boys would walk up and down in the bath stamping the socks in a similar manner to stamping grapes to make wine. The stamping was a fun thing to do because Albertina would have her transistor radio tuned to the BBC home programmes, but whenever the opportunity arose we would re-tune it to one or other of the pirate radio channels, and listen out for the latest pop hits.

Although this was a slightly smelly task, all the boys enjoyed doing it as it gave some respite from the mundane and disciplined daily routines that we all followed. Sister Albertina was always happy and upbeat during these sock-washing activities and all 6 boys involved would have a treat to look forward to after the 2 hour operation was completed. Stamping the socks gave us the opportunity of catching up on news and gossip, and there were always a few incidents of horseplay taking place, especially if Albertina had to leave the room for any reason. This would be an especially pleasant task in the middle of winter when our feet were always cold or damp, and one was glad to get out of the cold for a brief spell. The 'stamping of the socks' always had a lot of ready volunteers and I was a regular contributor to this strange but compelling activity, only on the basis of reward, and not for any perverse love of stinky socks.

Chapter 5
Charges, eating disorders, bullies to bait and wheeling dealing

As a boarder at Ponsbourne Park many tasks were allocated according to your age and ability. While the infants or 'cottagers' were not required to carry out any of these tasks, they were slowly trained to shoulder some responsibility and some work ethic even in their earliest years. Such tasks were known as 'charges' and these would vary in size and intensity from simple ones like ensuring dirty washing was in the correct basket, to major tasks like polishing the dormitory floors or filling coal scuttles for use in the dormitory stoves during winter nights. I quite liked doing simple charges; one of my favourite's being the ringing of the school bell to summon the pupils to classrooms and study periods. This responsibility was given to you when you had mastered a full understanding of telling the time. At the same time you were often required to clean and polish shoes and rugby boots for your seniors, or even warm up a toilet seat for them first thing in the morning. The 'stamping of the socks' also came under the list of charges that most boarders were required to perform.

All of these tasks were throwbacks to the so called 'fagging' system that was practised in many public schools in England including Eton and Harrow. While 'fagging' was not practiced at Ponsbourne Park it existed unofficially for younger kids under the charge of a house captain or prefect. My first role was to put toothpaste on one of the older boy's brushes every morning, or make his bed before doing my own, and leaving the dormitory. It didn't bother me too much to carry out such tasks providing there was no hitting or bullying involved. Warming the toilet seat was not my favourite task, the toilet block was always freezing cold, and this often delayed my own preparations in the early mornings. I soon wriggled out of this task when I found out that the prefect giving me my orders was slightly scared of my bad temper, and feared getting on the wrong side of this aggression. My least favourite task was the fetching of the milk crates containing the free school milk which was handed out at morning break times. Not only were these crates very heavy, but if the weather was cold, your hands would stick to the icy cold metal of the crate and give you a nasty frostbite. These crates had to be carried a fair distance and then returned to the same place with all of the empty bottles cleaned out. Often the cold weather was so extreme that every bottle in the crate would have popped its silver cap and a large lump of frozen cream would stick out of every bottle like a small volcano. In extreme cases the expanded frozen milk would crack and often break the glass bottle itself, I remember a trip to the infirmary having encountered such a bottle and impaling the palm of my hand on a shard of glass.

Some of our charges were very popular, as they allowed us to rough and tumble away from the discipline of the school buildings. One such task was collecting hay from the meadows and fields around Ponsbourne Park. The school caretaker Mr. Beard would hand-scythe these areas with two Italian helpers. (Apparently these two men were Italian prisoners of war who were rounded up and interred for the duration of the war, they were then employed by the Dominican sisters as general handymen, and decided to stay in England rather than return home to Italy) The hay was either sold or donated to the neighbouring farmyard after it was collected. We would help them gather all of the hay in pull-along trolleys and place them into small piles, scattered around the various fields. Such distractions were quite rare however as over eighty boys would be competing for the favourite tasks, and quite a lot of bribery and corruption was employed in securing favours with the Captains or vice Captains doling out the tasks. As my brother and I were poor by definition, we had to explore other avenues to ensure selection for some of the more popular charges; this required a great deal of 'ducking and diving' on our part. What we lacked in material resources, we made up for in various subversive, creative and scrounging talents. The 'sly Ruths' were never short of ideas and initiatives to ensure a fair slice of the action and cake at Ponsbourne Park.

It was quite easy to manipulate favours from our peers, especially if you could discover their weaknesses and then act upon them. When it came to dining, there were strict rules attached to one's presence in the refectory.

The main rule required that every single morsel of food had to be finished before your plate was removed. Like most kids, there were likes and dislikes when it came to meal times, and an unofficial 'barter system' had grown around the swopping of food. If I hated my Welsh rarebit that was served for Thursday supper I would trade this off with another kid who maybe hated his fried bread on a Friday. If you were caught 'bartering' in this manner, by either the nuns or the House captains, you would be punished beyond all description. This punishment would entail your loss of several meals for a few days, and a good strapping into the bargain. Both my brother and I became adept at dealing in these sometimes complicated trade-offs, and we soon became known for such practices among our friends and peers. A lot of the wealthier kids could be relied on for their laziness, in almost anything, so there was always a ready-made demand for our services in bed-making, boot-cleaning, shoe-polishing, letter-writing and any other tasks that we could get rewarded for.

One of my classmates was Peter Collins, a bright student in every way. Peter shared a dormitory with me and apart from the usual little worries that we all lived with, he had one major hate that was never going to go away. Peter's big dread was the morning breakfast where he would be required to eat a reasonably large bowl of porridge. Peter hated porridge. Every time a bowl of porridge was put in front of Peter he would complain of having a 'funny feeling'. Every morning he would be force-fed mouthfuls of the stuff often resulting in his vomiting it up several times. It was quite clear to me that there was no way he was ever going to acquire a liking for porridge, and the more they forced it on him the more he hated it. Peter always repeated his usual message that porridge gave him a 'funny feeling', what he really meant was that porridge made him feel sick. I remember him telling me that he wished the three bears would come along each morning and steal his fucking porridge, just like in the story. I felt very sorry for Peter because of this, they would often take him up to a series of pictures that were hung in a line along the refectory walls that told the story of Solomon Grundy. They convinced Peter that he would end up like Solomon Grundy if he continued to hate his porridge. The 19th century rhyme read as follows:

Solomon Grundy
Born on Monday,
Christened on Tuesday,
Married on Wednesday
Took ill on Thursday,
Grew worse on Friday,
Died on Saturday,
Buried on Sunday.
That was the end of Solomon Grundy.

In every other aspect of school life, Peter was an excellent pupil and excelled at everything both academically and physically in his school life. One day, I ate half of Peter's porridge before the nuns came along to force it on him. When the nuns saw that he was obviously making an effort to eat it, they agreed that as long as he ate half a bowl each morning that would suffice. Every morning I gobbled down my porridge and put my half empty bowl in front of Peter. I would then eat his porridge as well. In return for this big favour Peter would give me a bar of chocolate out of his tuck box twice a week, and also drink my coffee on Sundays- I hated coffee. Peter and I became firm friends from quite an early age and he also helped me with my reading and writing homework.

This then was how we managed to avoid eating anything we didn't like. There were, however, very few dishes that my brother or I disliked, but there were lots of other things that we liked a lot but could not get our hands on. Items like Heinz tomato ketchup, Daddies brown sauce, Hartley's blackcurrant, raspberry and strawberry jam, lemon curd, Marmite, peanut butter and marmalade. Drinks were also big on the demand lists and these included Robinson's lemon barley water, Ki Ora orange juice, Ribena, Tizer, lemonade and Corona drink varieties. In mine and my brother's case, all of these were just a few luxuries that we simply didn't possess, but we found many imaginitive ways of acquiring them by both fair and foul means.

Such efficacious items were only possessed by the rich kids, and the rest of us would look on in envy as they imbibed these wonderful things at mealtimes. A lot of serious bartering had to be employed if we were ever to enjoy 'goodies' like these, and we were determined, under fear of serious chastisement, not to get caught scrounging-but scrounge we did. Of course we were not always fortunate enough to put jam on our bread, or lemonade in our glasses. So many of us acquired an appetite for salt sandwiches, sauce sandwiches, and in the most desperate of cases apple or orange sandwiches. So odd were some of our concoctions that we often recited one of our little rhymes that went like this:

Yum, Yum Pigs Bum,
Mixed up with Chewing gum,
When it's nice take a slice,
Yum Yum Pigs Bum

Yummy, Yummy, my Mummy,
Can't afford to give us money,
Daddy's also short of cash.
So all we eat is soggy mash.

I can't remember who taught me these rhymes, but I had learned them long before leaving Ireland and arriving at boarding school, I spent my life reciting them to my friends who thought it was very risqué at the time. I used to recite them to Peter all of the time and he would lose himself in absolute hoots of laughter every time he heard them. Thankfully his days of 'funny feelings' were now behind him and he no longer had nightmares over his dread of the morning bowl of porridge.

Charges were always a good source of reward for us, most kids hated doing charges, and would try and avoid doing them at all costs. My brother and I would happily carry out their duties in exchange for some of the 'goodies' previously mentioned. You could also rely on the lazy kids to help with the above; some of them were so useless at doing things that we would willingly help out for a small fee. This would include the previously mentioned bed-making, polishing shoes, cleaning rugger or football boots, writing letters home or doing bits of prep for them. The nuns, of course, were always suspicious of us, and while some of them admired our tenacity, others would look for every opportunity to catch us out. We always chose our benefactors wisely, swearing them to strict secrecy and confidence in any dealings that they had with us, and never sharing our secrets with anyone. We did get caught out on a few occasions, but this was normally our own fault for being discovered with contraband that they knew we could not possibly have acquired by honest means.

We operated a kind of barter system between all of the boarding boys at Ponsbourne Park. As well as bartering there was a great deal of swopping going on which included everything from foodstuffs and sweets right up to expensive toys including Corgi cars and Airfix models. This practice was always frowned upon by the nuns, but it was often very hard for them to discover because we would simply describe these transaction as loans or borrows from the original owner and certainly never a swop. This was our currency in the absence of ready cash, and I made some amazing deals with various kids for some of the most diverse objects and toys that one could find. The school had its own tuck-shop which carried a limited range of penny sweets, none of which my brother and I could ever afford. The wealthy boys received parcels on a regular basis, which always included the top range of sweets, cakes and comics. My father would send us a threepenny bit or a sixpence attached to a letter with sellotape. These letters were not very regular as money was very tight in our family, but we were thrilled whenever we received them. Our pocket money would not last very long especially when compared with the ten shilling notes and postal orders that a lot of the other boys would receive. We realised from our very early days that our family was considered poor by the nun's standards, and Aloysius was constantly reminding us that our father worked in a factory, which was a far cry from some of the parents who were diplomats, bankers and company directors.

Notwithstanding the above, we realized that our parents were paying a lot of money for this privileged education, and both of them were doing second jobs just to keep the bills paid. We never ever complained to our parents about the school, and we certainly wouldn't tell them of some of the ill-treatment that we put up with during our early days at Ponsbourne Park. We were quite happy to keep our heads down, study hard, and manipulate any deals we could make with the other kids. There was always some guy who would want a favour doing, and a lot of them knew where to come. Any friends that you made at school were very special ones, as we all knew that we were in the same boat and faced the same challenges. There was an amazing camaraderie that grew up in the boarding school environment, and you could rely on your chums beyond almost anything. It was an unwritten rule that you never told on your friends, and it was better to take the blame yourself rather than betray a confidence. No one ever 'splits' on his mates no matter what the circumstances.

Of course, there are always exceptions to every rule, and one of these exceptions was the treatment of 'bullies'. There were not many bullies at Ponsbourne Park, but if you found one, you could guarantee that he would be a bad 'bastard'. My 'nemesis' was a guy named Paul Barnfield, who bullied anyone he could get hold of. Barnfield was the worst kind of bully, because he was a coward as well, but that didn't stop him beating up on the smaller kids around him. Barnfield was also extremely lazy, and would always avoid doing his charges by pushing them on to others. His normal bullying was to extract sweets or money from his victims, but not before giving them a good hiding.

I fell foul of Barnfield on two occasions. Once, when I refused to hand over my piece of cake at teatime one day, he gave me such a punch in the stomach that I was doubled up for about an hour afterwards, and I thought he had done me some real damage. Then a few days later when he ripped up a special project that I had spent days compiling for my art class. From then onwards, I vowed that Barnfield was going to go down in a big way for those incidents. I decided to bide my time and let the dust settle on it all for a few weeks. I knew that I had to be really careful not to raise either his suspicions or indeed the suspicions of any of my own classmates or friends in my dormitory. I was going to make sure that I got the opportunity to repay him threefold for all of the misery that he had caused me and all of the other kids around him.

My first plan of action was to get back at him in such a way that he would not even realise what was happening. I set about planning a series of sabotages that would ensure that he was never out of trouble with the house captains, the teachers, and the dormitory nuns. He was going to rue the day that he ever 'fucked' with a Ruth brother. I realised that anything I did had to look like a natural occurrence, so that he could not apportion any blame to anyone around him. I was also aware of not sharing these events with anyone, not even my best friends, because you can guarantee that a secret shared could easily come back to bite you on the bum. My first opportunity came about in the classroom one day, when he left his fountain pen unattended on the top of his desk to go for a toilet break, I quietly grabbed hold of it and spread the nib with a compass, the resulting blobs ruined his joined up writing for that day and earned him a brown star and an hour in detention. That one literally blotted his copy book for him and gave me a lot of satisfaction, I hadn't even got started yet.

One of the biggest crimes at meal times in the refectory, was to be found with food under your seat. Not only were you blamed for dropping it there, but you would also forfeit points for your house and meals for yourself. As I walked past Barnfield's seat one lunchtime, I dolloped a big spoonful of custard on to the floor underneath him and waited patiently for the fireworks.

It was the head boy's task to check down the lines of all the tables to make sure that no one had dropped food. Imagine my pleasure as Barnfield got hauled off his seat by the ear and dragged up to face his house captain. The house had to forfeit ten points and Barnfield spent yet another hour of detention paying for his misdemeanour. He was later docked a breakfast and a supper over the following two days. For the first time in his school career, Barnfield was getting plenty of stick from his elders and the other people around him. I knew that I had to keep the pressure up for just a little while longer. Barnfield had to realise that he was just as vulnerable as any of the other kids in the school, and 'he who lives by the sword, dies by the sword'.

During the following weeks, skid marks were appearing on his underpants just before the Saturday night inspection. Items stolen from the teacher's desk were mysteriously turning up in his own desk. His homework which he had completed at prep the previous evening was totally missing from his exercise book the following day. His white shirts were turning up at the laundry with serious ink stains on the pockets and cuffs which was also a major misdemeanour. His tuck-box was being constantly raided, and nice sweets were being replaced with cheap rubbish and rotting fruit. After a month of this sustained mischief, Barnfield presented a very sorry state to both the teachers and the house captains. More importantly, he was losing face with most of his fellow classmates. He had earned so many negative points and detentions over such a short period of time that he was now looking like the last pupil one would ever want in any of the house activities or teams. I almost felt sorry for him at times, but then I would remind myself that this was the same Barnfield that would kick the crap out of anyone without the slightest hesitation and, more importantly, the slightest reason. He lacked any kind of empathy with his peers, and was spoiled rotten by his doting parents. His was always the best birthday party, and he possessed all of the best toys and books, he was never without a large amount of pocket money, and his place at table was easily spotted by the large amount of jams, cordials and squashes at his exclusive disposal. I was going to drive this guy absolutely nuts at every opportunity!

He confided his frustration to a few of us one day at break time. We subtly planted the idea in his head that "maybe he had upset just one person too many with his persistent bullying, and that they were now getting their own back on him very effectively". We suggested that "maybe if he started being less of an 'ogre' to the people around him, then all of his problems might quickly disappear". Alas it fell on empty ears and a leopard never changes his spots. Every time Barnfield assaulted or 'bullied' another lad, he would be on the receiving end of more and more incidents of revenge, but he didn't have a clue where it was all coming from. He was so busy trying to get himself out of trouble, that there was soon very little time left for bullying on a large scale. Eventually his vice-Captain took him to one side and pointed out to him that he was "obviously upsetting a lot of his 'peers' and if he didn't buck up his ideas he would be in for a life of misery". The penny did finally drop and the message finally got through, because Barnfield became much better behaved, and thought twice before giving any of his peers any grief. As a result of this his life eventually returned to almost normality and his only worries were the ones we all shared- keeping out of trouble with the nuns. This however, would not be my final chapter as far as Barnfield was concerned, because a little while later I would be dragged into a serious situation as a direct result of his stupid actions. For a short while he would be causing me more than a little grief. This, however, was all in the future and in the meantime there were deals to be hatched, peers to be exploited, goodies to be scrounged and nuns to be spotted and avoided.

Chapter 6
The Dormitories. Slipper fights. A boy on a cold glass roof and a fight to remember.

As I have previously mentioned, the school dormitories were situated on the first floor above the classrooms and directly over the glass verandas. These draughty bedrooms had been converted from what were originally stables. They were basic in construction and practical in design. The floors consisted of highly-polished boards that were regularly polished by the boys themselves. These boards had acquired a glass-like, high gloss finish as a result of years and years of polishing and shining. Bright orange liquid floor polish would be flung in huge lumps on to the bare wood and this would be mopped vigorously into every board leaving a dull and tarnished finish. The boys would then be pulled along by one another, chariot-style, on big polishing mats until a deep shine was achieved. There were also polishing cloths that were worn on the feet over your normal shoes, and these were preferred by most of the boys as one could run and slide on these things just like a pair of real ice skates. These activities were part of our daily charges although the polishing was only carried out twice during the term time. Everyone loved this activity as it gave us the opportunity to 'horse around' and as the floors became shinier and shinier we would fling each other from one end of the building to the other using the shining mats as skis. We used to organise mock chariot races on the larger dormitory floors with four or five lads roped together with twine and flying around on the highly polished surfaces. The chariot racing was derived from a playground game that came into existence as a result of the Ben Hur film, I will re-visit this in a future chapter. We also loved to slide solo on these boards in just our stocking feet, and apart from the occasional splinter, or banged head, we had hours and hours of fun. Of course there was always the odd more serious accident to contend with during some of these sessions, but the odd split lip or head was a little price to pay for such a great time.

The dormitories were also mice infested and you could often lie awake at night and listen to them scampering and sliding across the polished floors, or rummaging in the waste-paper baskets for any dropped morsels. These mice were not shy, they had no hesitation in running across your path in broad daylight, and they always had a good supply of food courtesy of the tuck storage lockers that were also housed in the dormitory blocks. The mice provided a great target for slippers, balls or any other missile you could find to fling at them, and in spite of many of them ending up in traps, the population never seemed to diminish - there were just too many of them. We became so used to them sharing our environment that they came to be regarded as friendly intruders in our lives, one or two boys even managed to tame a few of them and keep them as constant companions. I befriended a small brown one that I fed on a regular basis from my hand, but I drew the line at carrying him around in my pocket as so many of the other kids did. They were great pets and inspired several of the children to care for them.

In the centre of each dormitory was a coke-burning stove similar to those seen in old 'prisoner of war' films, and this gave the dormitories the appearance of old Nissen huts. These stoves were the only source of heating within the dormitory blocks, and in the mid-winter we froze our 'bollocks' off in spite of their presence. We would often steal bread from the refectory, and toast it on the outside of these stoves as a special treat. These stoves were also put to good use in warming up your pyjamas on cold nights before going to bed. The exterior cast iron of these stoves would often glow red hot on the outside, and one had to be very careful not to get burned or singe your clothes and pyjamas as you were passing by. The stoves were ideally situated in the centre of each dormitory, and they cast a warm glow around the room all night. They were gainfully employed as the meeting place for illicit after- hours activities, and these included the legendary boarding school pastimes of story-telling and midnight feasting.

Midnight feasts were always held in the dormitories, but special care and caution had to be taken, because if anyone was caught out of bed after 'lights out' they would be severely punished. A series of lookouts were always deployed during these midnight feasts, and each boy took a turn in order to ensure that we were not discovered or captured. Loads of activities took place under the cover of darkness, and lots of mischief was also expedited in the small hours as well. Slipper fights were one of our favourite pastimes, and I was very capable at aiming a good slipper at any opponent in my line of fire. Unfortunately, some of the kids were not such good shots and on one very cold night my own slipper was inadvertently thrown out of the window on to the veranda roof below.

This was a major problem to me, as a missing slipper could get you a good 'strapping' by the nuns. The veranda roof was nearly eight feet beneath the dormitory windows and was constructed of thin wired glass puttied into metal frames. Not only would the offending slipper be spotted at some stage by an over-zealous nun, but the offending owner would be in big trouble as well. Getting my slipper from the veranda roof was to prove very difficult and costly, but it had to be retrieved at all costs. Brooms were hurriedly tied together to see if we could reach the slipper and retrieve it. Not only could we not reach the slipper, but now the poorly-tied brooms separated from one another and we were adding to all of the contraband lying on the veranda roof. The only solution was to climb out of the dormitory window on the end of a sheet and try and reach all of these items without breaking through the glass panes. It didn't work very well, and one of my legs plunged through an un-wired glass pane as I grabbed at the slipper and broomsticks. A shard of glass cut into my shin and the rest of the glass went crashing on to the paving below, alerting every nun to my situation.

All of the kids in the dormitory went scuttling off to their beds like cockroaches in a suddenly-lit room and I was left half hanging from the sheet and half sitting on the veranda roof like a 'sitting duck'. Within seconds the underneath of the veranda was awash with nuns running out of the T.V. room and heading straight in the direction of the previous commotion. As they walked towards the broken glass I knew that my 'goose was cooked' but then the strangest thing happened. Instead of looking up to where I was now precariously perched on the veranda roof, one of the nuns bent down and picked up a piece of roof tile that was lying on the paving right next to the pile of glass.

I was absolutely terrified of being discovered, and the boys in the dormitory felt sure that any second now I would be spotted and then there would be hell to pay for all of us. For what seemed hours, but was probably only minutes, I stayed stock-still while the nun turned the tile over and over in her hand. Some of the others that had joined her were now looking around the floor for bits of broken glass to be picked up. Amazingly not one of them seemed to look directly up to where my leg was dangling precariously through the broken glass. I was thankful that it was a moonless night and that the veranda was cloaked in darkness. They did not see my silhouette through the glass veranda, yet I could see them as clear as daylight from my position right above them. I remained absolutely motionless for what seemed like hours while they discussed the pile of glass and the piece of roof tile that had caused it to break. One of them went off, and returned to the scene with a dustpan and brush and cleaned up the broken glass. By this time my leg was bleeding profusely and I was shaking with both the cold and the fear of being discovered. The rest of the boys in the dormitory were waiting for an opportunity to yank me back up to the window, but were sensible enough to stay very quiet while the nuns were around. They were equally puzzled that not a single nun had spotted me sitting like a garden gnome on top of the glass veranda. The darkness of the night had certainly helped my predicament, but I also realised that years of dirt and grime and just a small amount of green moss had effectively 'camouflaged' me and my silhouette from view, I would just have to sit and wait it out until they moved away.

After a few minutes the nuns dispersed back to the TV room and I lay very still on the veranda roof waiting for some of the boys in the dormitory to rescue me. It seemed to be hours of waiting again before a few faces appeared at the window above me and made ready to haul me up on the end of the sheet. I carefully passed the brooms back up to them and retrieved my slipper. Having made the safety of the dormitory once again, and in full possession of the offending slipper and brooms, I was relieved and 'over the moon' at not getting caught. One slight problem was the wound on my leg which looked like it might possibly need stitching. There was no way that I could turn up at the infirmary that late at night without a bloody good story for the cause of the injury, and anyway, this would certainly give the whole game away. I decided to wait until the following morning when the dust would have settled on the whole exciting affair. We dressed my leg with some flannels and sheets and then we all settled down for the night.

The following morning at breakfast Sister Vincentia, the refectory supervisor spotted my injured leg and an inquisition began as to the cause of the injury. I lied very convincingly that I had ripped it on a piece of barbed wire on the way to the chapel in an effort to recover my school cap which had blown into the bushes. I could see that she plainly had her doubts about my story, but thankfully she gave me the benefit of the doubt with a swift clip around the earhole for being so stupid. Sister Vincentiaa was a tall moody nun with quite a heavy Northern English accent, she was also quite an enigma from a 'mood' point of view. We could never tell what kind of mood she was in until she confirmed it by either whacking you around the earhole with the back of her hand, or smiling sweetly while she complimented you on a particular action or happening that she had witnessed. You knew she was in a very bad mood however, if she splashed your hands with scalding hot porridge as she served you in the refectory. The trick then was to get the plate and the scalding hands back to your place in the refectory without dropping the bowl on the floor.

After breakfast I reported to the infirmary, where old Sister Albertina debated with Sister Oliver whether I should be taken to the hospital for stitches to be put in. After a lot of deliberation on their part, Albertina opted for dressing the wound and she doused it in her usual copious amounts of bright yellow iodine which stung like hell. She then applied several layers of lint and cotton wool to my leg, and finally wrapped it all up tightly with a crepe bandage. I was instructed to report to her every day to have the dressing changed until she was happy that the wound was healing alright. Thankfully there was no further discussion about the broken veranda from any quarter, and I was impressed with the discretion that my friends had exercised in keeping the whole affair quiet. As a result of this adventure my reputation as a tough guy with plenty of 'front' circulated around the junior's dorm, and in the classroom I was gaining a lot of respect from even the bullies and the day pupils (today this would probably be known as 'street cred').

Later that week, Mr. Reardon, the caretaker was busy fixing the broken veranda glass. He could plainly see that there was a large amount of blood around the broken shards of glass and that the dormitory window sill also had some smears of blood on it. It didn't take him long, looking at my freshly bandaged leg, to work out for himself exactly what had occurred. Like the 'true troubadour' that he was, he kept his comments to himself and feigned agreement with the sisters' theory about the broken roof tile. Weeks later, when my leg had finally healed, I told Mr. Reardon the complete story of what had happened that night. He listened very carefully, and nodded very knowingly, as I related the happenings of the 'slipper fight' and how I had ended up on top of the veranda roof, trying to retrieve my slipper and a couple of brooms. At the conclusion of my narrative, he reminded me how dangerous the roof of the veranda actually was, and how easily I could have fallen through it. Lighting up his pipe for about the fourth time in succession, he smiled broadly, gently patted my head and delivered those immortal words, "boys will be boys". He then sauntered off, leaving a trail of smoke from his old briar pipe, and the familiar 'clack' of his wellington boots making contact with the gravel underfoot.

Mr. Reardon became a particular favourite of mine, not only because he enjoyed listening to the various happenings of the boys, but because he was always completely discreet with the knowledge of our misdemeanours, In many ways, I imagine that he almost encouraged a little bit of disobedience on our part, especially as he was fully aware, that we were living in a very strict and oppressive environment. He would always have a friendly smile and lots of good advice for anyone that might seek his council. He would often repair broken toys for us in his free time, and he maintained our footballs and cricket kit without a single complaint. There was never any occasion when he wouldn't offer very sound advice to the kids who asked for it, and at Christmas time he was the most amazing Father Christmas, doing a complete round of the dormitories in the full festive attire. Mr Reardon was to figure very big in my life during a future event that would once again feature Aloysius as my main protagonist, but that was still a few years away.

A lot of our fun was centred around dormitory life and many pranks and practical jokes were planned and executed after lights- out and under cover of darkness. In fact, the dormitories were a hive of activity after dark not just for secret meetings and illicit gatherings, but they were also the place where daily gossip was discussed and delivered. Anything that happened during the school day was digested at night in the school dormitories, and even the odd outstanding score would be settled with a quick exchange of fists in true 'Marquis of Queensbury' style Invariably, these fights were carried out in front of the rest of your peers and siblings, and in spite of any outcome and whether or not you were winner or loser, a handshake always concluded every fight, this ensured that friendships were always interrupted on only a temporary basis. The vanquished was always at risk of another beating especially if they were to receive a black eye or facial bruising which would immediately alert the nuns that a fight had taken place. Although the nuns would not tolerate fighting, they were the first to put the boot in if they ever discovered that one had taken place - What a bunch of hypocrites these people really were.

Any fights that I got involved in were always private affairs away from prying eyes. If ever there was a dispute to be sorted out, a mutually agreeable venue would be chosen between the parties and these venues included the boys' toilets, the boys' dormitories, the boys' locker room, or a quiet part of the playground which could not be scrutinised by either the teachers or the house captains. Marquis of Queensbury was always the adopted rule, and once a man was down and stayed down, then the one left standing was declared victor. Hands were always shaken after a fight and this effectively ended the dispute for once and for all; Occasionally, if a handshake was refused this would indicate that the dispute was not settled and that other actions would occur at a future date. I was fortunate that in all my tussles and fights there were never any hard feelings, and often you would make a firm friend of someone who maybe just a few days earlier was trying to kick the 'crap' out of you in a playground fight.

Such a fight occurred with myself and a lad named Kieth Mellors when we were both about six years old. Kieth and myself were 'Cottagers' or infants at the time, and the fight was caused by Kieth throwing my monkey (the one that Sister Ambrose had given me on my first night at Ponsbourne Park) out of the top floor window onto the frosty playground. I retaliated by grabbing his own cuddly toy(a teddy bear, I think) and tossing it out of the same window. We both 'tussled' and fought on the dormitory floor to the delight of the other kids looking on. As we were both fairly evenly matched and gave a good account of ourselves, it is hard to say who got the better of who. One thing, for certain, that I remember was that we were both reluctant to go and retrieve the toys from the playground, as we were both probably pretty frightened of the dark at that time. We resolved the situation by taking each other's hand and making the long journey down several flights of stairs to the playground together. We were firm friends from that time onwards, and it was Kieth that I frequently accompanied with Sister Ambrose to

Moorfields Eye Hospital in London whenever he had an appointment for his sight.

Chapter 7.
Running away, My big dilemma and the cruellest of consequences.

A regular part of boarding school life and its strict regime was the taking of a register at the beginning and end of each day. At meal times, the pupils would assemble in lines behind their house captain, and each house captain would establish that every boy was present before ordering a march down to the school refectory which was about 500 yards away from the main school buildings. These marches would occur at any journey to either the school refectory or the chapel and strict discipline was applied to all of us by the various house or vice captains.

Often there would be a marching tune played on the school record player, that reverberated via loudspeakers around the school quadrangle. The speed of the march would be dictated by the particular choice of military music being transmitted. On many occasions we would be taught the slow drag march often used by the guards at Buckingham Palace. This march took a lot of learning and everyone was required to learn it without exception. The vice captains would follow behind the line of boys to ensure that no one stepped out of time, and more importantly that no one left the line. On arrival at the refectory each boy had to remove his outdoor shoes and put on a pair of soft plimsolls in order to enter the dining area. This ensured that the highly polished floors, so vigorously embellished by the pupils under the strict direction of the nuns, were kept in the optimum condition at all times.

The rigid marching routine occurred four times a day for each mealtime, and so by the end of each term everyone knew if anyone was caught out of line or step, or wearing the wrong shoes, they would be severely 'strapped'. Needless to say there were very few occasions when this would happen, because to be caught once was the only incentive needed, never to make the same mistake again. Of course, the reasoning behind all of this nonsense would become crystal clear to any boy within a very short time. If you were missing from the line, you would be presumed to be a runaway, and the word would go out very quickly in order to foil your attempts at making it very far from the school perimeter. It was, after all, nearly half a mile's walk just to get to the main gate at the school's entrance. If you made it to the school gate without being spotted, you were assured a good chance of making it a great deal further.

All meals eaten in the refectory had to be eaten in silence. Any boy caught talking by a captain or vice-captain, was sent to stand at the top of the refectory by the door. They would wait there for Aloysius to appear and receive three whacks of the strap. Needless to say, you could almost hear a pin drop during meal times. I did, however, find my self standing by the refectory door on several occasions and I acquired a good few sore bums as a result of my folly. Gestures and gesticulations replaced verbal speech in the refectory and this allowed us to communicate with each other without the risk of being pulled out by a house captain. Whispering was another alternative, but this was regarded by many as talking, and received the same punishment.

The school refectory was planned into four different rows of tables and benches each housing one of the school houses. If you were caught slouching on the benches at mealtimes, the house or vice captains would run down the row of benches and deliver a sharp punch to the unsuspecting 'sloucher' right on the side of his body. We soon learned to sit up straight at all mealtimes for fear of receiving a massive whack to your kidneys. The Dominic's house which was made up of just day pupils only occupied their tables and benches at one meal which was lunch, there is no doubt that they enjoyed a much more relaxed atmosphere than the boarders who occupied the other three lines of tables housing the Patricks', Andrews' and Georges' houses.

Loneliness was a big factor in boarding school life, and one would regularly hear sobbing coming from the dormitories after lights out. These were the kids who really missed their parents and their home life. Needless to say, we all at one time or another cried ourselves to sleep. Such occurrences were particularly common after the return from school holidays and half term breaks, and the crying would go on for several days until the kids concerned had settled into the school routine once again. There was never any real empathy or support offered by the nuns on these occasions, with the exception of the infants or 'cottagers' who had the kindly Sister Ambrose or Sister Oliver to comfort them a little. Most kids were left to their own devices, but the strict regime of learning to live life in the boarding school system soon taught you to forget about your parents and start coping with your new situation. I had quite a few nights like this myself, as did my brother and sister but as you got older and progressed into the higher classes in the school, you learned to control your grief because of the effect on younger and less experienced kids. The older children often became 'mentors' to the younger ones especially those who had become boarders for the first time in their young lives. Apart from the grief of loneliness, there was also a massive learning curve of rules and regulations to get your head around.

Most kids, at one time or another, talked of running away, but given the extremely remote location of the school, and the regular checking of the numbers, it would prove to be a very difficult place to escape from. Even if the opportunity to run did present itself, one would find it extremely challenging to make any kind of escape without money or directions. Most of the kids who boarded at Ponsbourne Park came, not only, from all over London, but many more had parents living in different parts of the country and even abroad. There were children from all walks of life whose parents' occupations varied from diplomats right down to working class factory workers. While at the school we were all supposed to be regarded as equals, but it was quite obvious to myself and my siblings that money definitely talked, and we were all made plainly aware of our own unique social differences. We had no illusions about where we stood in the pecking order and we were put in no doubt by the nuns, that our parents were simply working class. Most of the nuns, both teaching and lay staff were from Irish backgrounds themselves, and yet some of them treated the Irish children, much more strictly, and in a few cases, with complete contempt. All of this was self-evident to me, even at the age of six or seven years old, and I had no illusions that there would be any concessions to my Irish background. Does your father still work in a factory? was a regular enquiry from Aloysius and some of the more offensive nuns at Ponsbourne Park. We, of course, had no idea of the class-system which still existed in the England of the 1960's, but we were soon made aware of it on almost a daily basis.

My brother and I often talked about getting out of there, but even at our young ages, we were very aware of the difficult logistics which would present themselves in such an endeavour, especially as our parents lived miles away in North London. We would need to walk about 5 miles to the nearest station, and then without money or tickets we would have to catch a mainline train to Kings Cross. Finally we would have to find our way around the underground system and catch a train to Neasden. The whole journey would take us hours, and there was no guarantee that we would be able to sneak in and out of the various stations unseen. Such a task would be absolutely enormous and we were finally cured of any such ideas by an incident that happened to three of our peers who decided to do just that. Any further discussions of running away were quickly expelled from our thoughts by the events that were about to happen.

I have described earlier the various charges that each child had to undertake as part of his school activities. It was one of these charges in the midwinter that was to lead me to one of the most worrying and shocking incidents that I have ever witnessed. It was after tea on a normal Tuesday afternoon that I and three other pupils were filling coal scuttles for the dormitory fires. The three others were the aforementioned Paul Barnfield, and his two friends John Belmont and Michael Hepstall. We each had two coal scuttles to fill with coal and then deliver these to the various boys' dormitories before the evening rounds of supper and prep work. This was an activity that took us outside of the school boundaries where a large pile of coal and coke was deposited. While I was filling up my two scuttles I realised that the other 3 boys had simply dumped theirs by the side of the coal pile and were 'legging' it down the lane away from the school. At first, it did not dawn on me that these three were actually running away. I also realised that if the coal scuttles were not in place in each dormitory before supper-time then there would be hell to pay. All of the three of us would be in big trouble at bedtime if the fires were not equipped with enough coal to keep them burning through the night. I was in an awful dilemma, should I go and report the runaways and face the consequences of squealing on them? Or should I just complete the filling of all of the scuttles and say nothing? Whatever my decision, I knew that at suppertime I would be in big trouble. That would be the time that the runaways would be missed, and by then, they would have had nearly a three hour start on any pursuers. I was really 'pissed' at them for lumbering me with such a sudden and unwanted predicament.

I realised very quickly that my only option was to fill all eight scuttles and place them in the various dormitories. This was an absolutely exhausting process and I needed to make sure that there were no witnesses to my carrying out the scuttle duties by myself. Fortunately because this was mid-winter, and it was normally dark by about four o clock, I was able to do all of the scuttle deliveries under the cover of darkness. I could complete the task without being spotted by either teachers or prefects alike. I had a few close shaves while man-handling the heavy coal scuttles up the various flights of stairs to the dormitories, and I ducked in and out of doorways and corridors to avoid being seen by anybody. At the end of this little escapade I was absolutely 'knackered' out. I also had a great big ache in the pit of my stomach at the impending discoveries which would be revealed at suppertime. This was a serious situation to be confronted with and I knew that I would have to lie very convincingly at the inevitable inquisition that would follow. I was severely 'pissed off' at Barnfield and company for putting me in such a 'shitty' situation, and I surmised that they must have been planning their escape for quite a long time- they also knew full-well that I wouldn't be running to the nuns or house captains to report them missing. I had completed the scuttle task very quickly and efficiently, and then made my way to the classroom for afternoon prep. Several other boys were doing their homework, and I made sure that they saw me at my desk just in case I had to later rely on their testimony about the events of the afternoon.

Suppertime came around, and it was immediately discovered that three people were missing from their places at table. An excited hum went around the refectory, as people realised for the first time that Barnfield, Hepstall and Belmont were all missing from their places at table. I knew that it was only a matter of time before timetables were looked at, and they would see my name on the scuttle rota along with the three others. Everyone was speculating about how far the lads might get before being caught, would they all manage to make it home, or would circumstances work against them? It was obvious that a lot of the kids were really excited at the prospect of three of their number escaping from what was to most of them a kind of prison. Shortly before the end of supper I, along with a good few other lads, was summoned by the various House captains and questioned exhaustively as to the whereabouts of these missing boys. I tried to remain as calm as possible as I stated that we had all filled our coal scuttles and that I had then gone on to do my afternoon prep in the classroom. This explanation was accepted for the time being, but I knew that immediately the nuns found out and the boys were officially reported missing, I would be questioned at a much greater length by them. I would need to stick to my story at all costs.

I stuck rigidly to my story right up until bedtime, by which time the local police had been informed of their truancy. I was by now terrified that if and when the boys were picked up by the police my story would be denied by them and I was in for a 'shit-load' of trouble. The hours passed by until about 11.30 p.m. when a police car swept into the school quadrangle with the 3 missing lads sat in the back. Almost every dormitory, by now in total darkness, was buzzing with the news of the arrival of the police. As we peered through the upstairs windows, we could see the three lads being led into one of the ground floor classrooms by several nuns and a couple of uniformed officers. There was no doubt in my mind at that point, that I would soon be dragged into the whole 'sorry' affair once the detailed story was extracted by the nuns from the three boys. Far more however, was going to happen before I would have to face the nuns. I had little idea of what was to follow, except that it would prove to be the most shocking thing I was ever to experience in all my days at Ponsbourne Park.

When the Police had left the school, having been assured by the nuns that the boys would be reprimanded only, Aloysius marched the trio of 'runners' upstairs to their shared dormitory and then began to brutally assault them with a combination of belts, straps and her favourite hitting tool the infamous green cricket stump. Whether the other nuns were complicit in the punishment seems very doubtful, because the level of violence used would not have been sanctioned by any of them. I have no doubt that Aloysius took this upon herself to satisfy her own sadistic and brutal tendencies.

I, for my part, count myself very fortunate that I did not personally witness this awful event, but my brother witnessed every tortured minute of it. He recalled how the three boys were literally marched into the seniors' dormitory, stripped of all of their clothes by Aloysius and then belted and battered black and blue over a period of about 15 minutes. There was not an area of their backs, legs or buttocks that was not covered with cuts, welts and bruises. After the severe beatings, the boys could be heard sobbing for several hours, so bad was their pain. For several days afterwards they could hardly sit down or even walk properly. The other boys in the senior dormitory, who witnessed the beatings that night, were all in a state of shock at the violent and sustained nature of the attack, and they described every moment of the event as frightening and shocking. Aloysius was as violent as anyone had ever seen her. None of them could believe the level of cruelty that had occurred at the hands of this so-called religious person. In the past she had 'strapped' the whole dormitory because no one would own up to a certain misdemeanour, but this beating was in another dimension in both delivery and the level of violence.

The news of the beatings soon circulated throughout the school, and left no one in any doubt about the consequences of running away. I was grabbed by my ear the following morning as Aloysius continued her enquiries into the events surrounding the running away. I stuck to my own story in spite of a few good hard slaps across my face and head. I was fortunate that she had not delved too deeply into the coal scuttle duties of the previous few days, as she was much more concerned in finding out about who knew of the boys' intentions. I later caught up with the three lads and we confirmed all of our stories just in case Aloysius decided to follow up on the events at a later date. The boys showed me the scars and bruises that they had all received, and I realised that the stories circulating about the ferocity of the beatings had not been exaggerated. I was absolutely shocked by the bruising that they had all sustained, it was hard to believe that a nun could inflict such violence on kids of seven or eight years old. I was more than relieved that I had not been implicated by them in any way, and I was reminded of the loyalty and secret code of conduct that we all possessed in protecting our peers during such incidents. The bruises from Aloysius's assault lasted for a good few weeks after the beatings, and the most surprising thing to me was that no parent was ever made aware of what had happened from either the school or the boys involved. I often wondered what may have happened had the boys actually succeeded in getting to their respective homes. I have no doubt that Aloysius would not have been permitted in any way to punish them like she did, and this was the general consensus among many of the pupils at that time. To say that those three boys were walking around in a state of shock would be an understatement. Apart from the physical scarring that they carried with them for quite a few weeks, there was probably a much larger dose of mental scarring which I doubt they have forgotten right up until the present day. There was certainly a lasting impression on all of the kids that had witnessed this cruelty on that particular night, and my brother often refers to it right up to the present day. It was this incident that improved my relationship with the 'bully' Barnfield. For the first time in many months I felt genuinely sorry for him. This incident changed his whole demeanour and his relationships with the other boys that shared his surroundings. I was convinced that he would never forget his boarding school days as a result of just this one incident.

Chapter 8
Confession. Holy communion. How religion works and A very special gift.

At the age of seven, it was customary for all Catholic boys and girls to make their first confession and then receive their first holy communion. Prior to this, one had to have a knowledge of the complete Catechism which is a book containing all of the rules and regulations required to be a good Catholic. At Ponsbourne Park we were required to learn the Catechism off by heart, and be able to recite it whenever a question was hurled at you by either a nun or a priest. The Catechism is a very scary book, not the least, because it made you aware of what an appalling sinner you really were, and that if you were to follow all of its rules, you would be treading on eggshells for the rest of your mortal existence.

Even more frightening was the thought that even if you did manage to get to the end of your life without too much sinning, there was still a very good chance that you would not necessarily end up in God's Heaven. This prognosis does not bode well for the average Catholic, and it certainly scared the shit out of me. I'm not sure if any other faiths require confession as part of their doctrine, but given it's intimate nature, one can perfectly understand the nervousness and trepidation that a seven year old boy or girl might experience on their journey to faith. How much wrong can kids of this age actually be responsible for anyway? In my particular case I was probably guilty of a lot of small misdemeanours normally in the guise of scrounging, swearing and stealing the odd little bit of jam or lemon curd from another pupil's table when they weren't watching. I never regarded such things as stealing, preferring to regard them as my own contribution to the re-distribution of wealth. Robin Hood would have been proud of both myself and my brother, as we managed to re-distribute quite a bit of wealth in our young days at boarding school. We were first class 'scroungers' mainly because we didn't have a 'pot to piss in' and the only way of easing that situation was to become adept at extracting such luxuries from other people. The consequences of all of this activity however, left me in no doubt that I was headed to Hell without any doubt.

The first confession was also a very frightening experience for this seven year old. Not least because it required you to list your sins and misdemeanours to a priest, who would then administer a penance for you to carry out as a punishment for your sinning. Sinning was categorised in two separate categories. Small sins such as swearing without using the name of the Lord, or losing your temper were classified as 'venial' sins, and these sins only carried a punishment of time spent in a place called Purgatory. On the other hand sins including stealing, murder, adultery, taking the Lord's name in vain or missing Mass on Sunday were classified as 'mortal'

140

sins, and these sins would get you straight into the fires of Hell. All 'mortal' sins were direct transgressions of the 10 Commandments, and if you died in 'mortal' sin you went straight to hell for ever. I learned my 10 Commandments very quickly and could reel them off without any hesitation at all. The only worrying thing to me was that even as young as I was at the time, I had already broken one or two of these commandments and so was definitely reserved a place in Hell at some time in the near or distant future. This was not a good situation for my young mind to comprehend, and I spent a lot of my young life worrying about my fate in the next life. I envied those who did not believe in an 'afterlife' as they were free to enjoy the present one without any worries. Much later on, John Lennon described such a scenario in his song 'Imagine' and it struck a lot of valid chords with many of my generation who grew up worrying about the consequences of their past indiscretions.

Purgatory, on the other hand, was described as a place somewhere in between Heaven and Hell where sinners went to be cleansed before being allowed into heaven. There was no guarantee how long one had to spend in Purgatory before being allowed into Heaven, but it was described to all of us as a very long time. Now the way around all of this 'fire and brimstone' was going to confession. You simply went to the priest, confessed all of your sins, and apart from doing a little penance 'Hey Presto' you were absolved from all of your sins. Most penances consisted of saying a few prayers by way of cleansing your soul of sin, and once this was completed you were once again in what the church describes as a 'state of grace'. In broad terms, this allowed you to go out and commit a few more sins, in the knowledge that at your next confession you would be forgiven all over again. This was like a 'get out of jail' card, imagine our present penal system working on that basis....who the hell would need prisons? Just send all of the 'offenders' to confession and all of their problems are solved. We could rely on all of the rapists, muggers, robbers and muderers to go see the priest and then let them loose in the certain knowledge that, now that they were all in a state of grace, they would be no further problem to society.

Confession somewhat resembled the life of a washing machine, in which you threw your dirty washing every so often, and penance was akin to the washing powder that quickly and efficiently removed all of the stains. Even at the young age of seven, I could already deduce a few contradictions and perhaps even a small degree of hypocrisy in the wonderful ways of confession. I realised that you could become the biggest offender on the planet, doing all kinds of mean, nasty things to other people and then simply absolve yourself from all responsibility with a simple visit to the confessional.

Prayer was also another way of earning 'Brownie' points to get you out of Purgatory. Various prayers carried a certain amount of deductible days from your time spent in Purgatory. If you said these prayers regularly you could accumulate several days, weeks or months off your time. Known as 'plenary indulgences', they were akin to receiving luncheon vouchers which could be cashed in against your particular crimes. If prayer is the way to salvation, then we should all have earned our freedom a very long time ago. We spent our whole lives praying, with daily visits to the chapel and morning and evening prayers as well. There were prayers before and after every meal known as 'Grace', there were prayers getting out in the morning and returning for bed at night. There were prayers before and after every lesson in the school rooms and there were prayers before any sporting or competition event in the school calendar. We spent more time on our knees than in any other posture. In spite of all of this praying, I still calculated that I would have to spend an eternity in Purgatory just to make up for my daily 'ducking' and 'diving'.

Preparations for first confession and first communion took over your whole life for many weeks. There was a lot to learn, and everything would be examined and re-examined to ensure that you were fully prepared for those very important days. There would be rehearsal after rehearsal with the nuns to ensure that you knew every word off by heart, and they were not shy in whacking you around the head if you made any mistakes. My ears were often singing after receiving a good clout from one of the nuns, and I often wondered if they ever bothered to confess their own cruelty when they made their own individual confessions. It seemed somewhat ironic that these people could be the biggest tyrants in their treatment of their young charges and then go and get forgiven so that they could do it all over again. This religion had some very weird anomalies but the biggest of all were the nuns and priests that were responsible for our education and so-called spiritual well-being. How did they justify such actions to themselves, let alone their church and their God?

Another problem that I had at this time, was the need to produce my birth certificate, and I wrote frantically to my parents requesting that they send it through as soon as possible. Day followed day and week followed week, but still my birth certificate had not arrived. I was getting really worried that if it did not arrive, I would not be able to make my first communion - more seriously than this I was getting daily 'bollockings' from the nuns and teachers about the missing certificate. I tried to reassure them that I had indeed been born, and in the conventional way. But without that certificate I was 'persona non grata' in the eyes of the teachers, in the eyes of the church and in the eyes of the school - what a fucking mess!

When the offending certificate did eventually arrive, only about three days before the communion day, there seemed to be an even bigger problem, and this was brought about by the fact that on my birth certificate I was christened John James Marion Ruth, but the school knew me as Seamus Ruth. Rockets went up in all quarters especially as the nuns had by this time made up our first communion certificates and, of course, my one was now printed with the wrong names. Aloysius, along with a few other tyrant nuns berated me for days, and I couldn't pass her in either a corridor or the playground without feeling the back of her hand around my ear. Urgent phone calls were made to my parents for clarification about my names, and an explanation as to why I was not called

John James Marion Ruth as per my birth certificate. I was asked the same questions, but could not even venture an explanation for this puzzling riddle. I was seven years old, for Christ's sake! I was more concerned about losing my teeth and ending up with a 'gappy' mouth. What the feck did I know about the use of names as applied to the Irish race?

Now, when a child makes their first confession it can be quite unnerving, especially as you are telling your private secrets to a complete stranger, and then relying on him to be a bit sensitive when he hands out your penance. It's even more unnerving when the priest that you are about to confess to is known to you. In our case, we all knew the priest who would be listening to our future confessions very well indeed. This priest was Father George Leeson who was the resident chaplain of St Dominic's Priory, and who lived in the convent with the rest of the nuns. George Leeson was an imposing and kindly man who loved to gather the children around him. He visited the playground every single day and so he got to know most of the boarders very well indeed. He had been a naval chaplain during World War II and after completing his bit of 'soldiering' on the high seas he was now living an idyllic, quiet and innocuous life at the priory school. He had a pronounced limp which, we were told, was a result of injuries that he sustained during the war, and the rumour was that he had rescued some of his fellow shipmates when his ship was sunk by enemy U boats. George Leeson didn't have an offensive bone in his body and he was as far removed as one could possibly be from the disciplined and oppressive regime that was propagated by the nuns who shared his church. He was a quietly-spoken man, who never lost his temper and never ever berated the children that surrounded his every visit to the playground.

Be that as it may, we knew very little of the war years because we were born just a little bit later, and very few people seemed keen to discuss the war with us. Father George Leeson was such a person, we often asked him about his war stories, but he always managed to avoid the questions put to him. I think he was probably aware of how disturbing some of these stories may have been, or perhaps he had his own compelling reasons why he did not want to be reminded of such a time. I remember, around this time, being very interested in building models of aircraft and ships and I spent a lot of my pocket money on 'Revell' and 'Airfix' model kits. At one stage I brought a pack of balsa wood back to school after the holidays with the intention of building a flying model of an aeroplane. I struggled for weeks to build something that would actually fly, but I had no great success and discarded it into my locker in disgust. Father Leeson was aware that I was trying to build the aircraft and would often inquire about its progress, I had to finally admit to him, one day, that I had given it up as a bad job, I simply couldn't do any more with it.

One of the main reasons that the aeroplane had proved so hard for me to build was the lack of proper tools and glues. I didn't have enough equipment to do the model justice in spite of many hours invested in its construction.

There was no way that the nuns were going to allow us to possess Stanley knives or hobby tools of any kind, and as the school did not have many craft subjects in its curriculum, such items were almost impossible to obtain. I also had to hide my efforts from prying eyes, especially those of the nuns as I had no doubt that they would immediately confiscate it and that would be the last I would see of it for ever. I was also becoming far too busy learning my Catechism for the upcoming holy Communion tests that were a regular part of our routine, and we were only weeks away from the actual day of our Communion.

Father Leeson was well aware of all these facts, but he always encouraged and admired youngsters who took the initiative to create things, no matter how badly they might turn out. He insisted that I brought the little plane to him on his next visit to the playground so that he could take a look at it, and that's exactly what I did. As he studied the construction of my little aeroplane and moved it around in his big hands, he must have been suitably impressed with the progress I had made. He slipped the model carefully into a small box and told me that he would take it away and see what he could do with it. "Don't tell the nuns" I said to him alarmingly "or I'll be in for it". With a knowing smile and a little tap of his finger on his nose, he winked at me and slipped the aeroplane into the pocket of his big black cassock. That was the last I heard of the little aeroplane, and as the weeks counted down to the Sunday of my first Communion the whole episode had been forgotten by me in a frenzy of rehearsals, guilt trips, and religious tests for our big day.

First Communion Sunday finally arrived, all of us were very excited that all of the work of the last several weeks was now firmly behind us, and that apart from a few bruises inflicted by Aloysius and company we had come through it all virtually unscathed. The other exciting thing was that we would be seeing our parents for the first time in weeks.

As the big day dawned, eight small boys were dressed up in white shirts and white trousers, and I also had to wear a pair of horrible white plastic sandals that, not only, cut into my heels at every step, but also, gave me blisters on my feet at every point of contact. Despite this, I carried on regardless, and the thought of seeing my parents for the first time in weeks more than compensated for the army of blisters that were now growing across both of my feet. There were fourteen of us taking our first holy communion that day, six girls were also included in the line-up and all of our parents were invited to both the service itself and the breakfast which followed.

Of course all of us were on our best behaviour for such an important occasion, having been warned in no uncertain terms what the consequences would be if we were found lacking. That morning we had all ben 'scrubbed' to within an inch of our lives, and while some of us looked 'contrite' and 'saintly', others looked like they had survived a few rounds in the ring. My own appearance was one of 'tussled' hair and several missing teeth, and this ensured that my communion photo was never on display at any time in our household. Strangely enough the nuns were also on their best behaviour, I guess they had to play up to the parents and give the impression of one big, happy family – it worked very well and our parents were blissfully unaware of what a cruel crowd of hypocrites some of these people were.

The church service went without a single hitch and this was followed by a beautiful breakfast laid out in the main reception area of the convent. When it came to putting on a show for the parents, the Dominican nuns excelled in every way. The food was excellent and my parents were very impressed with the presentation of the room and the serving of the food which was carried out by some of the elder girl boarders. Little did our parents know, that for the previous week leading up to communion Sunday, a small army of kids including myself had been busy polishing the highly-varnished floors and cleaning and shining all of the brass and silverware that were in abundance on all of the tables. I remember my mum and dad commenting on the hard work that the Sisters had put in to achieve such a wonderful standard of cleanliness, but I decided not to bother enlightening them about the reality of how this wonderful transformation had come about. If the term 'child exploitation' had been coined in those days, we would certainly have been the epitome of it! Thankfully, we knew no other way and so these exploitations were simply the norm to us at the time. Regardless of all of this, we had a really wonderful day to look forward to, and our bad thoughts were put on hold for a short while.

After breakfast, all of the new 'communicants' were ushered out onto the grand palisade steps where a photographer had assembled all of his equipment in order to record the special day. The photographer busied himself in preparation for the shots that he was planning, and we all giggled incessantly as he covered both himself and the camera in a big black cloth in order to take his pictures Most of us lads with the large gaps in our mouths as evidence of missing milk teeth, made sure that we smiled broadly. I had two big gaps to show off to the photographer but this didn't stop me from opening my 'gob' as wide as possible. The tooth fairy did not exist at Ponsbourne Park in spite of several lads placing their teeth under their pillows at night. He or she had obviously embargoed our school, because in all of its history not a single sixpence was found under any pillows in our dormitories.

Notwithstanding the above, we were now assembled in three neat rows on the school steps, so that everyone could be seen in the pictures that were about to be taken. Father George Leeson joined us all for the photographs, and we were then all lined up to receive our commemorative communion medals from the kindly priest. As I waited for my name to be called, Father Leeson whispered to the nun assisting him with the presentation and she disappeared into the convent returning with a large shoe-sized box. As I waited for him to pin my medal on to my shirt, I noticed the nun passing the box to Father Leeson, he turned to me and said "here is your communion medal, I hope you will always remember this day, and in this box is a little something to remember me by." I was completely puzzled by the box, as were all of my peers, they had all received their medals, but not one of them had been given anything else.

As we returned to the breakfast table where our parents had now assembled for coffee, my Dad asked me what was in the box, I explained that I had no idea and as we both opened it I was absolutely thrilled to see this beautiful model aeroplane that Father Leeson had built with his own hands. The detail on the model was incredible, and one could see that a lot of time and patience had been invested in its construction. Every component, from the wing flaps and cockpit, right down to the individual propellers, had been beautifully carved and painted. I had never ever received such a beautiful gift from anyone in my whole lifetime so far, and I knew that it must have taken Father Leeson many, many hours to build such a special toy. To call it a toy would probably be an injustice, for it was now more a work of art, and was far too special to fling around in the school playground. I knew that this lovely gift had to be cherished in a very special way. There was no way that I could have constructed such a beautiful thing on my own. I was really touched by the whole event.

When, a little later on, my Father got the opportunity to talk to father Leeson and thank him for the gift, the priest explained to him about my own efforts in trying to construct the aeroplane. He had decided at that moment that those small efforts should not go unrewarded. I walked around all day with the aeroplane in my hands and was certainly the envy of all of my friends. This had been a happy and memorable day for so many wonderful reasons. The only 'downside' in all of that day were those horrible plastic white sandals that had almost ripped my feet apart and given me more blisters than a sunburnt plank.

Such episodes in my life reminded me that, in the harshness and cruelty of those times, someone special and kind would always turn up and create an event that would make the times so much more tolerable. Such a person was Father George Leeson. I asked my father to take the aeroplane home with him and for many years later it took pride of place hanging from the ceiling in my bedroom. It was later joined by several other Airfix models of various aircraft from the Second World War – I suppose that this was my first serious hobby, and one that would last for many years to come.

Chapter 9
Scrounging. A Load of frozen Rubbish and the Kennedy Intercession

On the 22nd of November 1963 President John Fitzgerald Kennedy was assassinated in Dallas Texas at about 12.15 local time. The news of this momentous tragedy was quickly flashed around the world in a series of news broadcasts, and Dallas became the centre of everyone's world for a good few weeks. At the precise time of the shooting, I was, for reasons best known to my stupid self, busy rummaging through several smelly dustbins in the corner of the school playground. It was tea time in England and I recall it being a severely frosty evening at Ponsbourne Park. I had been rummaging through the school bins for about two and a half hours dressed only in a light pullover, short trousers and very light socks and shoes. My friends and peers had all gone off to tea in the school refectory, and the 'lucky blighters' would now be on their way to a warm supper. The reason that I was 'rummaging around' in those dustbins on this cold and frosty November day, was to search and recover a sweet wrapper to produce as evidence of a misdemeanour that I had committed earlier in the afternoon. Once I had found and recovered it, I was to report to Aloysius for a 'damn' good strapping for 'scrounging'.

The actual search was devoted to the recovery of a wrapper from a Caramac chocolate bar that I knew I would be unlikely to recover on the basis that I had already flushed the 'offending' item in the boy's toilets. There were about seven very large dustbins to search in, and this was now proving to be both a mammoth and very cold and smelly task. Caramac was a brand of chocolate bar that was beigey brown in appearance and was caramel flavoured. I had previously scrounged the Caramac bar from Stuart Matthews, a day pupil, while we were playing in the school playground just after the lunchtime break. Stuart had befriended me some months earlier, and I had even visited his parent's farmhouse just outside Cuffley for Sunday afternoon tea on a couple of occasions. Stuart was probably the only day pupil who I had struck up a firm friendship with, and I had helped him a lot with various homework tasks in the preceding few weeks. The deal on this particular day was that he provided me with the chocolate bar in exchange for me finishing his composition homework. This had to be completed in advance of the afternoon English lesson. Academically, composition was now my strongest and favourite subject, and apart from doing deals with my peers to help them out with compositions, I was also gainfully employed writing letters for them to send home to their parents at weekends.

My fees for these activities ranged from receiving sweets, fruit or cakes (commonly known as 'tuck') right up to receiving jams, sauces and beverages at meal times. Occasionally my brother and I would do deals for 'Dinky'

154

or 'Corgi' model cars, so there was very little in the way of material assets that we couldn't lay our hands on. These items were simply luxuries which my parents just could not afford to buy for us, but the wealthier kids possessed them in abundance, and we were always on the lookout for new customers who were willing to swap our services for these valuable rewards. As far as the school was concerned, such activities were still classified as 'cadging' or 'scrounging', and the 'sly Ruths' were right at the top of the heap when it came to deals and trade-offs. Not a day went by without some 'dodgy transaction taking place. Of course, we were not the only ones plying our trade in the school playground. There were always little deals going down in and around the school, and the name of the game was never to get caught. Kids would trade almost anything for either swops or favours, and a whole network of 'opportunists' were busily taking advantage of the trend.

We were always very careful and secretive about these little deals, and we took a lot of time and trouble to ensure we were never caught unawares by unwanted prying eyes. Unfortunately for me, on that particular day, I was spotted taking delivery of the offending chocolate bar by a very strict and, as it turns out, very observant and 'nosey' nun named Sister Corletti. I had never had any dealings with Corletti up until this time, although my elder sister, Brenda had previously been in her class and had told us several stories of what a strict 'bitch' Corletti had been. Corletti could be as cruel as Aloysius and although she was not as loud and in your face, she was capable of intimidating her victims with a mixture of steely-eyed resolve and a large amount of sheer malice. Brenda told me that she was as terrified of Corletti as we were of Aloysius. So it came as no surprise to me that Corletti would be quite happy to report my illicit dealings , and she didn't waste any time in getting stuck in.

It was Corletti who had previously given my brother and I the unflattering title of 'The sly Ruths'. She had made it her business to find out how we, as two of the poorest pupils in the school, were always in possession of, not only, the latest toys, but also more than our fair share of sweets and 'goodies.' She was blissfully unaware how hard both I and my brother worked to keep our various enterprises and 'illicit' dealings away from prying eyes. We shared our secrets with no-one in the certain knowledge that a secret shared could quite easily bring a whole pile of 'shit' down on your head, especially in this place. We resolved never to get caught out by careless talk on our parts, and employed this 'dictum' in all of our manoeuverings.

Most of the boarding kids we had dealings with were aware of the unwritten rule of secrecy, but this particular incident would be the exception that proved the rule. This silly little transaction with Stuart would be my undoing, because I had not warned him that the deal had to be in the strictest confidence. He was blissfully unaware of how much trouble I would be in for taking the chocolate bar. There was no doubt in my mind that Stuart would unwittingly 'spill the beans' if put under any pressure by the nuns. Needless to say Corletti applied plenty of pressure to the naive Stuart.

An investigation of the incident was instigated by Sister Aloysius who had been informed by Corletti of my 'scrounging'. Both of the nuns had already interviewed Stuart at great length, and extracted his version of the events. I was dragged out of my classroom at about half past two in the afternoon and marched into Aloysius's classroom for interrogation. Any dealings with Aloysius were always bound to be painful. Today she had the bright red face of a 'raging bull' and an intimidatingly loud, booming voice that would scare the 'crap' out of anyone. Her loud verbal abuse was normally accompanied by a smear of spittle on both sides of her mouth, and as this condition increased, you would also be on the receiving end of a tirade of accusations and a shower of spittle. Her eyebrows moved up and down in time with her temper. Just one look from her intimidating eyes, which were magnified behind bi-focal glasses, was enough to turn your legs to jelly. So intimidating was she that she had the ability to get kids to admit to things they hadn't even done. Imagine the fear then, that she placed in those who had been caught fairly and squarely. I knew immediately that 'my goose was cooked', especially when she produced a piece of paper with a complete series of notes on the incident as reported by Corletti and the terrified Stuart Matthews. My mind was working overtime to try and mitigate the situation back into my favour, but she was already in full possession of all of the facts relating to the incident. I was desperately looking for a way to wriggle out of trouble, but there was one fatal flaw in all of my thoughts and calculations, and that was in the realisation that we were dealing with an offence involving a day-pupil.

Now, day pupils did not possess the same set of codes or values that the boarders did, especially when it came to wheeling and dealing. They were not schooled in the nuances of never telling or 'splitting' on another pupil. They had no idea of how much trouble that would get you in to. This unwritten code was not practised by the 50 odd day pupils that arrived on a coach every morning from the surrounding villages and hamlets. In many ways, they were encouraged to keep away from the boarders, and were even segregated from them during mealtimes. This day-pupil was no different from any of us in his fear of Aloysius, in spite of the fact that Aloysius would never raise her hand to hit a day-pupil. She would fear any reprisals or repercussions from angry parents whose kids went home to them every evening. Nevertheless, she still instilled an innate fear in them just by her scary presence and, of course, the various stories that would have circulated around the school about her. Poor Stuart Matthews was simply another victim who capitulated under the severe stress that both of these nuns were laying on him – and who could really blame him.

As I reported to Aloysius' classroom in the firm grip of the very smug Sister Corletti, I realised that this, without doubt, would be another day to remember. The inevitable first slap arrived out of the blue, long before any discussion had commenced. I knew that I was proven guilty by that one action alone. I was going to get a fair trial, and then they were going to fecking hang me! In that instant I realised that I must never ever put my trust in a day pupil ever again.

My nine year old ears were ringing in that now familiar way, as the slaps rained down on me in true Aloysius style. The story of the Caramac deal was played back to me by both of the nuns in a state of heightened excitement. Aloysius was in her element at being handed a culprit of 'blatant' scrounging, and she ranted and raged in her customary way, for what seemed hours. There was very little I could do to soften the situation, it was almost impossible to deny the facts or put off the inevitable consequences that would be manifesting themselves very shortly. Fortunately I had eaten the Caramac bar during my lunch playtime break. This had angered Aloysius even more, because she now had nothing to confiscate. She called me a greedy little tyke" and sent me back to my classroom with a tirade of abuse which included a brief description of my forthcoming punishment.

The first part of my punishment was that immediately after school and without going to tea with the rest of my class, I was to go to the school dustbins and recover the wrappers of the chocolate bar. When these were recovered I was to report to Aloysius with the wrappers and exchange them for the aforementioned 'strapping'. I was 'gutted' by the prospect of meeting up with her later. I was even more upset to see my friends heading off for the refectory and a lovely warm teatime, while I climbed in and out of dustbin after dustbin to try and find the wrappers that would later seal my fate. It was somewhat Ironic, but I knew that even in spite of sifting through tons

159

of 'shit' I would never be able to find the offending wrapper, I would be happy just to find any old Caramac wrapper to produce, but typically in all of those piles of rubbish there was not a single one to be had. As this was late November, the daylight was fading fast and a bitterly cold wind was 'whipping' around the dustbins. To think that one 'measly' Caramac bar had cost me my place at both tea and supper that day, filled me with anger. I was also starting to feel very cold because I had, stupidly, left my school blazer in the classroom which was now firmly locked. So, as well as being tired and hungry, I was about to freeze my 'bollocks' off in that 'smelly' corner of the playground which housed all of the school's rubbish..

As time marched on and darkness settled on the playground, I became increasingly aware of the night growing colder and colder. My hands and body were getting numb with the surrounding cold, and a fine coating of frost was now settling on the surfaces of the stainless steel dustbins. I was puzzled that no-one had come to find out where I was, and it dawned on me that none of the kids had returned from what was now the supper break – something very unusual had happened. Usually another kid would be sent by Aloysius to fetch you and it was now way past the time when most of the boarders would be finishing prep and making their way to the various dormitories. There wasn't a sound in the night playground now and the cold darkness sent me into shivers, I was becoming very cold, very tired and very hungry having now missed both tea and supper-this was not a good situation to be in. There was also an added problem and that was the lack of a Caramac wrapper. I had sifted through piles and piles of putrid garbage and other offensive waste products, but was unable to find a single wrapper of that description. How unbelievable that a chocolate bar as popular as Caramac was letting me down in such a big way-surely some other pupil had eaten one today.

Just when I thought that things were really hopeless, I heard the sound of someone moving around outside of the dustbin storage area. I was suddenly dazzled by a torch beam shining directly into my face, and a large hand was lifting me bodily out of the dustbin. I was scared 'shitless' until I realised that Mr Reardon the school caretaker was on the other end of that big hand, he had heard noises coming from the bins and had stopped to investigate. He probably thought that he would find an inquisitive fox or rat rummaging about for scraps of food, and certainly not a 'scantily-clad' little lad. I was shivering with both the cold and the shock of my sudden extraction, and Mr Reardon hurriedly wrapped me up in his big coat and walked me across the playground to his boiler house.

The sudden heat from the two vast boilers was a wonderful change from the freezing cold of the dustbins. I shivered on a chair in the welcoming heat, as Mr Reardon handed me a steaming enamel mug full of sweet hot tea. Mr Reardon was firing questions at me about the events of my afternoon. I related the incident of the Caramac bar, and my reasons for being in the school dustbins. He explained that all of the other kids were down in the church praying for President Kennedy who had been assassinated. Although I knew who John F. Kennedy was, I had never heard the word 'assassinated' before and he explained that the president had been killed by shooting; I was quite shocked by this news as even I knew that Kennedy was a very popular president.

I could see that Mr Reardon was angry and saddened by the News from America but he was also livid at finding a young boy in such circumstances. He told me that he would be talking to the headmistress and Aloysius in no uncertain terms. I told him that I would probably be in much more trouble if he said anything, "don't you worry about that my lad, I'm taking you straight to the infirmary, you could have frozen to death in those dustbins". An hour later I was cosily tucked up in the school infirmary with a kindly nun named Sister Centonni providing hot cornflakes and cocoa. I had previously heard Mr Reardon and herself discussing the whole incident and for the first time in my life at Ponsbourne Park, I realised that Aloysius might not always be able enjoy the cruel and vicious autonomy that was her erstwhile domain. Both Mr Reardon and Sister Centonni agreed that my treatment at the hands of Aloysius was completely unacceptable on this cold November night, but then their conversation drifted on to the events which were unravelling in Dallas, Texas.

Notwithstanding all of the above, my fear of Sister Aloysius was not diminished by the events that had just taken place. I knew that at some stage the incident of the Caramac bar was bound to raise its ugly head and come back to bite me. Strangely enough, it never did. I was back in the classroom the following morning and apart from a few questions and comments from some of my friends it was never referred to again. Even Corletti threw a glancing and knowing smile in my direction as she sauntered through the playground on route to her classroom, I figured that maybe she and Aloysius must have got the 'dressing down' of their lives, if not from Mr Reardon, then, perhaps from the headmistress and Mother Superior of the convent. I secretly hoped that the pair of them had received a really good 'bolloking'.

As the days went by, the threat of retribution from Aloysius still figured heavily in all of my waking hours. I was careful to avoid bumping into her and took every precaution to ensure that I was never long in her presence. The attention of the whole school seemed to be focused on the events in America and I managed to convince myself that perhaps Aloysius, in a state of temporary shock, had completely forgotten about the Caramac incident. Everyone's time and attention seemed to be taken up with the ongoing reports of the assassination of President Kennedy and then the shock revelations of the shooting of Lee Harvey Oswald the accused assassin.

We recited rosary after rosary and spent many more hours on our knees in both the dormitories and the chapel. Daily masses and evening benediction were increased during that week leading up to the state funeral. Our lessons and daily routines seemed to float out of the window amid a torrent of praying, mourning and reading the newspaper headlines. I realised that I was a lucky lad to get away with the scrounging incident, and resolved to be a lot more careful in the future.

In the weeks following this incident, Mr Reardon would often talk to me in the playground and make sure I was okay, he took a special interest in all that I was doing, and very occasionally I would re-join him in the boiler room for an illicit cup of tea. I never did find out whether he had taken Aloysius to task or not, but I had my suspicions that he certainly must have made some comments in the right ears. All of my questions to him were responded to with, a knowing wink and, very little comment.

President Kennedy's death created a massive impact in every newspaper of the day and there is no doubt that most people can remember exactly what they were doing when they heard the news of his killing. I have no doubt in my mind that if Kennedy had not been assassinated, I would definitely have received my 'comeuppance' from Aloysius on that cold November night in 1963. I was so grateful that both Mr Reardon and President Kennedy had come to my rescue both physically and, in the case of Kennedy, spiritually. I was also very aware that I would certainly remember what I was doing on the evening of the 22nd of November. As to the 'wheeling and dealing' that put me in that situation in the first place, things returned very quickly to normal, and I, for one, continued to illicit rewards in return for my writing services which were always in demand. I have no doubt that other little deals were being transacted by various pupils throughout the school, just as they always had been.

When I met up with Stuart Matthews, a few days after the incident, he was very contrite and told me that he had been worrying about my situation. He had even discussed the matter with his parents and had brought a letter written by them. I told him to tear the letter up as it would probably cause even more problems. The last thing I needed at that time was Aloysius being reminded of the incident, and my getting captured again. As I recounted the complete story of my night in the bins, we both laughed profusely and Stuart seemed relieved that the incident would not create a rift in our friendship. We remained firm pals right up until the end of our schooling, but I never again relied on any day pupil for favours or contraband, and I also went right off Caramac bars.

Chapter 10
Wet beds, a good hard slap on the back, The Marx Brothers and a set of flying teeth

The boys' junior dormitory was run by an elderly nun named Sister Albertina., the same Sister Albertina who previously worked in the laundry and regularly recruited us for the 'stamping of the socks. On the whole she was a kindly old soul, and while she still operated a strict disciplinary code of conduct, she was nothing like the 'ogre' of her colleague Aloysius. Sister Albertina was probably the eldest among her colleagues, and she had a kind of empathy that none of the other nuns seemed to possess. She wasn't big in the 'smiling' department, but then many of the nuns walked around with a half scowl on their faces, as if it were a prerequisite of their training. If you found a smiling nun in those days, she would turn out to be, either a very kind and genuine individual, or indeed, perhaps verging a little on the insane – there was no happy medium and the safest policy was to trust no one. I admit that it was one of my ambitions to try and get these nuns to smile a bit more often. Now that I was making some good progress academically, I was also starting to build a 'cheeky chappie' disposition that, for the most part, was beginning to work with a few of the more serious people around me.

I had moved into the junior dormitory in my third year at Ponsbourne Park and I was extremely excited about, not only, leaving the 'Cottagers or infant section, but also, the prospect of joining my elder brother who was in his last year in the juniors. He had advised me that Sister Albertina was not a bad old 'stick' and providing you kept on the right side of her you wouldn't go far wrong. It was a big help having my elder brother in the same dormitory, as he advised me of all the do's and don'ts of life in the juniors and also, of the likely pitfalls that could occur. He also made me aware of all of the 'troublemakers', bullies, and other undesirables to be avoided at all costs. My move to the juniors also allowed us to see a lot more of each other than in the previous two years of our schooling when we were virtually segregated from one another. I realised that life at Ponsbourne Park was getting slightly easier, and I now had an ally that I could put my trust in. The junior dorm seemed to be a happy place on the whole, and 'old Alberta' as she was affectionately known could show bouts of kindness that were rare and unusual in those days. Albertina's mission in life was to turn young boys into young men, and she achieved this by teaching the more practical skills of deportment and grooming. She would cure everything from uncombed hair, to getting rid of your slouch (if you possessed one) and she had no tolerance of 'scruffiness' or 'sloppiness'.

The junior dormitory held about 35 boys and our beds were arranged in neat rows along both sides of a long room. The room was divided by a central bulkhead which housed the obligatory dormitory stove and a hanging area for toilet bags, towels and dressing gowns. At the top of the dormitory was a washing area with a row of about 10 sinks where the boys would strip off and wash every morning. The highly polished floors provided a great sliding area for stockinged feet, and a lot of fun was had by all of us on this shiny surface. These were the same floors that would provide us with hours of fun during the polishing and shining process described previously. The bare floorboards were shone to a high-gloss finish, and if you were foolish enough to wet your bed, the resulting puddle would form a neat lake on the surface of the boards under your bed. Like I said before, there was no hiding place for bed-wetters, but in fairness to Albertina, she always made sure that the 'usual suspects' were woken from their sleep at regular intervals throughout the night to use the toilet. Persistent bed-wetters were provided with horrible rubber under blankets that protected the mattress and floors, but this meant that the poor 'sods' would be sleeping in a river of their own urine for hours and hours. Most dormitories had a fair share of bed-wetters and these guys suffered more than their fair share of ridicule, not just from the nuns, but also from their peers and house captains. My brother and I were fortunate that we were not 'bedwetters' per se, but there was always the possibility of the odd accident.

I remember wetting my bed one night and waking up in a state of sheer panic, I ran to my brother's bed and woke him up in a terrible state to get some help with my predicament. Between the two of us we stripped the sheets from my bed and rushed down to the boys toilets with them. I washed both sheets and my pyjamas in a real hurry, because there was always the possibility of Albertina arriving in the dormitory to wake up the usual bed-wetters. We washed the clothes and decided to rush them to Mr Reardon's boiler room which was situated a very long way from the dormitories. Having hung the sheets in front of one of the large school boilers and the pyjamas on a radiator in the toilets, we then had to return to the dorm to take care of the lake-sized puddle that was now under my bed, we also had a very wet mattress to take care of and it looked pretty likely that we would not enjoy much sleep on this particular night.

We were barely back in the dorm when Albertina appeared out of her room with a large torch which she used for her nightly inspections. Myself and my brother scuttled under a row of beds, like a pair of cockroaches, praying that Albertina would not discover that we were missing from our own individual beds. She clumped up and down the dormitory waking the bed-wetters who walked in a half stupor to the boys toilets. All the while we were terrified that at any moment Albertina would discover the two Ruth's were missing. The other worry was that she might go into the boys toilets and find my wet pyjamas. It seemed like hours that we lay there on the cold shiny wooden floor waiting for the dormitory to go silent again. Finally we heard the boys returning to their beds, and Albertina's footsteps receding back into the distance and her own room. We continued to clean the puddle from under my bed, and then wait to retrieve my sheets and pyjamas. My saving grace that night was that there was one empty bed in the dormitory which belonged to a lad that had been taken to the infirmary with measles. We quickly stripped the mattress off this bed and replaced it with my own wet one. It took hours and hours for my sheets and pyjamas to dry sufficiently enough for us to retrieve them, and having made a few return trips to the dormitory we swopped all of the sheets on to the empty bed. This whole operation took us almost until dawn to complete and certainly did no good for our individual nerves. We had no doubt that the damp, empty bed would soon be discovered by either Albertina, or the poor sick individual who resided in it. This would all occur at some time in the future, but we figured that the blame for this would probably fall on one of the bed-wetters – the 'sly' Ruths had triumphed again, but only through mutual cooperation and the ability to keep a secret and share it with no one.

Personal grooming figured high on the dormitory syllabus, and each boy had to learn how to make their own bed properly as well as maintaining their day clothes and shoes to a high standard. Bed making was regarded as one of the most important skills that a boy in the juniors had to learn. The bed was made using several techniques and skills that were apparently used in the nursing profession. Sheets were applied and folded in a certain fashion, and the top eiderdown was always neatly folded up and tucked under the pillow before being folded back to cover the pillow at the top. This gave the bed a very nice appearance as well as a uniform look all round, and ensured that the special folding of the bottom sheets and blankets would result in a bed that never became untidy. We had to practise this bed-making procedure for hours until every aspect of it became automatic to us, after that the standard had to be maintained at all times. Each boy had to make their own bed immediately after getting up in the morning, and before even washing or dressing. The younger lads were coached by their elders in all of these activities and many of them would be coerced into serving their masters in bed-making and other little jobs. We all knew our place.

When it came to personal hygiene there was no hiding place. Every morning we lined up in front of the dormitory basins and gave ourselves a complete wash-down from head to foot. Teeth had to be cleaned for at least two full minutes every morning and evening and hair had to be combed or brushed with a side parting. At weekends large amounts of Brylcreem were applied to our hair, especially on visiting Sundays when our best uniforms were handed out. Wrights Coal Tar soap was the brand used by the school and they frowned on any other scented soaps including Camay, Cussons Imperial Leather and Palmolive. We all smelled like washing machines on such occasions, and if you ever got caught falling below the standards there would be hell to pay. Shoe cleaning was carried out on Friday evenings in the boys' cloakroom and each boy was responsible for cleaning his own shoes, sandals and football boots. These were inspected regularly and had to be polished to the highest standard. I got very good very quickly at the shoe and boot cleaning, and it wasn't very long before I had launched another little business in this activity. I was cleaning boots and shoes for the wealthier and certainly lazier boys in the junior dorm. I was well rewarded for these services in the guise of tuck (sweets and chocolate) or jams and preserves at meal times. My brother had his own agenda for such activities, and between the pair of us, we were moving up in the world of 'wheeling' and 'dealing'. The Ruth brothers were slowly becoming the Ronnie and Reggie Krays of the barter system at Ponsbourne Park, the only difference was that no one was being threatened or murdered as part of the deal.

Every Saturday evening Sister Albertina handed out two shirts (one grey, one white), two pairs of socks one pair of trousers, two neck ties in the colours of the school (black and white) and in the colour of your house (green, red or blue.) one vest and one pair of underpants. These clothes were now your complete responsibility, and Sister Albertina enforced a strict rule of cleanliness and tidiness on her weekly allocation of uniform. Her biggest obsession was with personal hygiene and she had a big problem with soiled underpants. Each boy would line up to receive his change of clothes for the following week, and these were exchanged item by item. Punishments were doled out for damaged or filthy clothes, but the biggest event of the evening was Albertina's underpants inspection. Everyone lined up in the dormitory, and with both hands firmly holding your underpants open, you walked past Albertina who took a good look into them before allowing you to throw them on the washing pile.

Now, as I have mentioned in an earlier chapter, soiled underpants was a capital crime in Sister Albertina's world and anyone caught with dirty underpants got two whacks on the hand with the back of a wooden hairbrush. While this was a painful punishment, it wasn't anywhere near the pain of being strapped by Aloysius, and there was certainly no sadistic elements attached to Albertina's punishments. Nevertheless, it was unpleasant enough not to want it repeated in the future, and so the boys took very good care to avoid 'skid marks' in their underpants. I did fall foul of Albertina's hair brush on one occasion, and that was enough to convince me to keep a good eye on the condition of my underpants at all times. My brother had given me a tip of wearing them inside out and that way any little accidents would not be noticed by Albertina on a Saturday night inspection. A few of the boys who were likely to fall foul of the underpants inspection spent a lot of time not wearing them at all, but if you were caught without pants you would also be in a lot of trouble. Many of the boys would wash their soiled underpants in the boys' toilets on Friday evenings during shoe polishing duties. They would hang them in Mr Reardon's boiler room overnight, but if you were caught by a house captain or prefect you would be reported immediately. There was also the added problem of large amounts of other dirt appearing on your pants because of the filthy condition of the boiler room, or more fatally, the chance of burning them completely due to over -exposure to the boiler heat.

Occasionally Albertina would call an impromptu underpants inspection perhaps in the middle of the week and on those occasions she would find more 'skid marks' than the Brands Hatch racing circuit. If you were caught on any occasion that Albertina didn't have her 'trusty' hair brush with her, you would end up getting a big, hard smack of her hand on the bare back. These smacks would leave a big red map of her handprint on your skin for several hours afterwards. If you were on the receiving end of one of Albertina's hand slaps you certainly knew it, they were really painful and you then had to suffer the indignity of all of the boys laughing at the big red handprint that was now temporarily imprinted on your back for the next few hours. It was almost like having a 'whacking great' tattoo imprinted on your back. Having quickly recovered from the initial shock and pain, we would all laugh ourselves silly at this visual display of a hidden misdemeanour.

No one ever regarded Albertina as a cruel nun. I guess because her parameters and rules were well known to all of her charges. She was always very even-handed and treated every kid with respect. If you were unlucky enough to fall foul of her rules you were aware well in advance of the resulting consequences. Many months after joining the Juniors, I stole some underpants from a pile in the laundry, and these were in big demand prior to the Saturday night inspections. Lads who wished to avoid a big slap on the back or perhaps two slaps from Albertina's wooden hairbrush, would take advantage of my underpants rental business. Part exchanges were always welcomed and these would be washed and recycled with the aid of Mr Reardon's boiler house. On bath nights we were often required to share the same bathwater which was alright if you were one of the first few kids to jump in. It wasn't such a bundle of laughs however, if you were five or six down the list. By that time the water was so cold and scummy, that it resembled a stagnant mill-pond. There was a poem on the bathroom wall which we all had to learn off by heart and recite on demand. It was called the Bathroom Poem and went as follows:

> **Please remember, don't forget.**
> **Never leave the bathroom wet.**
> **Nor leave the soap still in the water,**
> **That's a thing you never oughta.**
> **Nor leave the towels about the floor,**
> **Nor keep the bath an hour more.**
> **When other folk are wanting one,**
> **Please don't forget, it's never done.**

Bath nights were always great fun however, as there was always high jinx going on. Competitions were regularly held to see who could keep their head under the water the longest. There were games around blowing soap through your face flannels to create artificial beards and moustaches. Towel and water fights were common occurrences and of course, boys being boys, there was always a lot of comparisons of each other's anatomies and in particular penis lengths. You never wanted to be the subject of any jibes or criticisms of your personal appendages, but we all got our fair share of these, especially from the older and slightly more mature boys. It was just another part of boarding school life. Nothing was sacred when it came to such activities, and if you were a 'shrinking violet' it soon got knocked out of you one way or another. Whenever anyone insulted me about the length of my penis (It was, by the way, quite a normal one in every way) Iwould reply, "It may not be large, but would you want it on the end of your nose as a wart?" This normally took care of any further insults.

My move up to the juniors coincided with a move of classroom and I would now join my peers in class 3 which was run by a lovely nun named Sister Joseph. Joseph was a very kind and quietly spoken individual who inspired all of the children in her care, I suppose that she could almost be described as 'saintly' especially when compared with some of the other tyrants that shared our space. She was an amazing artist and her teaching methods ensured that every pupil would attain a very high standard in both English and Maths. Sister Joseph walked with a severe limp and she always used a walking stick to help her along, this walking stick was made of Irish Blackthorn which had been highly polished and varnished, and you could hear her coming for miles because of the distinctive 'clacking' of the stick on the floors. We jokingly called her 'Long John Silver' which was probably a little cruel at the time, but then Treasure Island was one of the books that she introduced us to.

Her biggest talent was in the teaching of 'calligraphy' and as this would be the first time that we, as pupils, would be learning how to use a fountain-pen. She insisted that our parents provide us with a good quality pen fitted with an italic nib, together with one black and one blue bottle of quality ink. In those days there were two popular brands of ink one was 'Stephens' and the other more popular brand was 'Quink'. I wrote home to my parents explaining the need for a good quality fountain pen and, although money was very tight they bought me a Platignum pen. This pen was a very nice red one, with a unique self-filling ink reservoir and was still many years prior to the introduction of ink cartridges. I treasured this pen and it lasted me for the rest of my schooling at Ponsbourne Park. From this time forward, all classwork and homework was carried out by fountain pen, but worse than this 'italic' writing was the only acceptable medium in which written work was allowed to be submitted. If there was any hint of a 'biro' or 'ball point' pen you could guarantee a severe reprimand from all of the teachers. Italic writing is a slow process, as the nib of the pen is turned in different directions to provide varied thicknesses of script on the paper. The problem was that everything took twice as long to write and it was very easy to blot the copy sheet with too much ink. Homework and Prep became a real task using this slower medium of writing, but even I had to admit that the writing standards of all the pupils improved beyond recognition.

Sister Joseph's lessons were inspirational to all of her pupils, and she never raised a hand in anger at any one. She often rewarded good work with a Quality Street chocolate, and if you were on the receiving end of one of these rare delicacies, you knew that you were doing well.

During the course of my time in her class she inspired me into writing some of my most creative essays, and it was her influence above any other that instilled the desire in me to become a journalist. She marked all of her pupil's work very thoroughly and then allocated a coloured star according to the standard of the work. Gold and silver stars denoted a high standard of achievement and I worked really hard to ensure that nothing less than a silver or gold star was achieved.

During my time in class three Sister Joseph found out that my Mother was nursing in a General Hospital, and she wrote and asked my Mother if she could get hold of any old or discarded X-ray film. A few weeks later on 'Visiting Sunday' my Mother turned up with a big box of these used films and Sister Joseph thanked her profusely for them. We were all puzzled by such a strange request from the little nun and wondered what possible use she would put these to. We later found out that she had found a way of removing the images of broken limbs and other injuries so that the film was now perfectly clear. She then processed these films and fashioned them into framed religious pictures and many other kinds of artistic objects. These were then sold in the school shop to raise money for charity.

Sister Joseph also collected used stamps, milk bottle tops and silver paper, and it wasn't long before many of the parents were sending boxes of these items to her. She turned these items into cash and then provided money to several charities including Oxfam, Crusade of Rescue, and Cafod the Catholic charity. She was assisted in these activities by many of the boarder boys who would assemble in her classroom on Saturday mornings to sort out the stamps and silver paper. Needless to say, she was never short of volunteers, who had become more than aware of her rewards in the form of slightly stale buttered brown and white bread, Quality Street chocolates or Peanut Brittle.

I realised that the introduction of both Albertina and Joseph into my school life would change things for the better, firstly because I had found two more nuns that were not complicit in the cruelty and sadistic actions of Aloysius and her cohorts, but, more importantly, because they would become 'role models' in their care of the kids who came into contact with them. I never, however, eased myself too much into a feeling of security or well-being, because I knew very well that there waiting for me, in a future move to the senior part of the school, was Aloysius in all her 'demonic' presence.

For the moment however life wasn't at all bad and my peers and I were making real progress with our personal grooming and becoming more aware of our personal image.. We all tried to emulate the Beatles haircuts, but found this nigh on impossible because of the brutal haircuts inflicted on us by the visiting barbers. I settled for a more Adam Faith or Frank Ifield look with a little wavy 'quiff' to the fringe, and a nice neat parting. We were also avoiding, more and more, the instances of Albertina's large hand marks emblazoned on our bare backs like an ugly red tattoo. Girls were also beginning to figure more in our interests, and we never tired of trying to catch a glimpse of a girl in an uncompromising position. This was nigh on impossible, given the strict segregation, but we did get together in the classroom and on visits to the chapel.

Another aspect of life in the juniors, was the three-weekly visit of the barbers that I have just mentioned. Three of them would roll up in a small van and set up their temporary cutting room in the juniors cloakroom. Three tall teacher's chairs were carefully placed in the centre of the room and they would plug their electric cutters into three individual light sockets. We had no idea of their actual names, but they were given the nicknames of the 'Marx Brothers' due to one of them having an uncanny likeness to Groucho Marx. The three of them worked with quiet zeal with rarely a word being uttered by any of them, and they could cut nearly sixty heads of hair within a few short hours. The cut was pretty much American marine in appearance and we all felt like we had been attacked by a bunch of mad sheep shearers. For days after such a cut, your neck would be inflamed from friction marks administered by the clearly unsharpened trimmers that they employed. They also occasionally nicked the odd ear lobe with their sharp scissors, and the victim would report to the infirmary with profuse bleeding. I dreaded every single haircut for fear of one of these 'bastards' slitting my throat by mistake!

Groucho Marx, himself, was prone to a lot of sniffing during his visits, and if you were unlucky enough to be in his chair during one of these bouts, you could guarantee a neck full of 'phlegm' as his sneezes exploded behind your head. On one occasion the whole room went into mass hysterics when he managed to sneeze his top and bottom dentures right across the room like an aeroplane taking off. He calmly, threw a few 'fucks' about as he recovered his teeth from the ever-growing pile of hair. He then held them under the cloakroom tap to remove as much hair and grime as he could, and finally reinserted them as if nothing unusual had occurred. There were absolutely no exchanges of conversation from them to us, and if you dared to ask any of them for a particular style of cut, you could guarantee not only a cold silence, but an even more severe haircut than you would normally receive. Their glaring eyes said a thousand words, and their was little point in even trying to communicate with them. Many of us would try and pull our shirt collars right up towards our head, hoping that the barbers would trim less off our necks, but while this worked for a few of us, in the main, it was short back and sides for everyone without exception.

Life in the juniors was not at all bad, there was a more relaxed attitude here than would be experienced by boys moving into the senior dorms. Old Albertina was very generous with everyone providing her strict rules were adhered to. She would often allow a few select boys to sit up after lights out, and listen to the radio in her sewing room. Her chosen programmes would be the Archers or maybe the odd play on the BBC. If she ever left the room for any reason, we would all be busy spinning the dial to find a popular pop music channel like Caroline or Radio London just to keep us up to date with the latest hits. Albertina would often speak about the war years, and her anecdotes certainly captured the imagination of her young audience. She was also very generous with kids like myself and my brother who never possessed a great deal of pocket money. She would often just hand us a few sweets or chocolates during the tuck-time sessions, or encourage other more wealthy kids to share some of their spoils with those less fortunate. She liked to listen to the kids relating their day's activities to her, and loved a really good laugh whenever these anecdotes amused her.

Chapter 11
Ben Hur. A good hiding for all. The Beatles. A great big freeze-up and several new bumps and fads

Every school has its own fads and trends, and these are reflected in the games and pastimes enjoyed by the scholars. Ponsbourne Park was no exception, and games came and went just like the seasons of the year. The girls would be entertained with skipping ropes and hopscotch, and the boys would delight in British bulldog, cricket, rounders and, of course, football. Less active kids would be buried in stamp-collecting, card swops, jigsaw puzzles, chess, draughts and marbles. It didn't really matter which games took up your time and interest, providing you were enjoying them.

My brother Liam was beginning to turn into a bit of a trend-setter. He had started to tell stories in the junior dormitory after lights out, and the boys enjoyed them so much, that they got permission from Sister Albertina to have a story every night. His stories varied from the very silly, to the very scary and it wasn't long before ghost stories became the popular choice in the dormitory. While these stories greatly entertained most of the boys, there were a few lads that were literally 'scared shitless' by them, so much so that many of them would have difficulty getting off to sleep for fear of the darkness. These stories earned my brother a big reputation with all of the juniors, and he often struggled to find new story lines to share with his dormitory audience.

At about that time, he came up with a playground game called the 'Yankee Bumpers'. The game consisted of two teams of guys all running about with their arms folded in front of them. When either team spotted a member of the opposition they would run at each other at full speed, like a pair of mad bulls and try and bump one another out of the way. Needless to say, this was quite a violent game, and provided plenty of casualties for the infirmary. It became immensely popular however, and soon most of the junior and senior boys were making it their chosen activity at playtime. Anyone taking part in the Yankee Bumpers would be guaranteed a well-earned collection of cuts and bruises, and the game became popular for the loosening or loss of teeth, broken fingers and the occasional broken arm. The least one could expect from a good game of Yankee Bumpers was a series of bruises and grazes to every part of the body. These games became so intense that guys would literally lose their tempers and end up in a real 'fistycuffs' fight with their opponent. I don't remember how the game finally faded out of popularity, but like all of these fads, you just suddenly realise one day that they have gone out of fashion.

On one other occasion, my brother and I were throwing stones at a summerhouse while lining up for the dining room one lunchtime. This summerhouse was an amazing piece of machinery as it was mounted on a turntable and so it could be moved around to follow the position of the sun. It sat on a prominent mound at the back of the main convent, and we all took great pleasure in turning it on its axis to keep it in sunlight.

Several other lads decided to join in the bombardment, and soon the beautiful summerhouse had lost most of it's side windows. All of us were dragged out of line and made to wait for Aloysius who herded us into the scullery for a good strapping. She then made every boy sit down and write a letter to their parents requesting five shillings each for the repair of the summerhouse windows. My brother and I knew that my father would not be able to afford ten shillings so we both went to Aloysius and told her that we could not write such a letter home. She solved the problem by banning us from lunch for three days each and giving us another instant strapping.

We didn't mind missing a few lunches as we would have no difficulty pilfering a few extra slices of toast or bread from the breakfast servings,or scrounging up a few morsels from the other lads. The double strapping however was a little bit too much for both of us. We decided that being strapped twice for the same misdemeanour really was rough justice even by Aloysius' standards. We could quite easily have written to my father and asked him to replace the glass panes, after all, he did work for a glazing company. Instead we decided to take our punishment (not on the chin, but on the bum) and raise two fingers vertical to Aloysius for, what we saw as, a complete miscarriage of justice. We were both very proud of the fact that we were able to keep this away from my father, saving him the embarassment of writing to the school to pay ten shillings he really couldn't afford.

The sixties were a time of change in post-war Britain, they heralded a move from austerity and shortages, to new fads, new cultures and a general atmosphere of optimism. Rock and Roll was adopted by the young, but mainly influenced by American singers including, Bill Haley, Little Richard, Big Bopper, Buddy Holly, Fats Domino and, of course, the inimitable Elvis Presley. The music scene in England was still very much 'ballad' led, and singers including Tommy Steele, Adam Faith, Cliff Richard and The Shadows, Petula Clark and Dusty Springfield were topping the hit parade with their own musical contributions. The American music scene was still the main influence in those early days of the sixties, and it was very difficult for a British singer to make any headway in America. This was all about to change however, as a young Liverpool record store owner named Brian Epstein was about to launch a hurricane of a band on to the English and world-wide music scene. Out of this tame mixture of Pop and Rock emerged four young lads from Liverpool, who were to change the face of popular music for ever. The Beatles had arrived and with them a following so great that the press christened it 'Beatle mania'.

The Beatles sound was like nothing that had gone before, the lyrics were simple, the tunes were catchy, the harmonies were cheeky, but, most importantly, they were modern love songs which inspired a whole generation of kids, and even influenced great changes in the fashion and attitudes of the younger generation. John, Paul, George and Ringo exploded on to the Pop scene with mop-top haircuts, winkle-picker boots and clean cut suits. They were four cheeky chappies who, unbeknown to themselves at the time, would create a revolution that would change the face of youth culture forever. Songs including: Love Me Do, She Loves You, Eight Days a Week, Paperback Writer and dozens more, were churned out at a rate of knots unheard of before in the history of 'Pop' music.

Every kid in the country wanted a piece of the Beatles, and parents everywhere were at a loss on how to handle these new influences that were captivating their children. Most popular singers at that time would attract a teenage following, but the Beatles captivated little kids as well in a way that no one had ever experienced before. The swinging Sixties, were enveloping everything in their wake, and the music scene was going through a 'Renaissance' never before experienced. It was an amazing time of new hope and new beginnings, and even at our very young age, we became aware of this tidal wave that seemed to be cascading across our childhood years and influencing all of our attitudes and opinions. With the Beatles in full swing, there followed several other groups and singers including Gerry Marsden, Billy J. Kramer, The Searchers, The Rolling Stones, Sandy Shaw, Manfred Mann, The Troggs and The swinging Blue Jeans.

Pop bands or groups were springing up all over the country, but most prevalent among them were a bunch of Liverpool artists that became commonly known as the Mersey-Beat. Gerry and the Pacemakers, Dave Clark Five, Freddie and the Dreamers all followed in the Beatles success, and solo artists including Cilla Black, Lulu, Helen Shapiro all followed in the wake of the tidal wave created by The Beatles. The youth of England were experiencing a musical movement that was unprecedented at any previous time in history. Adults, parents, church leaders and politicians were at a loss in trying to stem this tide of musical-mania that was, in their opinion, corrupting the morals of the young and the whole mad affair was summed up in just one song by the then unknown Bob Dylan, called "The Times They Are A Changin". Across the Atlantic, the young Elvis Presley had reached, what is now described as, 'super star' status

At Ponsbourne Park the Beatles created a mini revolution that even the strict old nuns had difficulty in comprehending. Beatle magazines and comics were trashing the old traditional children's newspapers and popular comics, and parents were being swamped with requests for anything Beatle to be sent. Everyone was learning the 'twist and shout' dance and many kids were trying to grow their hair longer, although this was resisted by the school at all costs. Plastic Beatle wigs were being worn in the playground and the boys were picking up tennis rackets and turning them into pretend-guitars. The collars of blazers were being turned inside out to replicate the collarless suits that the Beatles wore in their early days. Pop bands were springing up all over the place and some kids were even writing their own songs and performing them in the play breaks between lessons. A three stepped portico at the top of the playground became an impromptu stage, and every playtime there would be a crowd of kids waiting to sing or be entertained by their peers - it was a great time to be young, but we still had to deal with a school culture that would want to preserve its old traditions at all costs. Resistance to the Beatles was being introduced to many of the school rules, and prefects and house captains were instructed to confiscate anything relating to the Beatles including chewing gum cards, posters, magazines and of course, the treasured Beatle magazines. There was a brisk and illicit trade in all things Beatle, and I made my own contribution in the trading and swopping of every imaginable Beatle collective. I was becoming quite the young dealer and entrepreneur, although the word had not even been heard of or coined back then.

Youth culture was dominating almost every media, and advertising was suddenly focused on the teenage market, which was turning normal singer-songwriters into overnight millionaires. The years of the consumer culture were exploding into the British way of life, and creating a whole new music revolution in its wake. The 'baby boomers' were finding a voice like no other generation before, while Bob Dylan was reminding everyone on the other side of the Atlantic that even solo artists, without particularly musical voices, were now being avidly listened to.

The main media for the growth of popular culture was radio. T.V. was still in its comparative infancy, but slowly and surely there were new T.V. programmes dedicated solely to the new pop culture. Programmes like Juke Box Jury, Top of the Pops, and Ready, Steady, Go. were attracting huge audiences of the young, and teenagers everywhere were buying up transistorised radios of every description. Of course, transistor radios were also becoming a lot more miniaturised, and several of us kept them well hidden under floorboards and above cupboards and wardrobes. At night, after lights out we would all cluster around someone's 'tranny' to listen to either Radio Caroline or Radio London. Both of these stations played all of the latest pop releases although the signals faded in and out because they were both pirate stations broadcasting out at sea.

Anyone found with a transistor radio would be severely punished, and a great deal of time and trouble were devoted to hiding these items very carefully. I found a good place under the boys' footlockers in the cloakroom and in this space I hid my illicit LP records and 45's, my marbles, and sweets and of course, my beloved GEC transistor radio. My catapult was now also housed there, but I was slowly moving away from the use of it, to explore more mature interests. This hiding place was mouse infested, so I had to keep everything I possessed in tins and wooden boxes, The mice still managed to get into some of the boxes, and it wasn't unusual to find the covers of your records and albums chewed through by the mice population. Some of the boys had their own crystal set radios, but these could only be used with earphones and they quickly faded away in favour of the latest transistor radios.

At the same time as the Beatles were propagating their own particular brand of magic, Hollywood was churning out some epic movies, and while our trips to the cinema were almost non-existent, the nuns did organise a few trips to selected films including Ben Hur, The Robe and King of Kings. All of these movies had a religious theme and were therefore regarded as suitable viewing for the school boarders. Of course nothing was ever cheap even in those heady days of the sixties, and if you desired to go and see a film, then your parents had to provide the five shillings fee. This included coaches to and from Hatfield or Enfield and, of course, your admission to the cinema. I wrote home for the five shillings knowing full well that my parents would not be able to afford such a luxury for us, but I was very surprised when the five shillings postal order arrived a week later. My brother complained bitterly that he had not received his five shillings, so he had to sty behind with the other poverty-stricken unfortunates. Ben Hur was certainly an epic film and Charlton Heston's performance as Yehuda Ben Hur was excellent. Of course, the most popular scene in the film was the great chariot race, and as soon as we returned to school it was decided that we would hold our own chariot races on a weekly basis every Saturday. A new fad was born.

Now chariot racing involved four guys being roped together with a few tied up skipping ropes and then a smaller guy would be towed behind them acting as the charioteer. This game required four fast runners to emulate the horses up front and the guy behind had to keep them together and in line, as they raced around an oval track drawn out in the playground. All of the kids enjoyed the chariot races, and they would bet sweets and occasional money on the various races. Obviously, if anyone was caught gambling, there would be hell to play, but the whole thing was very neatly planned to coincide at a time when most of the nuns were either at meals or in the chapel praying. The most risky part of chariot racing fell on the poor charioteer, especially if he wasn't a fast runner. As he got dragged around the playground by his four horses, it was very easy to fall over or get thrown sideways on the curves or bends. The rule was that once the charioteer had let go of his rope then that team were disqualified. Very often the charioteer would fall in the middle of a race and this always ended up in severely cut knees or worse still the odd broken limb. I knew of only one broken leg and a broken wrist during all of the time that the chariot races were a fad, but there was always a steady queue of guys reporting to the infirmary for attention to cut legs, cut hands, and grazed kneecaps. These injuries were always horrible, because invariably, the wounds would be full of grit and gravel from the rough surfaces of the playground. One could always recognise a victim of such an accident because his wound would always be daubed in yellow iodine, but we all wore our cuts with pride and showed them off like merit medals. As for the winning charioteers, well they were rewarded with crowns of laurel leaves fashioned from the hedges around the school. These winners looked like regular 'Julius

Caesars' and large amounts of sweets and contraband would change hands, courtesy of a few tuck boxes.

Another great fad came along very unexpectedly in the middle of winter, and this was as a result of the great freeze-up of 1963 which affected the whole of Britain. An unprecedented amount of snow fell in a very short time, and Arctic weather conditions prevailed for several weeks. Our school was literally cut off due to the enormous snow drifts and freezing surroundings. We were not alone in this as most of the country lay under massive snow drifts and frozen roads - things had literally come to a complete standstill. The day pupils at Ponsbourne Park could not be 'bussed' in for over three weeks and the school itself had to more or less abandon most of its normal timetables. We were confined to our dormitories most of the time, as the snow drifts were nine feet high in places, and all of the school driveways and bye ways were completely covered in what was described at the time as a 'white out'. We never wanted it to end, and were not in the slightest bit concerned that the country had literally ground to a complete halt.

School meals were greatly reduced as the weekly delivery of food could not be undertaken, and we were getting quite used to a diet of soup, bread and dry goods. We didn't go hungry as such, but our new diet was certainly having an impact on those lads who didn't particularly like soup. At one stage food was dropped into the school by helicopter as no vehicles could get near us, and even the local farmers gave up trying to move around in such dreadful conditions. Being confined to our dorms was becoming very boring and the daily activities had now been reduced to just a few lessons and a lot of sitting around, playing board games and looking out of the windows.

As the days passed, the school caretakers managed to clear away some of the enormous drifts that were entrapping us, and at last we could get out onto the main playground. The usual snowball fights and sliding around on the ice were soon in full swing and we all rejoiced in the temporary break from the school routine. Snow which can be a real hazard to people in general, was our opportunity to have some real fun. The snowdrifts were so high in places, that they completely covered doors and windows all around the school. It was clear from this amount of snow that no transport of any kind was going to be able to make it down the mile-long driveway to the school. We had hours of fun digging tunnels in the snow drifts and constructing snowmen. Of course there were the obligatory snowball fights, and while it was absolutely freezing being outside, most of us were too busy having fun to even notice the cold.

One day my brother Liam started to roll a giant snowball in the playground, and very soon he had recruited about twenty other lads to complete the task of rolling this enormous ball of snow until it became too cumbersome to move. Snow was packed all around the base of this enormous snowball, and several lads were up on top of it flattening it into a neat platform. Once the snowball was completed and stabilised, the boys hollowed out the centre of it and created what can only be described as an ice castle or barricade. This was an enormous piece of ice and had taken hours and hours to build and shape. It dominated the complete playground and became the focal point for all of the kids to have a rough and tumble for several days on end. My brother, as the architect and designer of this fine erection, decided to charge a fee for anyone wishing to play on it. It was an instant success, and he found that his wealth in 'tuck' and goodies was increasing day by day. He did of course share some of these 'illicit' contributions with me. The 'sly' Ruths were back in business for a while.

The guys on top of the barricade had to defend it like a medieval castle from the enemy, while the invaders had to storm the ramparts and try to remove the opposition from it. "I'm the king of the castle and you're the dirty rascals" was the war-cry of the incumbents on top of the ice block. Kids were being thrown in all directions and for days and weeks there were all kinds of games and challenges surrounding this enormous piece of snow. Over the weeks that followed this structure became more and more icy and much harder to climb on to, it took all one's effort to climb up its frozen walls and was even more hazardous to hang on to once you reached the top. Kids rushed from their classrooms at playtime to be 'kings' of the castle, and if they were unlucky enough in failing to climb onto the icy ramparts, they then found themselves as the invaders trying to capture it. Little accidents were beginning to happen, and there were more and more minor injuries resulting from the games we were playing. One day my friend John Willaby, who had spent days and weeks defending the ice castle with my brother and I, was thrown off the top of it and he unfortunately landed in an awkward position instantly snapping his collarbone.

A snapped collarbone is not a pleasant injury in anybody's book, and there is no effective way of treating the break except by immobilising the patient. Poor John was screaming in pain as they carried him off to the infirmary. His injury had to be dealt with by the nuns, as there was no chance of a local doctor or ambulance being able to get down the driveway into the school. When I visited him a few days later in the infirmary, he described how the nuns had to set the bones themselves and how they had created a figure of eight bandage to hold the injured bone in place. He had screamed for hours during and after this procedure and the only pain killers available to him were 'Paracetomol' and 'Aspirin' which were definitely not strong enough for the job. John just had to tolerate the discomfort in spite of a very painful injury, and being trussed up like a Christmas turkey. He nevertheless, settled into a quiet and comparatively pampered life in the infirmary. He later warned us that the nuns were now looking at banning the use of the ice castle, as it was clearly becoming too dangerous for the boys to play on. We knew that its days were numbered, especially after such a serious injury, and we waited for its inevitable condemnation.

After John's accident the ice castle was declared out of bounds by the nuns and the caretakers were told to break it up with pickaxes. The ice which the castle had been built from lasted for months after all of the snow had disappeared. When it finally melted away it took with it a lot of great memories of a winter that was like no other one in terms of fun and enjoyment. England has not experienced a winter like that ever since, and while it created chaos for people going about their daily routines, for us, it was an opportunity to enjoy some of the happiest times of our boarding school lives.

When the great thaw finally arrived, we were on our way home for the half term break, and we were particularly excited because my mother had now passed her driving test and had bought the first family car which was a brand new Austin 1100 4 door Saloon. This was the car in which she had taken her first lessons, and just before taking her test she had decided to buy her own brand new one, in readiness for that happy event. She would also be using her car in her role as a local district nurse, allowing her to get rid of her old pushbike which was, up until now, her only means of transportation. She had taken quite a few falls off her pushbike in the past, but I think this unprecedented freezing weather was the final reason for taking up the skill of driving. Unfortunately during that great freeze-up my Mother was out driving on a daily basis to her patients, and one day she hit a spot of black ice and skidded off the road into someone's front garden. The car was badly damaged and she was really shaken up, but she continued to do her daily calls by foot. The freezing conditions were unprecedented and almost everyone has a story or event connected to the weather at that time.

Mother's brand new Austin 1100 was duly repaired and she carried on driving it for quite a few years. I and my brother christened it the 'puke' mobile, because every time we travelled any distance in it we would get violently car sick. It turns out that Austin used a liquid suspension called 'hydrolastic' and this gave the car a floaty feel when driven, rendering some occupants sick as dogs in a very short time. It also had a vinyl interior which was freezing in the winter, and then stuck to you like glue in the hot summer days- all in all we were not too impressed with this car but it was apparently 'state of the art' for its time. I suppose the one good thing that we loved about the car was the super new 'Radiomobile' radio that was fitted to it. The tone of this radio was really sharp and we could now listen to our favourite pop stations while on the move, providing of course that we didn't have our heads hung out of the back windows 'pebble dashing' the side of the car with vomit.

Chapter 12
Drama-on and off the stage and Simon takes a Nicky laxative.

Once a year prior to the Christmas holidays, the school would hold their Christmas pageant and nativity play for the benefit of the parents. This would normally coincide with a visiting Sunday which occurred every two weeks, and was probably the highlight of the school year as far as the teaching nuns were concerned. Each class would have a role to play in the pageant, and this would normally take the guise of a well-known play or drama. Rehearsals for the pageant would start in early November and each child was required to take part in it, one way or another. For some reason completely unknown to us, the leading roles for many of these pageants were always being given to a day pupil, and the poor boarders always seemed to end up with the more basic support roles, better described by us as the 'dross' roles;

Whether this was by coincidence or design was a bit of a mystery, but we all suspected that the nuns had an alternative agenda in 'buttering up' to the parents of day pupils as they tended to be, firstly, more visible than the parents of the boarders, and secondly, moving and shaking in the more upper middle class echelons of society at that time. This later turned out to be a little bit of a misnomer, as many of the boarders parents' had very high positions in all sorts of professional, vocational and diplomatic careers. In fact the reason that many of the kids became boarders in the first place, was because their parents were pursuing professional careers in every location imaginable, including working abroad.

High on the agenda of the school's entertainment presentations would be the choral numbers performed by the school choir, and if you were fortunate (or unfortunate) enough to be chosen for the choir, you would have your work cut out for a few months in advance of the pageant, in learning the various songs and their individual harmonies. In fairness, the standard of singing was very high and it was considered a privilege by the nuns for you to be chosen to represent the school as a chorister. Strangely enough, there were no day boarders in the school choir, but we learned much later that this was due more to the fact that day pupils, were in the main, non-Catholic and would therefore not be in attendance at the Sunday masses and weekly benedictions that the choir would be required to partake in. Both my brother and I were members of the choir, not for our devotion to the music, but more because of the occasional treats that would accompany the various rehearsals. We did however possess good voices which was a prerequisite in remaining a member of the choir. Our love of choral music ensured that we were part of a choir right up until our late teens, and it provided us with some of the most fun and memorable experiences, especially in our later years.

A week before the pageant actually started, a big stage would be erected in the grand drawing room near the main entrance to the convent, and it was here that the final dress rehearsals for the pageant would take place. Each class teacher would be allocated a certain amount of time on the main stage to take their individual classes through their paces before the main event. I had managed for quite a few years to avoid taking very big parts in any of the productions, being selected occasionally to be perhaps a shepherd or maybe an angel in the 'nativity' play. Big roles were neither my desire nor 'forte' at the time, and I avoided being in any kind of 'limelight' as much as possible.

Unfortunately my role as a reasonable singer in the choir landed me one year with the leading part in the musical pageant, but I later found out (much to my great disappointment) that my leading role was to be that of an 'understudy' only. The thought of having to learn loads and loads of lines and having to sing various solo songs had already cheesed me off, but I was even more disappointed at the prospect of having to learn all of the lines just in case the main character fell ill or became injured. This was like a 'poison chalice' to me, but I knuckled down and learned all of the lines and songs, just in case the unimaginable happened, and the leading man broke a leg or something.

Now Simon Mollison was one of the brighter pupils in my class at the time, he achieved high marks in almost every subject and was being 'groomed' for greatness in the future. Simon would probably make house captain, prefect or perhaps even head boy in the coming years, mainly because he stayed out of trouble, was popular with the nuns (even the tyrant ones) and had a unique talent in 'sucking up' to anyone who could serve to further his personal ambitions. For all of that, Simon was not a bad lad on the whole, in fact I quite liked him. He was always ready to share his sweets with you in the playground, and his friendly demeanour made him quite a popular lad in our classroom. He was however, very vain and not a little self-centred as well. He knew that he was good at a great many things, and he made sure that other people around him knew that as well. The only problem that I could see with Simon, was that he was always being held up as a 'role model' by the nuns and teachers, and this would have the effect of upsetting the kids around him and promoting his reputation as a teacher's 'pet'.

One of the kids who particularly disliked Simon Mollison was another friend named Nicky Heatherton. Nicky was probably as talented as Simon, but, being a boarder, Nicky had never received the same recognition for his academic abilities, and his obvious acting talents. He always felt that he was walking in Simon's shadow and this inevitably 'browned' Nicky 'off' in a very big way indeed. Nicky had his own agenda when it came to his dislike for Simon, and it manifested itself in a surprising way to many of us. This particular year Simon was picked as the main character in the pageant, and I was unfortunate enough to be his understudy. The role of understudy is the most boring thing imaginable, because the understudy has to be present at every rehearsal and every performance of the show without ever taking part in anything.

There was no way that Mollison was going to miss any of the rehearsals, let alone the main performances, I was literally 'bored shitless' and even the small amount of singing, that I participated in with the choir, failed to relieve the tedium. I did however secure a minor role as a stagehand, moving props and operating lights, so at least my time would be put to some proper use and the boredom would be slightly allayed.

The pageant this year was based on a Romany Gypsy theme, and told the story of a group of Romany travellers and their journey around the Transylvanian foothills. The main character in this pageant was Romany Roff and he was the head of the tribe. This was the part that Simon Mollison was entrusted with, it was also the part that gave him his temporary feeling of superiority above his friends and peers. Nicky managed to 'wind' himself up to a point where any mention of Simon and his talents would result in Nicky slamming about like a mad dog, and it soon became apparent that Nicky's anger was sending him on a new course of mischief that was totally out of character in this normally cool and calm individual.

Simon, on the other hand, who was conceited and self-opinionated under normal circumstances, was now having a real good time. Now that he had achieved the leading role in the pageant, his 'narcissistic' tendencies knew no bounds. The costume that had been designed for the role was quite spectacular and very colourful. There was a bright red headband, a multi-coloured satin shirt and amazing black silk baggy 'doubloon' trousers with black suede boots. The sisters would put hours of work into the various costumes, and as seamstresses they were second to none. Mollison really looked the part when he appeared at dress rehearsals in this fantastic costume. As a day pupil he, like a great many others, tended to regard the boarders as 'a bit common' and his snobbery was more reinforced when he learned that I was his understudy for the role of Romany Roff. "What is the point of your learning all of my lines Ruthie, you're never going to get the opportunity of appearing in front of an audience", I actually agreed with him, but I was becoming more and more 'pissed off' with his condescending attitude and his superior stance. "You better make sure that you don't 'fluff' your lines or break your 'fecking' leg then" I replied with a wry smile on my face. Simon 'preened' himself like an overactive peacock in his fine costume and walked a way from me with a smug look on his face and a comment of "no chance" on his lips.

In the dormitory that evening I was discussing the Simon Mollison episode with a few of my friends including Nicky, and I assured them that there was no way that I wanted to play the leading role in the pageant, I was now having a bit of fun with creating sound effects and dimming the various lights up and down as a backstage helper. I was also a 'prompter' for people who had forgotten their lines, and many of them did indeed forget their lines. Nicky and the rest of the boys, however, on hearing Mollison's various comments to me, had a very different agenda in mind, and they were determined that Mollison was heading for the biggest fall from grace in the whole of his school existence up until now. The pageant was staged on three different days in front of three separate audiences. The first presentation was staged on Friday purely for the nuns, teachers and general school population, the second one was staged on Saturday for the parents and friends of the day pupils, and the final one was on visiting Sunday in front of all of the parents of the boarders. This was by far the largest presentation each year, and there were always far more people in the audience on the final day, due to the majority of children being in the boarding school section.

On the dress rehearsals day of the pageant everything went without a hitch, and the various classes went through their productions without a single problem. Mollison and the rest of the participants in 'Romany Roff' all came through the ordeal completely unscathed and not a single word or action was missed. The teachers and nuns were very impressed and I had no prompting duties whatsoever. Then came the first full production, and to my surprise Mollison 'fluffed' his lines on quite a few occasions, he also lost two or three props in different places on the stage, and I felt, justifiably, that his acting was pretty mediocre. He complained to me that someone had taken the missing props and hidden them, because they were not where they were supposed to be. I didn't take much notice of his complaints at the time, but a little later I got the impression that certain pals of mine may have introduced a little mischief into the proceedings to fluster Mollison in his finest hour.

After the first performance, Mollison paraded around in his Romany Roff costume like a 'prima donna' and basked in the praises and compliments from the nuns, teachers and everyone else that were around him. I must admit that I experienced a streak of jealousy at the attention that he was getting especially as I figured that, after seeing his performance, I was by far the better actor. For all of that, I graciously accepted that the opportunity for me to ever act as understudy would never arise, in spite of learning all of the lines and actions of the play. I was resigned and contented to be doing my own little jobs around the stage production, while allowing others to bathe in the limelight of their various roles.

As a school tradition, after the finish of the first show, refreshments were served to the children taking part, and this consisted of sandwiches, biscuits, cakes and orange juice. Mollison was known for his love of Victoria sponge cake and as everyone was allowed just one slice per person, I was very surprised when my friend Nicky Heatherton offered him a second helping off his own plate. I thought that this was a very benevolent thing for Nicky to do, especially as he had spent the previous days 'slating' Mollison to whoever would listen. I actually admonished him for sucking up to Mollison, and if anyone deserved a second piece of cake it should have been me as a fellow mate and fellow boarder. Nicky shrugged off my complaints, and winked mischievously at me as he walked away. I knew instinctively from that moment that something was afoot, but the plot would not be hatched until much later on in the dormitory, when I had the chance to talk to Nicky on his own.

That evening as the boarders retired to their beds Nicky confided to me that he had 'spiked' Mollison's cake with a couple of laxative tablets. He had crushed them up with a spoon and sprinkled them on to the rich cream and jam filling. Up until that day I had no idea what a laxative tablet was, but Nicky, who was a common user of them, explained in perhaps too great a detail what the expected result would be. "They should just be starting to take effect about now" laughed Nicky, "and I doubt if Mollison will be here tomorrow for the second show, and maybe not Sunday either". I was quite shocked at Nicky's actions, and really worried that Mollison would be quite ill as a result of these tablets. Nicky also admitted that himself and a few others had hidden the stage props to teach Mollison a good lesson and put him off his stroke, we all agreed that it had worked because his performance was pretty average, but I was worried that Nicky's pranks might somehow backfire on all of us.

The following morning, the news that we had all anticipated was announced. I was told that Simon Mollison would not be at the pageant that day as he had a very upset stomach and diarrhoea and I was summoned to the convent to be fitted with the costume for Romany Roff. I must admit that I did feel very guilty at the thought of Mollison moping around at home with a seriously upset stomach, but the guilt didn't last long when I reminded myself of what a complete 'arse' he could be at times. I warned Nicky not to let on to a living soul what had occurred, because if the nuns found out we would all be in very serious trouble.

My time to perform had finally arrived, and I knew that I needed to give the performance of my life in spite of being very, very nervous. As the curtains opened I was astonished at how crowded the hall was, but I immediately fell into the role and strutted up and down the stage delivering my lines and singing in all of the right places. Needless to say, all of the props were in the right place, and the performance went off without a single hitch. I realised at that very moment that I really enjoyed the acting and singing roles, and that perhaps in the future I might not be quite the 'shrinking violet' of before. It's strange how things come back to you when you bring them to mind, I can't remember much of the speaking part that I performed in Romany Roff, but I can remember clearly the 'finale' song as clear as day – it went like this:

Romany Roff, head of the tribe, is such a great man that he's hard to describe.
He's big and he's strong, he can sing a fine song.
He can set sapling snares to catch game unawares,
He can fish, he can shoot, and if you put a fruit.
At fifty yards distance he'll cleave it in two. with a knife that he throws,

All this only shows, that Romany Roff, head of the tribe.

Is such a great man that he's hard to describe.

That evening I basked in my own kind of glory, I had achieved my first dramatic success with more than a little help from my friends. Nicky and the rest of the lads were delighted that finally a 'boarder' had stolen the limelight from the day pupils. Even Aloysius was impressed with my performance, but any praise that she ever handed out to anyone was always tainted with a 'snide' comment like "don't you get too big for your boots my lad, because I will soon bring you back down to earth with the biggest crash you can imagine". I never ever doubted her for a moment.

The following day I was thrilled to hear that I had been chosen to carry on the role for visiting Sunday, which meant that my mum and dad would finally get the opportunity of seeing me performing in something a little more substantial than just a general chorus. I was more than excited at the prospect.

As for Simon Mollison, well he did recover his full bodily functions after just a few days, and he never ever suspected foul play at the hands of his friend, Nicky Heatherton. Simon continued to impress his teachers in every class that he went in to. He never did find out the full circumstances of the mystery illness that cut him down so suddenly that particular weekend, but Nicky Heatherton later summed up the whole incident with the following unforgettable words: "When the bottom seems to fall out of your world, take a couple of my little tablets, and let the world fall out of your 'bleetin' bottom." There's nothing much that I can add to that particular 'cockney' sentiment, but I will always remember Nicky's role in my first attempts at amateur dramatics.

Chapter 13
Let there be light. A very sick cow. Good vibrations and a visit to the school infirmary

To say that boarding school life was difficult would be a massive understatement, there were far too many skills to learn and far more pitfalls to trip you up on your journey to maturity. There were situations in my early experiences of boarding school life that constantly interfered with a smooth and constant equilibrium. By the time I was nine years old, I had become an 'old hand' at keeping my head down, and ducking and diving wherever and whenever possible. More importantly than all of this was my ability to fly under the radar of any possible trouble with prefects, house captains and teachers alike.

I suppose you could say that I had become totally institutionalised by life at Ponsbourne Park and in so being, had built up a good knowledge of every possible avoidance trick in the book. I was now old enough and wise enough to recognise when trouble was coming, and then take the necessary steps to avoid any of the consequences. Four hard years had elapsed, during which time I had shaken all of my memories of life in Ireland, apart from those which were being created on my various holidays back to the Emerald Isle. I had learned very effectively how to live my life in a strict, and oppressive environment, turning myself very quickly into the 'quintessential' English schoolboy and a typical product of the private boarding school system.

In my final two years at the school I found myself in a comfort zone that made life not just bearable, but also, quite happy and pleasant at times. I was now past all of the major difficulties of learning and achieving, I was less and less in the spotlight for getting into trouble in my day to day school life, and even Aloysius had moved on to find other new kids and unsuspecting victims to frighten half to death.

I was actually liking the experience of being educated, and while there were still many instances of 'snobbery' and 'racism' in the school, this was no different from the experiences of any other school around the country at that time. Racism in the 'sixties' was a fact of life and those of us who experienced it learned to live with it and deal with it in our own individual way. Taunts of 'thick Irish, thick Mick, Potato Paddy' were all terms that I had thrown at me during my schooldays. These taunts were so regular that I had given up taking any notice of them, and my fists spent more time in my pocket these days than sorting the odd comment in the school playground. It was around this time that my nickname 'Ruthie' was being shouted in football matches, cricket matches and even in the playground. I was becoming quite tolerant and certainly calmer in my approach to such things, and even when the odd racist taunt was thrown my way I would reply by reminding the 'taunter' that the English were invaded by the Romans, but the Irish scared the 'shit' out of Caesar's forces and chased them back into the sea.

Even on half-term or full term breaks, I found myself looking forward to returning to Ponsbourne Park, in the knowledge that I was now enjoying the school curriculum, and finding learning a very easy and pleasant experience. I thrived on the 'camaraderie' that I had built up with my many pals during the previous years, and it was getting hard to imagine a life outside of this environment. The friendships that I was forming in this unusual place were somehow more intense and certainly longer lasting. The addition of extra responsibilities and more trusted roles instilled an overwhelming feeling of well-being, and I found myself enjoying a little bit of extra power as well. My days of being constantly in trouble, and more importantly the fear of being severely punished had slowly passed me by. I was now in a position to avoid most of the daily troubles of my young life, and while these had by no means disappeared completely, they were now being visited on peers much younger and less mature than myself.

 Life was not at all bad, and I no longer felt the dread and fear of returning to school after the various holiday breaks. Wherever possible I tried to help the younger kids around me, especially those who were experiencing boarding school life for the first time. I knew what they were all going through having made the same 'harrowing' journey myself. In studies, I was doing very nicely and was no longer subject to hours of extra lessons or 'swatting up' to keep up with the rest of my peers. Sports-wise, I was enjoying being in the school teams for football, cricket and rounders, and having excelled at all of these activities, I was appointed Games Captain and Vice-Captain of Patricks House, a very rare appointment for someone still in their junior years at Ponsbourne Park. Along with these two appointments came a lot of 'kudos', a lot of great fun and just a touch of 'aggravation' to remind me that 'with great power comes great responsibility'. My spats of trouble with teachers and house Captains were now very few and far between, but I was always reminded by my Dad that there would always be those who out of resentment or jealousy, "make it their mission in life to take you down a peg or two". I was no exception to that rule and as my life of comparable ease progressed into my latter years at the school, I was beginning to acquire a few new enemies that could make things just a little difficult at times.

The angry little Irish immigrant was now maturing, and had become well versed in the English ways of living, and while I still retained much of my Irish attitudes, I could turn on the English reserve at the drop of a hat, and my accent was now very, very English indeed. I was also building up a few resentments and prejudices of my own, and some of these would manifest themselves in a few incidents that I would not be too proud of, but as the old saying goes, "all things happen for a reason". At that time of my life, I had a few of my own very good reasons to be less than satisfied with all of the things around me. I was acquiring a kind of social conscience that found me defending myself and others against prejudice, snobbery and greed and promoting the important principles of fair play.

Ponsbourne Park as previously described possessed a hierarchy of 'haves' and 'have nots', it mirrored real life in this regard. We had no illusions that we were without doubt the products of working class parents, and the nuns had no hesitation in reminding you of this on a daily basis. My father was now a factory worker and my mother was a nursing sister, a qualification which I would hardly have described as working class. My father had successfully run and grown his own business during the forties and fifties creating a great demand for the goods and services that he provided at that time as a hardware merchant. His business eventually failed, because he placed his trust in people who had no hesitation in deceiving him in the worst possible way. In my eyes my father was my hero and a self-made made man who would nowadays be described as an 'entrepreneur'. My mother was also a 'prolific' professional who had invested her time in studying medicine and achieving great things in her nursing career. To describe them as working class was, in my opinion, not only, derogatory to them, but also derogatory to the millions of honest working class people that kept these religious institutions in existence by their hard working ethics and their valuable financial contributions. The class system was alive and kicking in these the 1960's, but even at that age I was becoming aware of a great change that was sweeping through the country. This change was aided mainly by the popular bands and groups that captured the nation's mood in the lyrics of their songs. Footballers were becoming every schoolboy's heroes, and the whole youth culture was coming to dominance. Youth was finding a pwerful voice, andmaking itself heard at every opportunity.

I had already formed the opinion, even at this young age, that if some of these narrow-minded, 'snobbish' nuns and priests had any idea what people in the real world had to sacrifice in order to achieve their goals, they would perhaps realise what a bunch of non-achieving and self-indulgent hypocrites some of them actually were. I scoffed at institutions that purported to encourage equality and respect for others, while actually encouraging the complete opposite in the children whose care had been entrusted to them. Their support of a class system no matter how innocuous it appeared to them, was perpetuating a prejudice which should long ago have been thrown in the 'trash' can. Fortunately for me, there were also a few good people in this mixed bunch, who really did have the courage of their convictions, and who really did lead exemplary and worthwhile lives. It was these exceptional few that deserve true recognition for the care, influence and guidance that they provided to youngsters like myself, my brother and my sister. There were just far too few of them.

I was now nine years old, and fully understood the risks and consequences of any actions that I might undertake in all aspects of my school life. As an incumbent vice-captain, I was now required to shoulder some of the responsibility for the smooth running and future achievements of Patrick's house. Unfortunately the captain of Patricks was a peer that I completely despised, not because of his wealthy background, which he undoubtedly cherished and 'bragged' about at every opportunity, but also because of his total lack of empathy to his fellow boarders. This was a person that rode through life on the end of a silver spoon, a person that despised anyone from a foreign background sharing his environment, and a person that despised anyone around him that did not possess wealth.

My old adversary, Vincent Simson, had it all, the best clothes, the best toys, and the best approval from all of the nuns who benefitted by major contributions from his wealthy parents. He was anti-Irish to the core and anti every other race that happened to inhabit the same school playground at the time. I was puzzled very much by his appointment to captain of Patrick's house, which was predominantly made up of kids having a connection to or, in some way, being close to the Irish contingent of the school. I wasted no time in assuring him that his selection as captain was one of the biggest 'fuck-ups' I had ever seen the school make. How the hell could they select this lily-livered, jumped-up excuse for a human being to be Captain of a house dedicated to the patron saint of Ireland. Why instead did they not give him Georges house, then at least we, in Patrick's house, would get the opportunity of kicking the shit out of him at every opportunity on the rugger pitch, the football pitch and more easily on the school playground where everyone was 'fair game'. His Captaincy of the Patricks house was not well accepted by any of his peers, everyone felt that rather than earning the position, he had merely been handed it on a plate in return for his family's benevolence to the school. He excelled at absolutely nothing, his footballing and cricket skills were mediocre to say the least, and yet, he was in both school teams. Academically he was well below average in most subjects, and so bad were his English skills that I would charge him a small fortune to pen his letters home to his parents once a fortnight. I eventually withdrew these services as well, when I found out what a complete anti-Irish and 'snobbish arsehole' he could be.

The Simson family were responsible for donating TV sets, radio sets, books and pianos on a regular basis to the school. Nearly three generations of them had attended the school at one time or another, and they were known to be great providers of funds for the various projects that were undertaken by the Dominican sisters. On any visiting Sunday, the important nuns could be seen 'sucking up' to the Simson family while some of the other less wealthy parents would largely be avoided or perhaps, at the very best given 'short shrift' in any necessary conversations with the nuns. I hated the total hypocrisy of it all, and made it my future mission in life to take Simson and his indulgent family down a peg or two before very much longer. There were very few people that I disliked at this time in my school life, but Simson was certainly one of them.

Simson had the best of everything food-wise as well, his place at table was be-decked with the best in jams and preserves, he also enjoyed a choice of lemonades, cordials and squashes which the average pupil could simply not afford. Parents were already hard-pressed to find the fees to keep their kids in this privileged institution, let alone try and provide extra luxuries that were just not affordable. Noone ever resented another person possessing such 'culinary treasures', but when that person constantly refused to share just a little of these delights with a fellow boarder and peer, it really 'pissed' a lot of people off. One of those people was 'little old' me and as an adept scrounger and acquisitions expert it really instilled a sense of failure in me that I could not separate Simson from a single morsel of his several 'ill-gotten' gains. Simson gave me a really hard time during my tenure as vice-captain of Patricks, he berated my Irish background at every opportunity, and whenever there was trouble within the Patrick's house, he made sure that I was seen as the 'bad apple' on every possible occasion. He had opposed my appointment to the role at every part of the selection process, but fortunately for me, there were a few other influential voices supporting my position. He really was a selfish, small-minded, self-indulgent individual, and my resolve to teach him a lesson he would never forget was growing more and more urgent by the day. All I needed was the right opportunity.

One morning the 'infamous' Sister Aloysius came into the dining hall and silenced all of us in order to make an important announcement. The Simson family had very kindly agreed to donate a large light which would floodlight the main playground and driveway up to the boys' dormitories. This would be a very expensive donation from some very generous benefactors, and after the light was erected, there would be a small ceremony to turn it on. A few weeks later, a team of electricians and labourers turned up at the school to erect the giant floodlight and there was no doubt that this was going to be an enormous light. The giant pole was around 40 feet high, and on top of this was a large tent-shaped canopy which covered an enormous sausage-shaped bulb. I agreed, as did most of my peers, that this was an impressive looking floodlight, and whilst I looked forward to seeing the thing turned on, there seemed to be a lot of unnecessary fuss surrounding the plan to hold a 'lighting up' ceremony. You would have thought that the Trafalgar Square Christmas tree was arriving with people running this way and that to ensure that this was going to be a big event. Simson himself was relishing every minute of the fuss being made over the light, and bragged at the 'astronomic' amount of money that his parents had spent in donating the light to the school. No one likes a show-off and we had all had quite enough of Simson's daily 'blustering' about the big floodlight, anyone listening to him would have thought that he had, not only, funded the bloody thing himself, but that he had also erected it single handedly. I must admit that I was already hatching a plan to somehow sabotage it at some time in the not too distant future, and I'm sure that several other kids would be thinking the same thing. It just remained to see who would succeed in the plan, and when it would be carried out.

The lighting-up ceremony went without a hitch, all of the pupils and teachers from the school gathered in the main playground to witness the event. The Mother Superior of the convent, whom one rarely saw around the school, came and made a little speech about how the light was going to change our lives, and how the kindly Simson family would always be in the prayers and thoughts of all of the nuns and pupils at the school. Father George Leeson was also invited to get in on the act by coming to give it a blessing, and say a few nice words in praise of the donation. Simson himself took 'centre stage' at the ceremony, and preened himself like a Cheshire cat, he also had the honour of actually turning the light on by cutting a big red ribbon, a task which he performed with conceited pleasure. Most of us thought that he was a total 'plonker' at the time, but we had to applause with everyone else and give him yet another moment of glory. I was resolved, from that moment, to teach the self-righteous little 'fucker' a good lesson in humility and tolerance, and my plan to sabotage the light was growing more and more urgent as the days went by.

There was no doubt that the light was very bright and did illuminate the school grounds very well indeed. The playground was lit every night and we no longer required our personal torches to find our way down the shadowy drives and pathways. In many ways, the arrival of the Simson light ruined the perspective of the playground, dormitories and school buildings, and kind of polluted the whole place by its overwhelming brightness. Most of the boarders were unimpressed with its arrival claiming that it was now much easier to be spotted by the nuns and teachers, especially if there were illicit activities being planned or acted-upon under cover of darkness. It reminded many of us of the spotlights that featured in those war films of concentration camps that were so popular in the 60's. We really were under scrutiny now and we felt it as well.

Days and weeks followed during which time the normal school routines made me quite forget my previous intentions regarding the Simson light. By the time that the summer holidays had come around it had faded into my distant memory and all I had in mind was looking forward to the long six week break away from this place. Waiting for the coaches to arrive on the day of breaking up was everybody's favourite moment at Ponsbourne Park. We would all be sat on our suitcases in the main playground waiting to catch a glimpse of the buses as they meandered their way down the nearly mile long drive to the convent building. We seemed to be sat there for hours awaiting their arrival, but it didn't matter because we were all very excited at the prospect of a nice long holiday. It was like this every time term ended, we would count down the days until that final day arrived when our freedom would be once again realised. We would be busy packing our bags and closing up the dormitories for the summer holidays. All of the dormitory floors had to be polished and every window was cleaned inside and out.

On our final day, we would all dress our beds with brilliant white quilts that took the place of dust sheets, and all of our sheets pillows, blankets and pillowcases would be bundled up for laundering during the long school holiday. The dormitories took on an almost empty look as our belongings were boxed up in trunks and suitcases for the journey home to freedom. We were also dressed in our Sunday best uniforms with our brylcreamed hair stuck to our scalps and combed into oblivion. As the coaches drove into view, a massive cheer would go up accompanied by a hundred school caps being flung in the air in celebration. This was always the most exhilarating and exciting time, and as we passed our luggage to the driver for loading and took our allocated seats on the bus.

There would be a sudden and 'opressive' last minute silence as Aloysius boarded the bus to give us our final warnings and admonishments before releasing us. What normally followed, was a tirade of threats about our behaviour on the journey. The reputation of the school was paramount on such occasions, and we were reminded that heads would roll if there was any report of misbehaviour or 'playing up' on the two hour coach journey to Kings Cross bus station. Father Leeson would then board each bus and give us a blessing for a safe journey, and before we knew it we were all on the way to a 'glorious six weeks' of freedom. We felt like a load of freed convicts escaping once again from this oppressive and highly disciplined environment. Yahoo!!

After the summer break, there was always a lot of settling back in to the strict routines of the school, especially after several weeks of fun and a complete lack of threats and discipline. This wasn't to say that our parents were not strict - they certainly were, but when compared with the discipline at Ponsbourne Park we were comparatively free to do whatever we wanted within reason. On my return to school I had brought back with me one additional item which was not only banned by the school as an unacceptable toy, but could also lead me into a lot of trouble if I got caught with it. This item was a super, high - powered slingshot or catapult to use its correct name, and it had taken a few weeks pocket money for me to be able to afford. I naturally told no one of its existence, and like a 'would-be' assassin, I carefully concealed it in a polythene bag in a small hole below the playground wall, waiting for a future opportunity to put it to full use on the Simson Floodlight.

During the summer holidays we invariably returned to Ireland to visit our friends and relations. I always enjoyed staying with my Uncle Joe and Auntie Kathleen who lived on a large farm in Ardara, County Donegal. There were lots of cousins of various ages to spend time with, and I never tired of getting involved in all of the happenings on the farm. On this particular summer holiday I had taken my catapult to Ireland with me and had practised every day on various targets including my brother and five cousins who took it all in good heart. My cousins always looked forward to our visits from England, because it somehow made their daily life more exciting, and was a change from the usual routines on the farm. Chickens, sheep, hens, geese and cows were all terrorised by me on a daily basis, and my aunt complained that some of the hens had stopped laying their daily quota of eggs. My chosen ammunition was crab apples as they were round and light and very hard. Not only did these crab apples possess excellent aerodynamics, they were also just the right size for the catapult and, more importantly, my trouser pockets. I was shooting from the back of the tractor, the top of the barn, the top of the haystacks and even out on the hillsides as we collected the sheep for dipping and shearing.

My aim and shots were improving on a daily basis and one day I shot a cow in the arse as it was raising its tail to take a shit, the crab apple disappeared up the unfortunate animal's anus and it almost broke the world speed record as it took off like a rocket down the field. My cousins were falling over themselves with laughter, and I knew that if my Aunt or Uncle got to hear about the incident, or indeed, about the catapult, they would not be best pleased. Try as I might, I could not prevent my cousins from laughing incessantly, and even at the dinner table that same evening their amusement had not subsided. My aunt kept asking them what they were laughing at, and I was terrified that one of them might spill the beans. This was not a funny situation for me, but every time my cousins saw the cow in the field they would break into roars of laughter for no apparent reason.

A few days later my Uncle had to call the vet, as the unfortunate animal was in a great degree of pain and discomfort due to his sudden bout of 'uninvited' constipation and had even stopped giving his usual quota of milk at milking times. The vet duly arrived and it was not long before he discovered what was wrong with the cow and while he did not offer any explanation for the presence of a crab apple in the cows arse, I could tell that he knew that either myself or some of my other cousins knew exactly how this crab apple had found its way deep into the cow's rectum. I knew that I was responsible for this poor animal's discomfort and I felt really bad about it, but I was glad that the cow was now receiving the medical attention that it deserved. The vet stuck almost his whole arm up the poor cow's bum, and I couldn't look for fear of throwing up. What followed this action was an avalanche of cow shit which exploded from the cows arse like a giant waterfall. In amongst this debris was the offending crab apple, and the vet went straight to it as the cause of the blockage in the cows arse. A cow has several stomachs apparently, so there is no way, even if he had eaten the crab apple, that the cow would not have digested it. This was the explanation given to my uncle by the vet as he pocketed his fee. I'm sure that the vet new exactly how that crab apple found its way into the cows arse, but there was no further mention of it by either him, or my aunt and uncle. My cousins however, repeated the story at every opportunity, and the laughter increased with the frequency of the telling. I was so relieved that the poor cow was okay that I tried to make it up to him in the evenings as he came in for milking. I would give him extra oats and an occasional polo mint or brandy ball as a treat and he seemed to appreciate it very much. It was my way of saying sorry to him for all of the aggravation that I had caused. As for my cousins they just kept laughing about the incident for weeks afterwards, but they never ever let on to my uncle what had happened.

My uncle did eventually find out about the catapult on the last few days of my holiday in Ireland. Every evening he would sit down after supper to listen to the news and weather report on the radio. There was no T.V. In the farmhouse, so the radio was the only form of communication from the outside world. I had discovered that if I walked a few hundred yards down the hill from the farm there was a big pole with a large transformer sitting on top of it. This transformer supplied the power to the farmhouses that were scattered around the hills. I was constantly shooting crab apples at the transformer and if my shots made contact with one of the connections, I discovered, from my cousins, that the resulting vibrations would send interference down the wires and the radios in the various farms would lose their signals behind a barrage of interference and buzzing.

One evening I walked down to the transformer pole under the cover of darkness and I let rip at it with a few crab apples. Every time I hit the target, the radio in my uncle's kitchen would go haywire with interference and this would set my cousins into howls of laughter as my uncle shouted abuse and expletives at the radio set. He soon found out that I was missing from the room, and it didn't take him long to extract the truth from my cousins as to what the hell was going wrong with the radio. My last recollection of that evening was the booming of my uncle's voice as he shouted expletives at me from the top of the hill. His voice echoed all around the valley, and could be heard by every neighbour in the area. I returned to the farm to apologise and surrender my catapult for the

229

rest of my stay there. It was given back to me as I left for the return journey to England.

I was now fully competent and skilled in the art of firing a catapult. Here I was back at school, at the end of the Summer holidays, awaiting the opportunity of putting it to good use. I had made several aborted attempts to take out the 'Simson' light, but on every occasion there would be someone or something preventing me in completing my mission. On the few occasions that I did manage to practise with the catapult the crab apples would bounce off the enormous bulb, and I realised my choice of ammunition was not up to the job, I would have to find an alternative projectile, if I was to make a success of shooting the light into oblivion. After serious thought I decided to employ new ammunition and use a standard sized marble ball, as I knew that this would definitely smash the bulb to 'smithereens'. I now had to be very careful in planning a time to complete the action, because as a vice captain and games captain, I had a big responsibility to be a 'role model' for the kids around me. Apart from all that, I knew that there would be a massive 'hoo-ha' and inevitable investigation to catch the 'perpetrator' of such a serious offence.

The weeks flew by and we were now past the half-term break and heading for the Christmas holidays. I had just three weeks left to make my move, but the opportunity would just not show itself. On so many occasions, I had sneaked away at night and at quiet times during the day to try and get a pop at it, but the opportunities were always thwarted by someone's presence, or the chance of being seen from the main school buildings. The ideal time to hit the light would be in the daylight hours when the thing was actually switched off, but this was proving far too difficult, and there were far too many potential witnesses in the way of a daylight strike. It was going to have to be a night-time operation, but then I would run the risk of being caught out of my dorm after lights out, or, worse still, being seen in the act of sabotage.

Then just two weeks before Christmas Sister Albertina called me out of the dormitory to run an errand for her to the main convent building. She had dropped and broken her thermometer while trying to take a sick kid's temperature in the infirmary, and I was to go to the convent and ask for a replacement one. I ran down the school driveway to the convent, and collected a thermometer from Sister Angelica the school 'bursar'. I knew that this was my ideal opportunity to hit the Simson light and as I collected the catapult and marbles from its hiding place, I could feel the adrenalin rushing through my body as I prepared to put my plan into action. Everything outside was quiet and peaceful, there was a severe frost that crunched under my every footfall and a nice misty night had diffused everything into a gentle haze. I knew that no one would be able to see me from either the dormitory buildings or the top of the school playground, here was the opportunity to bring my plan to fruition, and I relished the moment standing there on this cold December night.

As I positioned myself underneath the Simson light, I was aware of how still and quiet everything seemed, and my hands had a slight shake in them as I drew back the leather and elastic tensioner with its marble missile right underneath the massive bulb. As I let go of the marble, there was an immediate, massive flash and a loud explosion that almost scared the shit out of me. The noise was so deafening, that I was frozen to the spot for a moment. Shards of hot glass and pieces of red hot filament were now 'raining' down on me like a volcano erupting, and the top of my head was being pebble-dashed with a million little pin-pricks from the glass and hot metal shards. I was hopping and dancing about throwing "fucks" in every direction, and cursing myself for not having a torch to inspect my injuries.

How stupid was I not to have worn my balaclava or a hood of some kind? I knew that I had sustained some bad cuts to the top of my head, as blood was already trickling out of my hair and down on to the bridge of my nose. There was now complete darkness around me, and it took several seconds for my eyes to get accustomed to the sudden lack of light. I ran like a mad thing from underneath the Simson light, and hurriedly placed my catapult back in its secure hiding place. The whole school playground was now in complete darkness, and I admonished myself yet again for not having brought a torch with me, with which to see. I stood outside the school building for several minutes like a wounded porcupine. Shards of glass were sticking out of the top of my head, and rivulets of blood were dripping copiously off the tip of my nose and the sides of my ears - this was not a good situation, and certainly not one that I had planned for.

Things had not gone to well and I now had to think of some very convincing explanations when I returned to Sister Albertina with her new thermometer. I knew that I had sustained several cuts to my head, but I had absolutely no idea how bad my injuries actually were. The mix of adrenalin combined with the freezing temperatures had, for the moment, suppressed a lot of the pain, which would later return with a vengeance. When I arrived back at the 'juniors' dormitory bedlam broke out as over thirty boys started shouting and pointing at me like I was an alien from another planet. Sister Albertina rushed out of her sewing room to investigate all the noise, and she looked at me almost in a state of shock. My whole head and face was now completely covered in rivulets of blood and debris, and shards of glass and metal were sticking out of the top of my head like hedgehog spines. She rushed me in to the infirmary where two young lads were awaiting the arrival of the thermometer to check if they were sick or not. I handed the blood-stained thermometer to Albertina who had already commenced the removal of several pieces of glass with the aid of a tweezers. Every piece of glass that she pulled out of my head was like a pin-prick of torture and her questions were coming fast and furious. All I could say to her between 'ooohs, ouches' and 'ows' was that the Simson Light had exploded as I was walking past it, and I had been showered in glass. In actual fact, this was the truth, the only difference was the omission, on my part, of the catapult and marble which had caused it to explode. I felt I was being quite truthful, and this added a lot of credence to my tale of woe. Albertina had completely accepted this explanation of the events for the moment, but I knew that immediately Aloysius got to know about the incident from Albertina, I would be in a totally different 'ball park'.

That night I went to bed with a head full of pain, for not only had she pulled every single bit of glass out of it, but she then went on to shave and wash it firstly with warm water which hurt like hell, and then with a basin full of TCP which was twice as painful. The final application of yellow iodine and a massive crepe bandage completed my transformation from schoolboy to Egyptian mummy. I was now the third visitor to the infirmary that night and would be kept there for quite a few days to come. I didn't mind the infirmary as much as the thought of the inevitable inquisition that was bound to follow sharply on the heels of this incident. Ruthie needed to come up with a consistent and believable story of the events, that would pass the test when I ran the inevitable gauntlet of questions, threats, theories and innuendos.

Three days after the incident I returned to the dormitory and normal classes and routines within the school. My head was still bandaged with a large crepe dressing and I had to report to Albertina every morning to have the dressing changed. Lumps of my hair had been removed by razor, and the more serious wounds were still being treated with yellow iodine. Workmen had turned up while I was still in the infirmary and they had replaced the massive bulb, they had also added a large piece of wired glass underneath the bulb, which indicated to me that perhaps they suspected that some kind of missile had caused the previous breakage. I was becoming more nervous by the day, awaiting a great big inquisition about how I had sustained my injuries, but one never ever came, it was as if the whole incident had been completely ignored. Of course I could never tell the truth to my friends, as I knew this would be far too risky, but I so wanted to let them know that this was my own little contribution of 'two fingers vertical' to Simson and his indulgent family.

As for Simson himself, He wasn't believing a word of my story,he knew instinctively that I was involved up to my neck in the sabotage of his precious light. I suppose it doesn't take a lot of working out, when you analyse all of the evidence. He certainly wasn't going to swallow my explanation as easily or willingly as the nuns had, and he warned me that the affair had not been forgotten by him and that I had better watch my back in the future. He didn't really have to warn me about watching my back, this was a complete given for me, as I had been watching my 'fecking' back ever since I arrived in this place. I knew however, that Simson would find a way of getting to me in spite of the fact that he had absolutely no conclusive evidence that I had sabotaged the light. Even the three days spent in the infirmary, having glass extracted out of my head with tweezers, would not suffice as punishment for this insult to his family, I had been warned.

Two weeks later I was on my way to Kings Cross station on the coach, and I knew that the Christmas holidays would be more than enough for the whole affair to be forgotten. I was later telling my brother about the incident (he had by now, left Ponsbourne Park for secondary schooling) and he was surprised that the nuns had not reported it to our parents, especially when I was required to be in the infirmary for three days. Such events were normally reported to parents as a matter of course. Our own thinking was that the nuns did not want an inquisition around the reasons for a nine year old boy being out of the school buildings after dark and unaccompanied by an adult. Whatever the reason, I was glad that the whole episode of the Simson light was now behind me. I never did get the satisfaction of actually telling Simson that it was indeed me who had sabotaged his precious light, but then again, it would have made no difference to the insensitive, self-centred idiot. He would remain as 'snobby' and 'indifferent' to all of the people around him for the duration of his days at Ponsbourne Park. There was no doubt in my own mind that Simson would have another go at me sometime in the future, and I would need to tread carefully around him in the meantime, he was fully convinced that I and I alone was responsible for the damage to the light, and he would remind me of this at every possible opportunity.

Chapter 14
School holidays. Lost in London. The paint incident and a barrel full of trouble.

My ninth year at Ponsbourne Park was probably my most difficult one. While I was becoming well-educated and much more worldly-wise, I was also becoming much more aware of the realities of real life. It was probably the year when my childhood innocence was being replaced by the cruel truths and tough consequences of life. This was also the year when John F. Kennedy was assassinated and our quiet and naive existence was being replaced by the realisation that this big world was full of evil plots and evil people. My previously described dustbin adventure, had reminded me of how quickly one's fortunes could change.The newspapers incessantly carried pictures of the assassination and it seemed like the whole planet had put itself on hold for several months as a result of this event. Our age of innocence was slowly coming to an end, and I was aware of a great change in people's attitudes and opinions as a result of this one event. Of course, we still had our Beatles fads and musical interests dominating life in the playground, but the complete 'Kennedy thing' was still fuelling people's daily conversations. As the conspiracy story unfolded in the daily newspapers, one questioned whether the whole of America and its politics were involved in the plot.

In Ireland, Kennedy's picture was being placed next to those of the Pope or the Sacred Heart. it was as if a new saint had been created, and as an Irish descendant and Roman Catholic, Kennedy would certainly take his place among the angels and saints of a whole nation in mourning. My father was particularly saddened by Kennedy's demise as The Kennedy family had originally emigrated from County Wexford where my father's family were also domiciled. He always had a big sense of 'affinity' with the American president and took every opportunity to ensure that we were up to speed with all that was happening in politics in the early sixties. We lived all through 'The Cuban Missile Crisis', 'The Bay of Pigs Debacle', and the deteriorating relationship with Kruzchev in Russia. The horrible days following his assassination In Dallas, Texas. kept Kennedy at the forefront of all of our conversations, and resulted in our spending far more time on our knees in the chapel. His death changed the face of America forever and as 1963 became 1964 one could feel a complete deterioration in the so called "American Dream" as it started to call up many more of its young men to go and fight a futile war in South East Asia. Vietnam was the biggest waste of young American lives, and while Kennedy was loathe to get involved in any big way, his vice president Lyndon B. Johnson, upon taking up the role of President after Kennedy's death, immediately committed more and more American troops to the war front. It was a disaster from start to finish and all efforts by America to keep it from being a totally 'Communist' country were to fail dismally.

Here in England, the pop culture was slowly overtaking the cold war and politics in its news value, and a revolution in fashion and new appearances was invading the London street scene. Carnaby Street was the new Mecca for fashion and trends, and pop music was the new poetry of the younger generation. Twiggy, Mary Quant, Jean Shrimpton and a host of other unusual looking fashion models were becoming our 'pin-ups' and the music scene was pumping from every hidden radio in every dormitory around the school. Pop was replacing politics as the new topic of the day. On the streets of London, however, there were several protest marches against the Vietnam war, and an organisation called CND were organising 'ban the bomb' marches on a regular basis.

This was also the year when I would find myself in the most trouble I had ever experienced at home. I had already experienced a mountain of trouble at school with the 'scrounging' incident and the Simpson light plot still very fresh in my mind. As I returned home for the summer holidays I was very excited and very proud, because I had just won the top prize for the 'Annual Cadbury's Chocolate Composition Awards. I was especially thrilled to be able present my Mum with the large tin box of Cadburys assorted chocolates which was the prize for winning the competition. Most kids of my age would have 'scoffed' all of those chocolates long before getting them safely home, but I was so excited at winning that I purposely kept them as a trophy to present to my Mum.

I had entered the competition every year, and had always received a small box of chocolates and a certificate of merit for my efforts, which every kid did, but this year was special because I had finally achieved first prize. The large brown certificate bore the legend 'First Prize, Certificate of Excellence' and it took its place alongside the 'Merit' certificates which I had collected over the previous three years of the competition. I was really looking forward to seeing my mum's face as I handed her the chocolates and presented my certificate to her. This, however, would have to wait, because my mum was busy working and would not be making the usual journey to King's Cross to collect me from the coach station. This year my mum had befriended a fellow nursing colleague named Mrs Saville and she had two girls of my age group that would be making several visits to our house over the coming holidays. Mrs Saville had volunteered to collect me from the coach to save my mum from having to take time off from her nursing job. This poor lady didn't have a clue what she was letting herself in for, but she would soon find out!

My summer holidays began with the usual waiting for the coaches to arrive in the school playground, there was the same sense of excitement that followed this ritual every holiday, and the same euphoria as the two coaches drove into view. This holiday however, was going to take on a whole new life of its own as the dramas that were about to unfold will testify. Prior to getting on the coach for King's

Cross, the nuns had been notified by telephone, that my mother's friend, Mrs Saville would be meeting me off the coach instead of one or both of my parents, as was the norm. I didn't think too much about the arrangement at the time, but as the hours of the day unravelled, the whole family would be thrown into a drama caused mainly by bad timing, bad communications and a complete lack of proper arrangements. Today I would probably be describing such an event as a 'SNAFU' moment. 'SNAFU' translating to 'situation normal...all fucked up'. I had never met this Mrs Saville before, so I had no idea what she looked like, I naturally presumed and hoped that, as I didn't have a clue how to recognise her, that she would make herself known to me as I got off the bus at Kings Cross. Mum was bound to have shown her a photograph, or at the very least, described a be-freckled nine year old with 'gappy' teeth', 'Brylcreemed hair and a very 'cheeky' disposition. The trouble was that there were about twenty nine year olds arriving on the coach that day, all sharing the same disposition.

As the coaches pulled in to King's Cross coach station, there were the usual crowd of parents awaiting its arrival. I jumped off the coach and went round the back to collect my suitcase. I stood watching the other kids greeting their parents and then walking off to catch trains, buses and taxis to their various home destinations. Soon I was the only kid standing there and the nuns who had accompanied us on our trip to Kings Cross were eager to get back on the coaches and return with the drivers to Goff's Oak in Hertfordshire. There was no sign of this Mrs

Saville who was supposed to be meeting me, and the nuns were getting more and more anxious to begin their return journey back to their convent home.

There was no way that the nuns were going to leave me standing by myself in the middle of London and so they made some phone calls to my parents' house but there was no reply at the number. After an hour of waiting they decided that I would have to return to Ponsbourne Park with them where further arrangements would have to be made. I said that I would continue to wait for Mrs Saville, at King's Cross, but there was no possibility that they would allow this. With a heavy heart I re-boarded the bus for the nearly two hour journey back to school. Something had obviously gone very wrong with the arrangements, and I was very 'hacked off' at the prospect of returning to school.

It was strange being back at Ponsbourne Park when all of the kids had left for their summer holidays, the place was 'eerily' silent and as I walked into the large entrance of the convent building I was amazed to see it stripped of all its furnishings, while four nuns were busily polishing the floors and windows and cleaning down the pelmets and walls. I was ushered into the Bursars office where Sister Angelica was frantically making phone calls to our home address to try and locate any member of the family. She asked me if I had my father's phone number but I explained that he worked in a large glass factory in Neasden and would not be able to be contacted. As I sat there swinging my legs and becoming more and more frustrated by the proceedings, the nuns received a phone call from my mother who explained that Mrs Saville had gone to the wrong coach station in London, but was now making her way to Goff's Oak station where she would meet me.

This was good news for me and a few minutes later I was sat in the front of Father Leeson's Austin Cambridge heading for the local station at Goff's Oak. When we got there he said that I would be met at the station and he walked me to the waiting room with my suitcase. Before leaving he put his hand in his pocket and placed a half Crown in my hand, "when you get home tonight, buy yourself some sweets" he said, and off he went to the station car park. I sat in the waiting room for what seemed hours and several trains had come and gone and yet no sign of Mrs Saville. I went over all of the arrangements in my head, and wondered if they had meant me to be met at Kings Cross. More time went by and a few more trains came and went, by now I had convinced myself that this was the wrong station and that Mrs Saville was probably waiting for me at King's Cross.

I jumped on the next train now fully convinced that this was the right thing to do and forty-five minutes later I arrived at King's Cross, St Pancras. At this stage I was fairly pissed off with the messed up arrangements, and I also realised that I didn't have a ticket to hand in at the exit gate. As I walked towards the gate with a crowd of other passengers I was terrified that I would be caught with no ticket. I walked cheekily through the barrier with several other people and fortunately I had not been spotted by the ticket collector. King's Cross Station was enormous and I had no idea where to wait for Mrs Saville. While all of this was going on poor old Mrs Saville had arrived at Goff's Oak and was completely distraught that I was not there to meet her. She frantically explained to the Station Master that she was supposed to meet a nine year old boy and that he was now missing. The Station Master remembered me sitting in the waiting room for a long, long time, and he immediately phoned King's Cross Station and spoke to the British Transport Police. He explained that there was a missing child with a little brown suitcase, who was missing from Goff's Oak Station but may have boarded a train and who would probably be making his way to Kings Cross.

I, of course, was totally oblivious of the fuss and panic that was now ensuing, as members of British Transport Police were advised to keep an eye out for me. I had been to a kiosk on the station and bought myself a bottle of fizzy orange and a bar of chocolate with the money that Father Leeson had given me. I sat in the middle of the station on my little suitcase right underneath the big clock where Mrs Saville could easily spot me. Several times, while sat there, I thought I had heard my name being called on the station public address system but there was so much echo and hustle and bustle in this very large environment that I didn't pick up on it. It was now late afternoon and I had officially been missing for over three hours since leaving Goff's Oak. Half of London's police force had now been advised of a missing nine year old who was wandering somewhere in the Kings Cross area. I was feeling really hungry by now as it had been a long time since breakfast, and while the drink and chocolate were nice and refreshing I could do with something more substantial to fill my stomach.

I decided there and then, that I would wait just ten more minutes and then I would find my way to Baker Street and catch a train to Kingsbury where we lived. I had made this journey so many times with my parents that I wasn't in the slightest bit phased or concerned at the prospect. Just as these thoughts were going through my head, I was aware of a tall figure standing looking down at me, and as I looked up I was aware of the biggest policeman I had ever seen standing there with his hands on his hips. "Master Seamus Ruth I presume" said the police officer, I was now extremely confused and wondered how this policeman could possibly know my name. "Yes" I said, rather shyly, "that's me" The policeman explained that everyone was looking frantically for me all over London. He picked up my suitcase and gently guided me away with his big arm to The British Transport Police station. Unbeknown to me at the time, Mrs Saville was now in a state of total panic, and reduced to a tearful shadow of her former self. She must have been pretty exhausted herself by the whole sorry experience. Here she was doing my parents a favour by trying to pick me up, and here I was being escorted to the police station after a massive manhunt for a missing nine year old all around central London. The poor lady was half demented, and I have no doubt that she must have really regretted ever volunteering for this task.

When we got to the Police station I had a great time. Everyone there made a big fuss of me. I was given lemonade and Kit Kats and then a little later they treated me to bangers and mash for tea. They had also located Mrs Saville who had travelled all the way into Hertfordshire to try and meet me, but in the meantime my father had been contacted at his place of work, and he was now making his way from Neasden to King's Cross as well. In the meantime I was having a great time, a woman police officer was given the task of caring for me until someone turned up to claim me and she took me all around the station, visiting the stray dogs, sitting on a Police motorcycle and riding around the yard in a patrol car playing with the knobs and switches. I was given police badges, key rings and a single record of Tommy Steele's 'Little White Bull' which had been quite a popular song a few years earlier. This was turning out to be a great day out, and I even sang a few of my school songs for the police officers in their canteen which resulted in a great applause from all of them. With my pockets full of presents and souvenirs, I was hoping that the day would never come to an end. This, my first expereience of dealing with the police, was the best adventure I had enjoyed for a very long time.

Finally at around six o clock my dad and Mrs Saville arrived at Kings Cross to pick me up. I could see that poor Mrs Saville had been crying as her eye-shadow was smudged around her face, and she was shaking all over. My father was was very apologetic to the Police, and tried to comfort Mrs Saville in the best way he knew. The best way he knew, was to turn the whole thing into a kind of comedy of errors, which went down like a 'lead' baloon. The poor woman was totally distraught by the complete experience, and had been reduced to a sobbing shadow of her former self. Both of her daughters were with her and they had shared the same miserable and 'shambolic' day with their mother. They, however, had found it quite an adventure, and had enjoyed every minute of the several train journeys they had taken. I never did get to the bottom of how all of the arrangements had been so badly messed up, but it was all put down to a series of 'communication breakdowns' and the dust would soon settle on the whole incident.

The Saville sisters were very pleasant and well-mannered girls and over the next few weeks, we would go walking, swimming and take trips to the park on a regular basis. As the weeks of summer went by Mrs Saville said that before our summer holidays were over, she would be taking myself, my brother, and her two daughters to visit the London Zoo, and I must admit that I was really looking forward to the trip. I had never been to a zoo before and I had heard a lot about Regent's Park, London Zoo from various friends that had visited it in the past. You could say that I was very excited at the prospect, and one of the Saville sisters was definetely taking my fancy in a biggish way

At the back of our house in Kingsbury there was a long back alley where most of the kids from the neighbourhood would meet and play. Some parts of the alleyway were 'no go' areas because some of the local 'bullies' would set upon you if you were anywhere near their piece of territory. One day we were playing in the alleyway with the Saville sisters and a local lad named Keith Kittsaw who lived just a few doors away from us decided that he would create a little bit of aggravation by sticking his nose in where it wasn't wanted. Keith was an overweight, loud-mouthed individual who had a terrible habit of sticking his fingers up his bum and smelling them. I never understood his fascination with this activity, but whenever he partook of this weird and disgusting habit we would refuse to play with him until he went home and thoroughly washed his hands. Keith had a booming voice that could be heard all over the neighbourhood and he was forever in trouble with various residents for his outspoken taunts and bad language. Of course we could all use bad language, and often did on a regular basis, but we were always careful not to be caught by adults or parents. In Keith's case, he was just too 'uncouth' and 'stupid' to realise the difference, and he cursed and swore at anyone without the slightest hesitation. These bouts of unruly and loud expletives always ended up in complaints from neighbours directly to Keith's parents, and he spent a great deal of his time being confined to his bedroom for his behaviour, a term which they now call 'grounded'.

Keith had a very pretty sister named Christabell who I had developed a massive crush on at the time. Christabell was quiet, intelligent, polite and as opposite from Keith as one could possibly imagine. She was always pleased to see me on the school holidays and we would often try and steal some time together away from her loud and uncouth brother. Christabell was the first girl that I had ever kissed, and this would become a routine whenever we could find time alone together. Unfortunately most of our attempts at privacy were always invaded by her brother's loud and intrusive presence. We would also exchange little letters while I was away at boarding school, it was a kind of nice arrangement, but Keith didn't approve of his sister hanging around with either of the Ruth brothers. Christabell on the other hand was always pleased to see us, and she would often count down the days to our various school holidays when we would return home once again. Keith's grandfather would admonish us at every opportunity, especially at times when we would send his loud-mouthed grandson home crying as a result a good kick up the arse. "You don't want nothing to do with those bloody 'Arish'" would be the standard response from his 'bigoted. grandfather.

So Keith was never really encouraged to play with us whenever we would return home, but he clearly enjoyed our company as he would spend many of his waking hours calling for us to come and play with him. We tolerated him because of his sister, and we knew that Christabell would probably disappear from our lives forever if the fragile friendship with her brother was broken. Notwithstanding all of that, and because his grandparents, and to a lesser extent his parents, were completely anti-Irish, we restricted our contact with them to the very minimum. His grandfather was a real old 'racist' who treated Irish, blacks and every other race with complete contempt. Whenever Keith was going out to play his grandfather would remind him at the back door to "keep away from those 'bleeding' Arish". We would howl with laughter whenever Keith related these comments to us, and in spite of the prejudices that existed at that time, we merely shrugged them off as narrow-minded and hypocritical, and compared with our boarding school existence, pretty innocuous.

Christabell used to get highly embarrassed by her grandfather's and the rest of her family's prejudices, but Keith being slightly older had already been influenced by the rantings of his grandfather. On one occasion when Keith was berating the 'bleeding Arish' my father, who had overheard the comments, reminded him that it was the Irish and black nurses that were keeping the 'old boy' alive with their daily visits to administer insulin and other medications to his grandfather. He also reminded Keith that West Indian workers were keeping the complete London transport system running and without the Irish and the Blacks the whole country would probably come to a complete standstill. No doubt, Keith would go home a little later and relate this conversation back to his parents. I doubt if it would have made any difference to them or his 'bigoted' old grandfather, but I suppose that given the old boy's contribution as a soldier in the war years, he might be entitled to a little 'levity' and a few racist comments.

Keith would fall out with us regularly and one day you would be his best friend and the next he would be 'effing and blinding' your very existence. Year after year we would return home in the various holidays and Keith would be also counting down the days until our return, not because he was such a great pal of ours, but more because he had probably fallen out with every other kid in the neighbourhood. We would spend long days with himself, Christabell and many other friends at Kingsbury swimming pool and explore various places of interest in the areas around home. One minute Keith would be delighted to share our company and then he would suddenly turn on us for no apparent reason. Invariably he would be sent packing with another kick up the 'arse' only to return for more the very following day. We had been used to this for years, but it didn't really matter much to us because most of the time we would be away at boarding school and the friendship was merely 'transient' for the most part.

Things did come to a head however, when the Saville sisters arrived on the scene. Keith, for reasons best known to himself, took an instant dislike to them, and at every opportunity he would be extra rude and very, very mean to them; he loved to make them cry with his insults, and one afternoon he soaked the pair of them with a water pistol, which he filled regularly from a large water barrel in his back garden. I finally decided that the time had come to teach Keith Kittsaw a lesson in manners and along with another friend from the back alleyway, we devised a cruel plan which, if successful, would keep the Kittsaw family a little busy for a while.

Steve Stanley was another neighbour of Keith's and lived just a few doors away from him. Affectionately known as Stiffo, Steve, like many other kids around the area, spent a great deal of his time being 'pissed off' with Keith, and his constant belligerent attitude. We had briefly discussed a plan to put Keith in his place, and the aforementioned water barrel was to figure prominently in its execution. I knew, from the start that this plan, if attributed to me, would probably end our fragile friendship with Keith for ever, and I worried even more about losing my friendship with Christabell. Nevertheless, and with the constant badgering and encouragement of Stiffo a plan was taking shape. We had decided that enough was enough and that Keith's bad treatment of the Saville sisters and everyone else around him, warranted more than a little action on our part. We planned our campaign with precision and determination and we knew that this one incident was going to create more than a little trouble in the Kittsaw household. I was very worried about the effect of our plot on the rest of the Kittsaw household, and I warned Stiffo of the importance of keeping this event totally between the two of us at all costs.

The Kittsaws had a large secluded back garden that was easy to get into, as their house was the last one in a row at the end of the back alleyway. Secrecy and stealth were essential to the success of our plan, and it was imperative that the journey from my house to his house along the back alleyway was not witnessed by a single friend or neighbour. Steve, who lived just two doors away from Kieth, had the same priority, and we sneaked around like a couple of alley cats avoiding being spotted by any of the neighbours. Nobody worried about security or break-ins back then, so doors and gates were very rarely locked, and I knew for certain that Keith's back garden had no lock on the gate of any kind. We hatched our plan to make a very special, visit to Keith's back garden one evening in the very near future, to get our revenge on behalf of the Saville sisters.

One Saturday night after dark, we sneaked out of our respective houses, into the back alleyway, and crept stealthily into Keith's back garden. There was nobody in either the kitchen or the upstairs bedrooms, as they would by now be sitting in their front lounge probably digesting their suppers and watching an episode of a western called 'Bonanza' on the television. There was the big barrel just to one side his back door which was used to collect rainwater off the kitchen roof. This was the same rain barrel that Keith used to refill his water pistol from. Steve and I quietly and carefully manoeuvred the barrel across the outside of the back door and leaned it at an acute angle against the door of the Kittsaw's kitchen. We then ran their garden hose into the barrel and filled it right to the brim with water from their hosepipe located on the outside tap. If my memory serves me well, the average barrel held about 56 gallons of liquid, and so there was a hell of a lot of water leaning against the back of Keith's house, waiting for someone to open the back door. We left the scene as quietly as we had arrived, and sneaked back indoors without anyone noticing that we had been missing. The plot was firmly hatched, and there was now no going back. We had expected Keith's kitchen door to be open at some stage that evening but for some reason nobody went into the kitchen on that particular evening, and so the barrel was leaning there all night waiting for an unwitting victim. I retired to bed with an innate sense of annoyance that nothing had come of our plan that evening, and I was slightly worried that there was an outside possibility that someone may have spotted the barrel and put an end to our little plot, I didn't have to worry.

The following morning there was, apparently, hell to pay in the Kittsaw household. Keith's Mum had got up to make their customary Sunday breakfast, and she was the one unfortunate enough to open the back door for the first time that day. What followed was a deluge or tidal wave which swept through the kitchen and into the downstairs hallway. I wished that I had been a fly on the wall as Mrs Kittsaw screamed 'blue murder' with as many expletives as she could think of. The neighbours to either side of her described a scene like 'world war three breaking out' with the whole Kittsaw household screaming and shouting at each other for what seemed hours. Accusations were flying around the various households where any suspects could be imagined, and this, in turn, fuelled a deluge of insults and innuendos from all over the street. We, of course, did not get any of the news until much later on that day when Mrs Thompson, our immediate neighbour, related the whole story to my mum over the back garden fence. I remember I had to make myself scarce during that conversation, as I could not contain the laughter that was welling up inside of me like an erupting volcano. She had been told by Steve's mum, Mrs Stanley, that the barrel of water had created a mini 'tsunami' downstairs in the

Kittsaw household. There was not a single room that had not been affected by the wall of water that had unexpectedly cascaded through their back door in a 'deluge' of wet destruction. The dog and his basket had gone sailing down the hallway like the 'owl and the pussycat' and old grandad Kittsaw had thrown so many 'fucks' and 'cunts' about that they were scared he might give himself a stroke or a heart attack. Steve's mum questioned him at length to try and ascertain who, he thought, had done such a mean thing, never suspecting for a minute that her own son had been up to his eyeballs in the planning and execution of this awful act of vandalism.

No one in our family had a clue that I had been in any way responsible or connected to the morning's events, but I knew that the blame would soon come knocking on the door when the Kittsaw family started to 'tot' up further possible suspects. For the meantime however, I knew that they would all be too busy 'bailing out' the enormous amount of water that had come calling on that fateful Sunday morning. I did feel extremely guilty after this event however, especially as granddad and grandma Kittsaw who slept downstairs in the house, had to be moved out for a few days while their carpets and floorboards were being dried out. Neighbours reported a further cascade of foul language from grandad Kittsaw, as he was being driven away from the scene. I felt even guiltier as the story of the damaged food supplies and dry goods that had to be thrown away were related to us all. I didn't feel bad for very long however, as Keith later 'bragged' that the insurance company were renewing everything that was damaged, including a few extra items that his parents had added to the list.

Steve and myself stayed completely quiet about the whole event and did not even let on to close friends or family for fear of the news getting out. We both had perfect alibis as we were both in bed on Sunday morning as witnessed by our complete family, and no one had thought of the possibility that the barrel had been placed there the night before. I don't recall if the incident had been reported to the police or not, but I felt sure that Mr Kittsaw would have left no stone unturned in her search for the culprits. I could picture old grandad Kittsaw mouthing the memorable words "It was probably those fucking Arish".

Just one week later, on Saturday morning, we were due to take that exciting trip to the zoo with the Saville sisters. Unfortunately events were about to take a change for the worse, when an unprecedented disaster took place in our own household, with me right at the centre of it. If there is a thing called 'poetic' justice, then this incident was probably the qualification for it. I remember that it was a beautiful sunny Saturday and both my brother and I were very excited at the prospect of spending a day at the zoo. This would be my last outing of the holidays as I was returning to school the following day, so I wanted to make the most of it. My father had given us some pocket money to spend at the zoo, and we were now awaiting the arrival of Mrs Saville and the two girls. What was about to follow would bring absolute 'pandemonium' for my poor parents and in particular my soon-to-be heartbroken mother.

I was in my bedroom putting together an 'Airfix' model of 'the Golden Hinde' and my brother was downstairs watching out of the window for the imminent arrival of the Saville sisters. That morning, my dad had decided that while my mum was out working on the district, he would take the opportunity of painting the loft hatch at the top of the stairs. My dad was such a careful and competent painter that he rarely changed out of his normal clothes into overalls or scruffier attire. In fact he did everything in his collar and tie much to the annoyance of my mother who constantly admonished him for using his best clothes on such tasks. He could regularly be found doing various jobs of decorating in his normal daily clothes, even donning his usual tie and shirt, a habit that I myself later came to emulate. This particular morning my dad had placed his step-ladder at the top of the stairs on the main landing and having opened a very large can of white gloss paint, he proceeded to paint the loft hatch.

At that precise moment the doorbell rang downstairs, heralding the arrival of the Saville sisters. My brother answered the door and the two girls stepped into the hallway dressed in two very pretty matching summer dresses and bright red ribbons in both of their hairs. Before my dad had time to react or warn me that he was painting the trapdoor, I sprung out of the bedroom like a greyhound, and raced towards the stairwell. Not only was I completely unaware that my dad had commenced painting, but I was also totally oblivious of the giant tin of paint that was now balancing precariously on top of the newel-post at the top of the stairs. To say that I bumped into it would be a real understatement, I literally smashed into it at about a hundred miles an hour. I then watched it's progress, in stunned silence, as it tumbled down the stairs banging from one side to another following a trajectory towards the two sisters standing patiently in the hallway below.

It's very true that when people are describing a past serious event they refer to things happening in slow motion. Well I know where they are coming from, because to this day I have a slow motion vision of the events that unfurled on that memorable day as a direct result of that somersaulting can of paint.

My Dad rarely used expletives in his daily life, but that morning, I'm sure that I clearly heard the phrase 'fucking hell' as the paint tin began its fateful journey following the laws of gravity and spreading its contents over my mother's brand new red 'Wilton' carpet. The drama did not end there however, for as the can made its final bounce, on what was probably the bottom stair, a copious amount of paint shot out of the still spinning tin. It literally 'pebble dashed' both of the Saville sisters as they stood there in their best clothes waiting patiently for the Ruth brothers to accompany them to the zoo.

One of the sisters, Moira, had always worn those round pink 'National Health' glasses that were so popular in the 60s, and today was no exception. She received the full force of the tidal wave of paint, and as she carefully removed her glasses which were now covered in white gloss paint. She resembled a sad little Panda bear replete

258

with two perfectly round silhouettes where her glasses had previously sat. There followed a scene of complete carnage with my dad, myself and the unfortunate Saville sisters right at the middle of it. Fortunately my brother had been out of range of the splashing paint, but he stood there in a state of shock at what he had just witnessed.

From that moment 'pandemonium' broke out all over the house. My father shot down the stairs like a man possessed, and as he surveyed the damage all around him, he was heard to mutter these dreaded words. "Jesus Christ we'll all be killed when your mother gets home". The Saville sisters were quickly ushered out of the front door after my dad's futile attempts at removing the gloss paint from all over themselves and their beautiful summer dresses, My brother had the unenviable task of taking them home to their mother who was waiting for all of us to arrive at any moment, what turned up was a sight that I am sure she will remember for a long, long time to come. Her two beautiful daughters who just minutes earlier had eagerly skipped off down the road to our house in their beautiful Summer attire, were now returning from, what could best be described at that time as, a 'bloody war zone'. My brother later described Mrs Saville's reaction as one of complete shock, and the two sisters had to spend several hours in the bath being 'scrubbed' with massive amounts of shampoo, washing-up liquid and any other detergent that could be found to remove the paint. I remember wondering, as the girls left for home, if my brother would dare ask Mrs Saville if we were still going to the zoo in spite of the recent happenings.

I, of course, knew at the very moment the paint can started it's untimely journey down those stairs, that our trip to the London Zoo was now in total jeopardy and as my father ripped up the paint-stained carpets and laid them out on the back lawn, I began to realise the extent of the damage, there was not a single piece of carpet that had not been affected by the paint spillage, not to mention the various walls inside the hallway that had also been splashed in several places. My father, whose pallor had turned to a million shades of pale, rapidly disappeared down the road with my brother to town, and returned with what amounted to gallons and gallons of turpentine and white spirit. I later discovered that he had bought every available bottle and tin from one particular shop. He literally poured the spirit copiously into the carpet and then brushed it out again with a stiff yard brush. The carpet had turned from rich red to a warm pink colour.

It was at about this point in the proceedings that my mother returned from her morning's work visiting patients out on the district. To say that she was in a mild state of shock would be a gross underestimate, you could hear her 'wailing' from about three streets away. She paced up and down the back garden purveying the carnage with a look of total horror on her face. My father continued to scrub away at the carpet amid a 'barrage' of inquisition from my mother who, after a brief report around the morning's events, took herself off to her bedroom to contemplate the full implications of her current domestic situation, and shed a few hours more tears. During all of this time I was keeping myself busy in my own bedroom, preferring to avoid any possible contact with either my mother or my father for at least the rest of that day. Surprisingly, my mother was in too deep a state of shock to come and speak to me about it, a situation which I was very much surprised and relieved about. Hours and hours elapsed, during which time my poor father scrubbed the living daylights out of the red Wilton carpet. A deep depression had, that day, descended on the Ruth household which was not to be forgotten in a hurry. This little drama would traverse the years as an amusing conversation piece, but at this very moment in time it had merely provoked a silence and an atmosphere that that you could cut with a knife.

There is no doubt that my father took the brunt of the blame for the paint incident. my mother apparently cried for about four days after the event, especially as she had saved for months to purchase the carpet which was now adorning the back garden in such a sorry state. I was returning to boarding school the following day and for one of the first times in my life, I was grateful to be leaving this scene of absolute chaos. The only consolation, as my father dropped me at Kings Cross coach station, were his kind words when he told me not to worry about the carpet. I climbed on the coach that day, feeling really sorry for both him and my mother who had saved so hard to buy that red Wilton. The carpet was eventually restored to the hall, stairs and landing after several hours of scrubbing and cleaning, and several days drying out in the garden. We were always reminded of this incident, because for years afterwards there was always the faint smell of white spirit emanating from it. My father did a 'sterling' job that day however, and I was lucky that, apart from a good stiff telling off, I managed to extricate myself from this awful situation with all of my limbs intact. My father, of course, continued to take the full blame from my mother as the events of that day were analysed and replayed on a minute by minute basis to neighbours, friends and acquaintances for many months afterwards. To say that he suffered 'brain damage' would be a fair description of my father's condition at that momentous time in his life.

The story of the damaged carpet was the subject on everyone's lips, not just over the next few weeks or months, but for years afterwards, and it eventually took on a 'comical' hue in which I was the main protagonist, while my father still bore the largest portion of responsibility.

As for the Kittsaw water incident, that became a very secondary event in the story of that particular holiday, and faded slowly in to my, and everyone else's, distant memory. Surprisingly, no one in that household suspected me of being the culprit responsible, they had identified several other possible suspects for that particular piece of work. My anonymity remained intact, and Keith Kittsaw, many months later, described to me a household in total turmoil and disbelief, that anyone would have the front to carry out such an attack on such 'kind' people as themselves. I wondered if I would ever share any more innocent kisses with Christabell, who seemed to be the only normal person in the Kittsaw household. My father did eventually question me about the water barrel incident, and asked me who, in my opinion, was responsible for the tidal wave within the Kittsaw household. I think I may have detected just a slightly knowing smile emanating from his lips as I 'reeled off' a few possible candidates from up and down the alleyway, who could be capable of such bad behaviour.

I never did find out the outcome of Mrs Saville's part in my being lost in London that last day of term, or of the Saville sister's brief visit to our house on that fateful paint day. I did however, often wonder if they ever eventually managed to make it to the zoo. I was also somewhat saddened by the fact that all through that summer I had been sharing a few illicit little kisses with Moira, the elder of the sisters, and now it seemed to be over. One thing is for sure, the invitation was never repeated for us to accompany them to any other outings. As a matter of fact, I think this was the last time we had ever spent in their company. Strange that, very strange indeed.

Chapter 15
My Move to the senior Dorm and a bad dose of Mumps

The journey back to boarding school after a long holiday was always a great big anti-climax, and the school buses were quiet and subdued in comparison to the homeward journeys where kids were noisy, animated and excited. As I climbed on to the bus at King's Cross Station, I was reminded of the big adventure that had ensued on my outward journey. This journey would not in any way compare with the excitement of that day which now seemed so very long ago. The holiday had been filled with events that were memorable to say the least, and would provide plenty of conversation to my pals back at school. In fact, my pals back at school would be the only people that I could possibly share those happenings with, as there was no chance of the stories being relayed to anyone back in my home town. Equally, I would never share my illicit school adventures with any of my peers here, for fear of the information falling into the wrong hands.

The first few days were always full of 'catching up' stories and discussions around the holidays in general. These discussions would start up in an animated chorus of 'guess what's' as each kid in turn related the happenings of his particular holiday. I did share the story of the paint episode with a few of my best friends, as this occurrence was basically an unfortunate accident, and I still had a lot of regrets around the expense and aggravation that the incident had cost my poor parents.

The prospect of returning to school didn't inspire a single one of us, as we watched the busy city traffic recede into the distance to be replaced by country lanes, country noises and countryside. I was particularly morose at the prospect of returning to Ponsbourne Park and a completely new living situation, but then, there were several others on the bus who were facing the exact same prospects. So I wasn't completely alone in my thoughts. As the bus pulled down the main driveway to the school, I reflected on what a beautiful setting we inhabited, the school buildings sparkled white in the autumn sunshine and the surrounding countryside was a mass of beautiful autumn colours. It's true that many kids would never enjoy such a wonderful environment in which to receive their education. This place bore no resemblance to the inner-city schools, where the constant rumble of traffic and a severe lack of greenery created a really unhealthy daily 'grind'. On the other hand, those city kids had the distinct freedom of being able to return to their own homes every night, and probably to parents who doted on them at every opportunity. They would not be feeling that extreme loneliness which we experienced every term upon returning to Ponsbourne Park. There would be very few tears in their bedrooms tonight as their mothers and fathers kissed them off to sleep, but here in our lonely dormitories there would be a lot of sobbing and crying, especially from the younger kids around us who had not yet learned to put a brave face on their feelings and do their grieving in complete privacy. What a shame for us, to be living in such a wonderful and idyllic setting and yet, being constantly fearful of just a few uncaring adults who inhabited this place with us.

The time had come for my move from the juniors' dormitory into the seniors. I was now to be exposed to Aloysius on a daily basis without the opportunity to avoid her in any way, and it was with great amount of fear and trepidation that I presented myself in the seniors section on that September day. My return from summer holidays and all of the upsets and adventures that had occurred already seemed an age away. The usual routines of settling back in to the disciplined day to day mundanity of school life were now upon me. The first task for every boarder upon their return from any holiday was to familiarise themselves with new situations. I wandered around the seniors' dormitory looking for any labels that might bear my name. These would be placed above beds, towel racks, sports cupboards, cloakroom hooks and every other place that one frequented on one's journey around the timetables and routines of our daily lives.

I busied myself unpacking all of my clothes and equipment in readiness for the coming school term. I knew from conversations with my brother that the seniors dormitories were probably the most threatening for newcomers, not least because you were now the lowest form of life to inhabit them, and you were 'fair game' for any of the older boys to kick about at their leisure. The best policy was to sort a few of them out in the early days, and make it known that, although you were a new kid on the block, you were not about to take any of their 'shit' lying down. I had a slight advantage in being a vice captain, but this ranking would not carry any favours from the elder senior boys that already inhabited these dorms.

A few of the older seniors were already busy throwing their weight around, establishing their authority over the younger newcomers. I had expected as much, and the odd kick up the arse from a senior was replied to, in my case, with two fingers vertical and a promise that if they wanted to try me out outside, they would regret every 'fucking' minute from this day forward. Of course there were some that you would not dare try to retaliate with, and the wise policy in those cases was to give them a very wide berth. All in all I was not fazed by any of the seniors that I would be sharing the dorm with, my brother had given me a blow by blow analysis of the ones to be avoided and the ones to put in their place straight away. It was not so much a 'dog eat dog' situation. It was more a "try anything with me just once, and I will kick the living shit out of you". Many of them already knew of the reputation of the sly Ruths, and treated me with due deference and respect. The rest would make themselves known during the course of the next few weeks, and hopefully, after a few well aimed kicks and punches, a mutual respect would follow shortly afterwards.

Fortunately for me, there were at least six or seven of my good pals also coming up from the junior dormitories, and we had resolved very quickly to be a little gang of

Musketeers with a mutual 'all for one and one for all' mentality. This should allay most of the 'crap' that could be thrown at us during those early days of settling in to the seniors' environment.

The first thing that I noticed about the senior dorms was that they were a lot 'scruffier' than I had expected. Clearly these accommodations were a lot more basic than the junior and infant environment, and everything seemed a lot more dirty and dusty. They also seemed much more crammed and oppressive with lower ceilings and less window light. Maybe I had grown too much in the past few years and was now seeing things from the perspective of a taller and more mature boy. With all of this in mind I set about creating my own tidy environment around my bed and locker, making sure that all of my kit was housed in the correct places within the dormitory building. My previous tenure in the junior and infant dorms had taught me to be fastidiously clean and tidy with both my clothing and all of my personal toiletry equipment. Cleanliness was certainly next to Godliness in this place, but more importantly, cleanliness kept you out of a lot of trouble with both the prefects, house captains and dormitory sisters. Clothes had to be neatly folded at all times, and every personal item that one possessed had to be housed in its proper place. Beds had to be made in the prescribed manner and suitable for inspection at any time. I double-checked everything just to be sure. The last thing I needed on my first day back was aggravation with Aloysius or any other senior that might come my way.

A sudden scuttling of feet, and kids running around in a panic, alerted me that Aloysius had been spotted in the building. It was almost like rats flinging themselves on traps at the sight of a big cat heading in their direction, "Annie Oakley on the warpath" was the message shouted from boy to boy and dormitory to dormitory as more and more kids joined the scramble to get away. I remained calm but nervous as I heard her distinctive footfall begin the journey up the long wooden stairs. This would be my first experience of being completely under her jurisdiction since leaving her classroom about four years earlier and while I unfortunately ran into her during various times through the previous school terms, I would now be much closer to her scrutiny on a daily basis. I didn't relish the prospect. My peers shared the same fears as, I'm sure, did all the boys in the senior dorms, it was ironic that without Aloysius around the place this whole school experience could now start to be a very pleasant one. Strange that one person can make so much difference to the 'ambience' and 'atmosphere' of a place just by their mere presence. Aloysius certainly wielded her power across so many aspects of our school life, probably because she enjoyed the status of not only teacher, but also of Seniors house mistress, she was everywhere at one time.

"Welcome to the senior dorm Master Ruth, I hope we see some great things from you this term". Her greeting took me off - guard and completely by surprise, I had never forgotten my first meeting with her, and I was quite taken aback by her apparent good humour as she shuffled towards me in her usual black and white attire. She somehow appeared less threatening than before and I thought that I might have detected a hint of friendliness in her otherwise familiar voice. The fact that Aloysius had greeted me so politely, and without a single threatening gesture, was a little unnerving, and her whole demeanour was one of pleasant informality and friendliness. I was careful not to be 'lulled' into a false sense of security and become too relaxed in her company, she was still a pretty dangerous antagonist as far as I was concerned. She questioned me about my summer holidays and enquired how my mother and father were keeping. She even managed to preclude her normal pointed question "does your father still work in a factory?" This was very strange behaviour indeed, and I wondered if she was perhaps suffering from a temporary lapse of memory, and that any minute now I would receive a smack around the earhole for old time's sake.

Nothing of the sort occurred, and here I was talking in a civilised manner to a nun who had, for many years, scared the living shit out of me and all of my peers. She intimated that she was expecting a lot from me this term and that my main aims in arriving in the senior dorms should be to "stay out of trouble and be a 'role model' to all of my peers, especially the younger ones". I thought I had landed on another planet, here was this 'ogre' who 'cowed' all of the kids in her care being friendly and civilised with a mere 'amoeba' such as myself-was somebody playing a practical joke? She sat with me for several minutes exchanging what can only be described as 'pleasantries' and even some of the other lads who had skulked away to avoid her, were timidly returning to listen in on the conversation. Something must have happened to her in the previous school holidays, perhaps she had been kidnapped by aliens and given a new personality or a 'charisma bypass'. Whatever had happened to her I was hoping that it would continue to influence her mood for a very long time to come.

Before leaving the dorm she put her hand into the deep pocket in her habit and pulled out a little red velvet box which she placed firmly into the palm of my hand. "I am going to trust you with a new role this term" she said, "and I expect you to take it very seriously indeed, as no boy of your age and in their first year in the seniors would receive such a privilege" I was puzzled by this strange gesture, and as I opened the little box in trepidation, there sat the 'Games Captain' shield, a beautiful red enamelled badge with gold lettering beneath it, in the shape of an unfurled scroll. She pinned this on the right hand lapel of my blazer and warned me "it can be taken away just as easily as it has been presented, so you better make sure that you make good use of the privilege and responsibility that comes with it"

I was absolutely 'flabbergasted' that she should think me responsible enough to take on such an important role in just my first year in seniors dorm, but I wondered whether this might also turn out to be a 'poisoned chalice' in disguise. I assured her that I would certainly take the role seriously, and that was the last conversation that I was to have with her for quite a few weeks to come.

My first few days in the senior dorms passed without further incident and I had now moved up to class five where, I had been warned, that the real hard education would commence. I wore my Games Captain and Vice Captain badges with great pride, and although there were the odd rude remarks from people who didn't rate my abilities, in the main most of my peers were happy with my appointments. Class five was the pre 'Eleven Plus' class where studying for that all important exam would commence. I knew that the pressure would be on me, and that a lot of serious studying would now follow. I was happy with my abilities in most subjects, but my weakness would be Mathematics, and always had been.

A new nun had been introduced to the school during the summer holidays and she would be our new form teacher, we wondered what kind of character she would be. Would she be the usual strict unsmiling 'ogre' that so many of them were, or would we finally meet a kind and sympathetic individual with a more caring side? Well, we were pleasantly surprised when Sister Mary Lucy walked in to our classroom on that very first morning. Not only was she quietly spoken and 'all smiling' she was also a stunning looking woman who smelled of scented soap and walked with a skip in her step. All of us were smitten by her youthful and pretty persona, and her brief introduction to us convinced me that here was a teacher that I could really learn a lot from, and who would take an interest in all of our learning endeavours.

She described a life spent in South Africa as a young novice and then her advancement into university and teaching. She was also quite 'trendy' and spoke enthusiastically about the 'swinging' London scene that was a fast growing part of the sixties culture. She reeled off the pop songs and bands that she particularly liked, and found common ground with us all from that first meeting. She expressed an interest in every pupil as she ticked off our names in the class register, but most surprisingly of all, she advised us that she would not be using the strap as either a deterrent or punishment, a statement that earned her a big round of applause from every kid in the room. We could hardly believe what we were hearing, and we were all delighted to have a teacher who would clearly use a very different approach in her dealings with us. The fact that she would not be employing the strap was the most amazing surprise to us all, I secretly hoped that she would be a reforming influence on Aloysius, but I imagined that I would probably wait just a little longer for that particular miracle to occur. Perhaps when Hell froze over.

The playground conversations were a mixture of excitement and admiration for the new teacher, and Sister Lucy was turning into a 'heart throb' with all of the boys who were lucky enough to be in her class. Things were really looking up. My classroom life was taking on a whole new experience of its own and it created a fantastic atmosphere that was welcomed by both the day pupils and the boarders alike. Aloysius maintained her good moods which was a puzzle to everybody, no one could understand her complete change of temperament, but we still chose to tread on eggshells around her as we were all aware that a leopard doesn't change its spots. Things in the senior dorm were a bit weirder for anyone who was a bed-wetter, in the juniors Sister Albertina tended to wake the offending kids up and make them go to the toilet at regular intervals through the night.

Aloysius however, had a much more imaginative way of keeping her bed-wetters on the straight and narrow. She simply moved them and their beds in to an annexe room next to the main dormitory. This annexe room housed all of the workings of the school clock including the Westminster chime bells that rang out every fifteen minutes. I know I have previously mentioned this, but the reality of witnessing any kid having to sleep under the clock was absolutely horrific when experienced in reality. They literally could not fall asleep under any circumstance, because the noise generated by the various cogs and pendulum of this enormous clock were absolutely deafening. The long pendulum creaked and groaned as it traversed its journey from side to side of the clock housing, this alone was enough to keep anyone from sleeping. I was now witnessing first-hand how badly treated were the kids who had the misfortune to wet their beds, this was the worst kind of ostracisation that anyone could imagine. Whether this cured any of the bed-wetters is hard to say, but it sure provided them with a lousy nights slumber, and even more, the incentive to go to the loo in order to avoid a wet bed in the morning. I knew a couple of the kids who literally fell asleep in the toilets through sheer exhaustion only to wake up a few hours later shivering with the cold.

Thankfully, I was not a bed-wetter and on the rare occasions that such a thing did happen to me, I always thought about those poor unfortunate kids that ran the gauntlet of Aloysius's cruel rules. As the weeks went by, I became increasingly aware of Aloysius's kinder attitude to the senior kids, and then she suddenly disappeared one day without any warning. She appeared to have just left the school completely without any of the pupils witnessing her departure. Something was definitely not right and we were all puzzled and bemused by these new circumstances that were literally turning our world upside down. With the old Aloysius, everyone knew where they stood, and ran like fuck away from her presence at every given opportunity. To have her change her character in such a dramatic way was absolutely mind-boggling, and just when we were getting used to the new non-hostile version of the same person they suddenly up and disappeared without explanation. The mystery was solved a few days later however, when a gentle nun named Sister Centonni was placed in charge of the senior dorm. She explained that Aloysius had returned to Ireland where her mother was seriously ill. While we all offered a certain amount of sympathy for Aloysius's predicament, we were also secretly rejoicing that here was some respite from the strict and oppressive regime that she had created. We all prayed that this state of affairs would last for a very long time, and the words on everyone's lips was 'freedom at last'. We wondered if her strange change of mood at the beginning of this term was tied in with her worries about her sick mother and surmised that this was definitely the reason for it.

Sister Centonni was instantly recognised as a pretty 'soft touch' she was the complete opposite from her predecessor in almost every way. Her relaxed approach to every aspect of running the senior dorm, soon created an environment of happy abandon among myself and my peers. Sister Centonni had been previously known to us as a 'kindly' lay nun who took care of the school gardens, we would often join her to assist in fruit-picking and help in keeping the seemingly acres of lawns that were a big feature of Ponsbourne Park. Guys were rarely admonished for any wrong-doing, and there was certainly no threat of a strapping from this likeable nun. Serious misdemeanours were normally punished by her in a very mature and 'grown up' manner. Kids would be excluded from certain privileges if they really misbehaved badly, but these punishments were so innocuous in comparison to previous ones, that most of the kids in her care gave her a lot of respect, and went out of their way to please her. This relaxed atmosphere spread throughout the whole school, and even life in the strict confines of the classroom took on an almost surreal existence for what seemed a very long time. Even the other nuns and teachers seemed to lighten up, there were far less punishments being meted out by many of them, and a nonchalant attitude seemed to pervade every aspect of school life.

It was during this period, that I enjoyed my most rewarding and satisfying times in my tenure as Games Captain. Although the role entailed lots of organisation of inter-school football matches and sports competitions, it also demanded large amounts of commitment in making sure that all of the sports equipment was in good repair and always at the ready. Tennis nets had to be erected and hung in readiness for any matches that had been organised; leather footballs had to be inflated to the correct poundage for use in competitions and practise days. School kits had to be stored in readiness for future matches and cricket equipment and kits had to be maintained for the same purpose. I threw myself into the role with enthusiasm and gusto, soon finding out that much of it was hard work combined with 'tedium' and repetition. Fortunately for me, I was able to obtain lots of new kit and the renewal of several ageing footballs and cricket balls.

The school teams were never better equipped, and this started to show in improved results both on and off the various pitches. I enlisted the help of several of the juniors to help with general cleaning of the kit, and the tidying out of the sports shed, which was housed in a little brick-built niche attached to the main school wall. Mr Reardon agreed to put a new roof on the little building, and within a few short weeks the sports equipment and its housing were in ship-shape order. The one frustrating thing about my sports Captain's role was the lack of competition with other schools, and competitions were restricted to inter-house ones only. Most of our competitive matches were played between boarders and day pupils, so it was really hard to decide what level of achievement our school teams actually slotted in to.

Given the above, it was very hard to measure just how high our standards were, we only had our own internal house matches and competitions, which, although we believed were to a high standard of acumen, were pretty unmeasured against other schools around Hertfordshire. The games Captain's role required that person to be strictly neutral in their support of the school teams, but I have to confess that my interest in Patrick's team leading in the various leagues was of prime importance to me. I did everything I could to try to provide an 'edge' for them mainly in the provision of coaching on Sunday afternoons, to bring them up to scratch with other teams in the school.

One particular Sunday afternoon, I had confided in Mr Best the football coach that I would like to see Patrick's house win the annual final which had not been achieved for over 10 years, and never in my own time as a boarder at the school. The most popular teams were Georges and Dominic's who seemed to share alternative years at winning the school football cup. The school finals and sports day were always held on the last visiting Sunday in July prior to the school breaking up for the Summer holidays, and it was no coincidence that George's house possessed the richest kids among the boarders and that Dominic's House was populated with day pupils only, who had the opportunity of much more coaching in their home environments. Many of the day pupils were playing in small Sunday league teams almost every week, while the boarders were only coached properly on alternative Sundays, and were thrown together as a large bunch of boys who were never individually coached. Many of them having not the slightest interest in sport of any kind.

Mr Best agreed to give additional coaching to Patrick's house, providing that I selected a team that would put in the effort. He also agreed to come on Saturday afternoons to provide more support in that area. There was just one little catch though, I somehow had to get permission from the nuns for Mr Best to attend, and while I knew that this was the ideal opportunity to request this, especially as Aloysius was away, I was not confident that permission would be granted. I approached Sister Centonni and she immediately agreed to put the proposal to the school headmistress,who would need to agree the monetary arrangement with Mr Best. Over the next couple of weeks I made myself busy approaching certain strong players in the Patricks House and outlining my plans for the Saturday sessions. Unfortunately there were only about five reasonable footballers among all of them and we would need a lot more if we were to form the basis of a strong future team. We would need to steal players from other houses, on the promise of extra coaching and other illicit rewards which we hadn't quite dreamed up yet.

The problem was eventually solved by singling out individuals who had no particular loyalty to the House that they were currently in, but were reasonable football players. The difficulty lay in relocating them from one house to another, especially in the dining hall where seating was allocated equally among the four houses. Moving people around was almost impossible especially as many of the candidates were involved in other House activities which necessitated them staying put.

Eventually I found five lads willing to move to Patricks and join the extra coaching sessions on Saturdays, we finally had the nucleus of a team for the first time in years. Among these lads was a very strong player named Barry Dania. Barry had suffered from polio as a younger lad and this left him with a club foot which necessitated him wearing a built up shoe that looked more like a boot. Barry was physically much stronger than his nine years and I had watched him hit cricket balls much further than anyone else. He was also brilliant at tackling and winning the ball on the football pitch. His biggest strength, however, was kicking the ball, he had a powerful left-footed kick that sent the ball sailing into the distance, and I had no doubt that Barry Dania would form the backbone of the new Patricks team. No one ever wanted to come up against Barry in either a tackle or a penalty kick, as he had such a powerful and muscular frame, and one kick from that built up boot would certainly render the recipient incapacitated for a good long time. All of the moves to Patricks were completed in a few days and the biggest disruption took place in the dining hall or Refectory to give it its correct name. In the Refectory kids had to swop places with the new recruits and this resulted in a lot of moaning and groaning by those who had to give up their place in the Patricks team. Every mealtime there would be dissent from two or three of the more vocal among them and sporadic fighting broke out within the Houses that they had involuntarily invaded. The whole thing was soon brought to order by the house Captains and vice Captains who solved the whole scenario with a few threatening expletives and some occasional well-aimed smacks in the mouth. Vincent Simson the Patrick's house Captain was actually on my side for the first time in our history, and while he didn't have a great deal of interest in football, he badly needed the improved results to make his life a little easier among the other house captains. I trusted Simson about as far as I could throw him, but I took advantage of this temporary truce, knowing that none of the good will he promoted would last for long.

The Saturday coaching sessions were going really well, and all of the lads were improving their game with the help of the extra training. I was really pleased with the progress of the team and felt that this year could be the year for Patrick's to win back the school cup. A few weeks later, on one of the Saturday training sessions, I came over all hot and dizzy and Mr Best sat me on the side-lines, I had this awful pounding headache, and my jaw ached all around my neckline. I didn't have a clue what was wrong with me, but as the day progressed I felt really rough and my temperature was soaring. At suppertime I took my usual place in the refectory and that was the last thing I remember. I had fainted in the Refectory, and woke up a few hours later in the school infirmary.

I had contracted the worst dose of mumps that the Sisters had ever seen, my temperature had been so high that they had literally sunk me into a cold bath in order to cool my body down. At this time there was a lot of debate around calling an ambulance and having me admitted to hospital. My face had swollen up so badly that I was struggling to breathe, and every morsel of food that they tried to give me was immediately ejected in a torrent of projectile vomiting. I had also been quite delirious over the previous 24 hours, so much so, that a number of nuns were keeping a constant watch on me which was unprecedented at that time. My temperature stayed high for several days and this was treated by my being immersed into those icy baths every few hours. This was not a pleasant experience, and I knew from previous stories that I would be isolated from the rest of the school population and in the infirmary for at least ten days.

During this time the nuns were administering the most awful medicine I have ever tasted and the local Doctor who had come to visit gave me an injection in my bum that was the most painful thing I had experienced in a very long time. I was not very happy in my new isolated environment and I felt completely cut off from the everyday activities and interactions of the school. No news got back to me about what was happening outside and the infirmary had now become my prison during this long and painful illness. My staple diet was warm milk and porridge interspersed with copious amounts of vegetable soup and all of these concoctions were cooked up on a little stove in the corner of the room. I could hardly keep a single solid morsel down, and my throat was so sore that I didn't want to eat anything. I knew that things were bad when my Mum turned up to see me, this was a highly unusual thing to happen in the middle of a school week, but clearly she was concerned about how ill I actually was and needed to see for herself.She brought with her copious amounts of antibiotic tablets that tasted disgusting, but certainly seemed to do the trick. I eventually spent 15 days in the school infirmary, and when I finally got out of there I had lost about a stone in body weight.

The weight loss was not a real worry to me, but given that I was a skinny 'runt' to start with, I was then fed a diet of high calorie foods and all of my portions became large ones for quite a time. I was also fed the usual supplements of Cod liver oil and Virol malt together with these strange red capsules that tasted utterly bitter, I think these were some form of iron tablet, but at every opportunity I spat them as they were disgusting. The lads later told me that at one stage the whole school had been praying for my recovery and that in the early days of the illness I was, apparently, quite delirious, and was using a lot of foul language some of which the nuns had never experienced before. I had been too poorly to move to the hospital which was miles away in Hatfield, Herts, so I was receiving daily visits from the local doctor. I had no idea how ill I actually was at the time, but I knew that I never wanted to experience anything like it again in my lifetime.

As I recovered from the mumps and was able to sit up in bed and gain some normality, I noticed a radio on the shelf in the corner of the infirmary, and when the nuns were away at meals or prayers I busied myself finding all of the pop channels and these helped while away the long hours of otherwise boredom. During the day I would amuse myself reading comics including the Beezer, The

Topper, The Beano, The Hotspur and of course, my favourite comic the Eagle. The nuns were quite critical of comic-reading and discouraged parents from sending them into the school, but this was a futile exercise and was soon forgotten about. I loved the Eagle, not only because there were fantastic comic strips, but because they always featured cut-away diagrams of, ships, tanks, cars, locomotives, and of course all of the war machines of the day. Late at night, after 'lights out' when the whole school had drifted off to sleep, I would find Radio Caroline, a pirate radio ship, and spend hours listening to all of the latest hits on the radio. The signal was always awful and would drift in and out of earshot as the boat was broadcasting from well out at sea, and being constantly jammed by the terrestrial BBC. During the day the radio signal was almost impossible to find, but late at night it came through much easier and clearer. The music choice was absolutely fantastic, and I spent many happy hours writing down the lyrics to all of my favourite pop songs and then singing them for hours on end. Life in the infirmary while recovering from any illness was always a lot of fun as you were exempt from all of the daily routines and disciplines, and this allowed you to enjoy some of the more relaxed pastimes that kids loved to pursue.

Towards the end of my illness, I was joined in the infirmary with two or three other mumps victims and finally having some good company to share the hours with, certainly accelerated my recovery process. We spent many happy hours playing board games, singing and larking around and listening to the radio for hours on end.

Of course, we always tried to feign illness to give us a few more days of enjoyment, but there was very little opportunity of getting away with this for very long. These nuns knew every trick in the book including how to recognise a 'faker'.

Chapter 16
My Great escape. Anarchy in the classroom, the return of Aloysius and another fight to remember.

Two days before my release from the infirmary, an incident occurred in the art and crafts class which was to have long-reaching repercussions for everyone involved. During a craft lesson which involved basket-making, wool weaving and 'papier mache' modelling, several lads from class five and class six got involved in a serious fight which escalated into a full scale battle. Copious amounts of paints and other materials were flung around the art room, and glue was both thrown and wiped into several heads and faces in a light-hearted moment that was to escalate into an 'altercation' that would get out of hand very rapidly. This event had started with an innocuous few incidents brought about by high spirits and the temporary absence of Sister Henry, the arts and crafts mistress, who had been called away from the classroom. What had started as a fairly harmless exchange of insulting words and 'banter' between two pupils, quickly deteriorated into loud exchanges with several kids flinging objects at each other and then attempting to kick the 'crap' out of each other and anyone else around them.

Within minutes the escalation embraced broken windows, bloody noses and a major riot between the warring parties. By the time Sister Henry had returned to the classroom she had inherited a situation that had gone completely out of control and had resulted in some pretty serious injuries and a completely wrecked form room that now resembled a 'war zone'. Unfortunately, many of the 'protagonists' were house captains and vice captains and even the head boy was involved, which was a big surprise to everybody. The resulting damage was so bad, that Sister Henry was left with little choice but to report the complete 'affair' to the Reverend Mother and Headmistress.

When the headmistress and both form teachers surveyed the resulting damage an hour later they were shocked to see how much equipment had been wrecked by the 'warring' parties. Pictures and frames were broken from the walls, paint and glue had been thrown all over the various surfaces of the room, window panes and wall charts had been smashed to pieces, and several chairs and desks had been wrecked into the bargain. What they arrived upon, was a scene of total 'carnage' with bloodied noses and split lips heading up the assortment of injuries that the various factions had sustained, there were also a few black eyes and a broken nose to be added to that list.

This was a serious incident in anybody's eyes, but given that many of the boys involved were in responsible positions in their own right, it was regarded as the most serious misdemeanour that had ever occurred at Ponsbourne Park in recent times. There is no doubt that some of the relaxation in discipline since Aloysius's departure may also have contributed in part to some of the reasons for the occurrence. There is even less doubt that had Aloysius been present at the end of it, there would have been a lot of very sorry faces into the bargain and not a few very sore heads and arses as well. She would have kicked the 'living shit' out of most of the lads involved, without the slightest hesitation.

News of the happenings flew around the school like wild-fire, and typically all of the blame seemed to be laid at the feet of the boarders only, while most of the day pupils, who had been present at the time, walked away from the incident without a single blemish on their characters, in spite of many of them being involved right up to their dirty necks.

I found out about the incident in the middle of the afternoon when a steady stream of victims were presenting themselves to Sister Albertina in the infirmary to have various war wounds attended to. I was now pretty well recovered from my recent bout of sickness, and I was looking forward to being released back to my dorm within a couple of days. The most serious of these injuries appeared to be a broken nose which later required hospital treatment, and the victim was my friend John Mallory who was quickly whisked in Father Leeson's car to the local cottage hospital. John described to me how he had been "flung across the classroom" during the incident and had collided with the corner of a radiator which snapped his nose like a stick of celery. He also described many of the other lads involved, and their part in the wrecking of the art room. John would not give the name of his attacker at the time, pretending not to know the identity of the individual. He later confided to me however that he knew exactly who was responsible and would bide his time until he could get his own back. I had no doubts that John would be true to his word, he was a hard-faced, ginger-haired Balham boy, who, though small in stature, was more than capable of looking after himself in a situation. He and I had got into a fight while we were both in the infants side of the school, and fighting Mallory was like getting mauled by an angry bear, if I could imagine such a thing. After that incident John realised that you didn't brawl with the Irish and get clean away with it either. I realised that smaller wasn't always going to be weaker and that John could certainly look after himself when required. We later became firm friends for the duration of our time at Ponsbourne Park, and it was John that taught me every possible South London swear word imaginable.

There is no doubt that, had I been present in the art classroom at the time, I would probably have been involved in the proceedings in some small way, because I later found out that some of the fighting had broken out as a direct result of lads exchanging insults over the changes that I had made in the football and house teams a few weeks earlier. I suspected that John may have been defending those changes in my absence, ensuring his own part in the resulting outbreak of violence. This however, was not the only reason for the 'fracas' because a few serious insults had earlier been exchanged between the basket weavers and the wool weavers, both sides casting aspersions on the perceived sexuality of any boy pursuing such an activity which was more suited to girls, 'sissies' and 'Nancy boys'. There were members from the various school houses in the room, a few of whom had been moved around to facilitate the changes in the football arrangements. This full scale row had erupted very suddenly, and had got more than a little out of hand very quickly.

A few days later I was back in the classroom after my long illness, and I realised what an effect the fight incident had wrought on both the pupils and Sister Lucy alike. The relaxed atmosphere had disappeared completely and what replaced it was an oppressive stilted silence in which both teacher and pupils had lost all semblance of interest in one another. Sister Lucy called me back after class to discuss my recent illness, but I knew instinctively that she wanted to speak to me in depth about the experiences of the previous days and how they had affected Sister Henry in the crafts class, and herself as the form teacher most aggrieved by what had occurred. She and I both knew that had I been present at the time, I would have been equally caught up in the events, and she reminded me that my absence from the class on that fateful day was probably the only thing that separated me from all of the other lads who were involved.

I had no doubt about the veracity of her comments and was now witnessing a teacher completely devastated by what had happened, I suppose it must have reflected on her own position as a new teacher in the school, and I felt very sorry for her situation, and kind of relieved that I had not been in any way involved on the day. I was also relieved that I was still in her 'good books' and secretly pleased that she would confide in me. It seemed like I was suddenly one of the 'goodie goodies' by mere circumstance, but I wasn't about to apologise to anyone for being a victim of the 'bloody' mumps. It wasn't exactly a bed of roses spending nearly three weeks in the infirmary and no contact with the outside world.

That, however, is the way the 'cookie crumbles' sometimes, and I intended to make best use of my new situation regardless of the opinions and actions of others around me. I reminded Sister Lucy that as well as many of my own peers being involved, there were also several day pupils who were present at the time of the incident, and yet not one of them had been taken to task about it. She agreed that the day pupils should not be exempt from any punishment or consequences that might later ensue, and I got the distinct impression that she would act positively on that information.

As a direct result of all of these happenings, one house Captain, two vice captains and the head boy were all suspended from their duties with their badges being removed. They and sixteen other lads, were forced to eat all of their reduced meals standing up in the refectory for the next several days. During school time the same 'miscreants' had to stand in the school quadrangle with their hands on their heads, while their various parents were contacted for monetary contributions towards the refurbishment and fixing of the form room. Our classroom was like the 'Marie Celeste' because so many of our peers were now domiciled in the outside quadrangle, somewhat resembling a bunch of scarecrows, or ballet dancers in the first throes of 'Swan Lake'. I felt very sorry for all of them, they were clearly very embarrassed about the whole affair, but they, and I, were also aware that had Aloysius been present, their predicament would have been a far more painful and devastating state of affairs for all of them.

As well as the mealtime and school time punishments, these lads also had to have daily meetings with the Mother Superior who admonished them relentlessly for their misguided and hostile behaviour. In the mornings before breakfast they were all gathered in the chapel to beg the Lord's forgiveness in repeated Hail Mary's and Our Fathers, while in the evenings they reported to the art and crafts class to help with the re-painting and repairs. By the time the 'poor sods' got back to their dormitories, it was well after 'lights out', and they were utterly dejected, hungry and completely exhausted. We all made sure that 'illicit' food and 'tuck' was available for them, which was the least that we could do in the circumstances-they were still our friends and peers in every circumstance, and we all shared a common bond in that respect.

A few days later they were all back in class, and although things didn't quite get back to normality, it had become relatively quiet and peaceful once again. Sister Centonni was still looking after the senior dorms, and with all the privileges and responsibilities having been removed from the head boy and house captains, there was an air of subdued expectancy and wonder at what the outcome might be for these lads. Would they be permanently removed from their positions in the school, or would they be reinstated having served their time and punishments over the previous two weeks. Their various badges of rank had been taken off them without a promise of return, and they now all occupied spaces well away from the top and bottom of the tables in the refectory, which were the traditional seats for Captains and Vice Captains.

In the dormitories they were no longer allowed to order other boys around, and the remaining house captains and vice captains took over all of their duties with regard to keeping discipline and dishing out punishments. I, for my part, shouldered a great deal of the extra responsibility having taken over the captaincy and vice captaincy for Patricks House. In spite of this being a temporary arrangement, I was very proud of the fact that not only was I the youngest vice-captain, and games captain in the school, I was now also the youngest House captain ever. I was going to enjoy all of this esteem for as long as it could possibly last, not because I felt superior to anybody else, but more because I had taken the House Captain's rank from that old protagonist Vincent Simson, and that really did give me a lot of pleasure. My school blazer now boasted three shiny badges in a neat row along the lapel, which made me feel almost like a five star general wherever I went.

I have to admit that my new roles added a hell of a lot of responsibility to my already over-burdened task lists and the worst part of being acting House Captain was the necessity to be out of bed a full half hour before anyone else woke up. The 'fagging' system had long since finished in most boarding schools by this time, which meant that you could no longer rely on a youngster to go and warm up your toilet seat in the morning, or lay out your clothes in readiness, or clean your 'rugger' or football boots. Like all boys of my age, I valued my sleep above anything else in the world, and here I was losing even more of it. The upside, of course, was the ability to ride ship-shod above all of the rules and regulations with an almost free reign, and with no head boy to 'mete' out any orders, I enjoyed a period of complete authoritative and self-indulgent impunity. In spite of all of this, I was careful to remain very even-handed in all of my dealings with both peers and teachers alike, constantly reminding myself that at any moment Aloysius would be returning from her travels fully armed with her own strict and unique agenda.

During this time I took the time and trouble to find out the exact circumstances of the riot in the craft room, but more importantly I collected a list of the day pupils who were present at the time, knowing that most of them were involved in one way or another. My sense of 'fair play' demanded that something be done to bring some of these culprits to book just like our own boarders. In the course of collecting these names and the stories attached to them, I inadvertently discovered who was responsible for throwing John Mallory across the room and breaking his nose into the bargain. The culprit was our own recently demoted House Captain, Vincent Simson, and it was no secret that Simson detested John Mallory, for reasons that went back years in both their histories. It wasn't hard for anyone to detest Simson, he made it his business to be obnoxious to almost everyone he came into contact with. In my later conversations with John Mallory, he still refused to either confirm or deny if Simson was responsible for his broken and now greatly misshapen nose. I knew from this that Mallory had his own agenda running, and any revenge or follow-up acts would be his and his only, I wasn't about to argue with this, but I did wonder just what John had in mind in getting back at this self-important individual. I was also more than aware that Simson had a bit of unfinished business with me being his main suspect for the breakage of his precious parents' playground light in the previous year. He had confronted me on several occasions since the incident and had quite rightly guessed that I was the only possible culprit. I continued to remind him that I was the only person injured on that fateful night and enquired of him whether I would be stupid enough to put myself through all of that for a mere act of vandalism. He replied that I was indeed stupid enough. What a 'tosser', but he was half right as well.

The day we all dreaded finally arrived. Aloysius's taxi pulled up outside the convent on a cold October evening. Two lads who had been serving on the altar at evening Benediction had spotted her stepping out of the car, and they saluted her as they walked past. Soon the news was spreading throughout the whole school, and an air of gloom and doom seemed to descend on everyone. The lads that were involved in the previous craft room riot, as it had now come to be known, were terrified at the prospect of having to deal with Aloysius, and they huddled in small groups discussing their possible future outlook. Many of them asked my opinion on what I thought might now happen, and I reminded them that they had already been punished for the incident, I also advised them that when questioned, they needed to make her aware that there were others involved that did not receive so much as a 'telling off'. I assured them all, that if I was given the opportunity to speak with her about the incident, I would also make her aware that not everyone involved had been included in the final tally of culprits.

It was quite a few days later that Aloysius returned to her duties, and this had the effect of creating rumours that perhaps she wasn't coming back into the school at all, but would be just living in the convent with so many of the other lay nuns. There was no such luck however, for one Monday morning in early November she turned up in the senior dorm to wake us all up for the usual early mass call. Nothing had seemingly changed in her voice or her energy level. She flew around the dormitories like a thing possessed, pulling blankets and sheets off the lads that did not wake up sharply enough. The procession to the hand basins for morning washes was the exact same as it always was and the supervision of bed-making and dressing was no different. What seemed to be missing however were the occasional slaps on the bare backs which normally accompanied Aloysius's morning ritual. Not one lad received as much as a push from her, and while the boys still lined up in the playground for the usual march to chapel, there was not a single shout or 'holler' from Aloysius' lips. Something had changed in the weeks that she was away, or perhaps Sister Centonni and a few of the other temporary carers in our dorm had had a quiet word with the headmistress about Aloysius's habits as described by the boys. This was not the 'ogre' that we had all come to fear and hate, and it was all the more unsettling to us, because no one could be sure if this was just a temporary state of affairs.

As we marched down to church that morning, there were stifled conversations among all of the boys about Aloysius' strangely subdued behaviour. Some were of the opinion that this was just the calm before the storm, and that given a few days of settling in, she would return to her own frightening self. Others thought that maybe the death of her Mother had suddenly brought her to the realisation that her attitude to the kids in her care needed to be improved. I didn't really have an opinion either way, I just remembered some of the misery that she had visited on myself, my brother and so many of our peers in our younger years. I reminded myself of the dictum that 'a leopard never changes its spots' and continued to act very cautiously around her, as did a lot of my friends.

Within days she had acquainted herself with all of the reports about the wrecking of the Arts and Crafts room and while she confronted none of the named individuals about the incident, she did make it known to each one in turn that she would be catching up with them in due course. A cloud of apprehension spread throughout the fifth and sixth classes, as each individual waited to be summoned to explain their personal role in that infamous event. Time had suddenly seemed to stand still, a lot of the usual playground activities had kind of died a death, there were no more marbles competitions, there was a severe lack of Corgi and Dinky cars being towed around on strings. The usual ball games including cricket, rounders, football and handball were missing from the daily list of activities, mainly because so many of the normal participants had been effectively removed from these privileges. A cloud had descended around the playground and dormitory areas, where just a few weeks earlier the sound of laughter and mickey-taking could be heard in every corner of the school buildings. The fun had been removed from school life, and I wondered, whether things would ever return to normality again - or at least normality as we knew it. Life in the junior and infant side of the school continued unabated and those kids were blissfully unaware of the serious atmosphere and mood changes that had been visited on their senior peers.

I continued to busy myself with the day to day running of the Patrick's house and my duties as Games Captain. The football team were making great strides with the extra coaching from Mr Best, and had won two of their last three matches against the other houses. I was beginning to think that we really did have a good chance of winning the football championship at the end of this year with weekly improvements rolling in fast and furiously.

Just one week after her return, Aloysius summoned all of the boys connected with the Art room riot (as it now came to be known) to a meeting in her classroom. All of the boys who had been involved were called out of classrooms five and six and filed hesitantly across the quadrangle to Aloysius's room. As the door closed behind them, there was immediate speculation of what kind of punishment they would receive for their misdemeanours. Top of the list was six whacks of the strap on the backside, or at best a more innocuous six whacks of the strap on their hands. The head boy, house captains and vice captains would probably get additional punishments including the removal of some meals, extra charges in the dormitories and other school buildings and a withdrawal of all school privileges like T.V. Tuck shop allowances and attendance at any school parties. These were the usual punishments which up until this time were 'doled' out to anyone found guilty of misdemeanours. I had received plenty of these punishments in my tenure in both the junior and senior dorms and the only one of these that I really dreaded were the missing meals, as the pangs of hunger lasted a whole lot longer than six of the best on either the arse or the hands. As for lack of tuck allowances, these could easily be replaced with a certain amount of cadging, scrounging or deal-making.

Aloysius was efficient and thorough in getting to the bottom of the story, and as each lad gave his version of the events she took copious notes of each statement presumably for later cross-interrogation. When everyone concerned had made their contribution she made each one of them sit down with a sheet of paper and write down the names of all of the pupils who had been in the room that afternoon, and was not a little surprised to find that twelve day pupils were not among the accused standing in front of her. When she asked each of the lads who they thought was responsible for the damages to the art room, every one of them raised their hand in unison, preserving the old school tradition of never 'splitting' on your mates. These lads were all sent back to their various classrooms without any further action on Aloysius's part, and they were temporarily relieved that no punishment had been dished out so far. Clearly Aloysius was appearing to be more democratic in interviewing the day pupils as well as the boarders, and this was what eventually transpired as the twelve other boys were summoned separately to her classroom. Nothing else transpired that day and all of our conversations took on a great deal of speculation as to what might happen next. We didn't have to wait for long before a few things started to happen.

Marching to morning mass a few days later, Vincent Simson was accosted by John Mallory with a flying tackle to the legs. Both of them disappeared over a small box hedge just outside the chapel walls. Simson's legs had buckled under the full force of Mallory making contact with them, and for a moment they were both rolling over one another in a vice-like grip. What followed was a vicious fight with no 'holds' barred. Mallory got quickly to his feet and laid into Simson like a thing possessed, fists were flying in every direction, and a large crowd of boys were now surrounding them shouting encouragement to both lads. By the time myself and the other house captains had run from the back of the line to separate them, the fight was in full swing, with Mallory delivering punch after punch to his opponent. Simson's face resembled that of a defeated boxer with cut lips, swollen eyes and a nasty gash on his left ear which was bleeding copiously. Mallory had taken a few return punches as well, but his injuries were nothing compared to the sorry mess that Simson presented. The two were quickly separated with both of them trading expletives and threats to one another. As Mallory walked away, in what can only be described as a 'cocky' gait, he turned to Simson and shouted "that'll teach you, you arrogant fucker, let me know when you're ready for some more. You've just been taken apart by the fucking Balham Bomber". Unbeknown to John at the time, and as a direct result of this incident, he would now be known as 'Bomber Mallory' for the rest of his days at the school. Simson and Mallory were quickly ushered away by some of the other lads and taken to the convent toilets for cleaning up, when they appeared in the chapel a few minutes later, they both resembled a couple of 'crash' victims. They stood out like 'sore' thumbs and were being scrutinized by not just their peers in the church, but also, by all of the nuns who had assembled there for Mass.

That same afternoon, both Mallory and Simson were summoned to Aloysius's classroom for an explanation of the morning's activities on the way to church. She didn't have to ask many questions about the general happenings, as both lads were now sporting faces that would be better suited to the aftermath of a heavyweight boxing match featuring Cassius Clay and Sonny Liston. Both lads gave their own distorted version of the events, and by the end of the interview Aloysius was made aware of many more of the happenings that occurred during the Art room riot, and its part in the subsequent fight which she was now investigating. Oddly enough, neither Mallory nor Simson were 'strapped' for their behaviour, but instead they were given a week each without dinner or tea, with several other privileges being denied them as well. No one could believe how leniently they were dealt with, and it was slowly dawning on all of us that the Aloysius of old, the 'Annie Oakley' in nuns clothing, had finally hung up her 'strapping' habits for a more innocuous form of punishment. Lads all over the school were breathing large sighs of relief at the knowledge that a monster had been tamed and that their life might just be a little more tolerable in the light of this change.

I for my part, was facing a slightly bigger fish to fry in the guise of the Eleven Plus examination. This exam had been withdrawn in Hertfordshire, but some bright spark decided that I might just be bright enough to sit it in London, which was still holding on to the examination... This would have been a good idea if I had covered any of the London syllabus, but unfortunately I hadn't. There was no extra tuition available, apart from a few past exam papers that were made available to me. Having worked my way through a few of these exam papers, I realised that I was going to struggle to achieve the required grade to ease my way into a good future Grammar school in London. Christmas was just a few weeks away, and while I was looking forward as always to the holidays, I guessed that most of my time would be taken up with trying to cram for the forthcoming exams, if, of course, I was made to sit them.

As I approached my last year at St Dominic's, I realised that although things had become a lot easier in my boarding school life, other challenges were coming along, which I certainly wasn't properly prepared for. The threat of a forthcoming Eleven Plus examination would certainly be a 'nemesis' to me, and like the man sitting on the deserted beach wondering where the sun had gone, It was all about to dawn on me!

Chapter 17
The 11 Plus. A new head boy, Mr Whitton and a slightly sexual encounter

January 1965 was not a good month for me, I had just returned from my Christmas holidays to be informed by my Teacher Sister Lucy, that I was going to sit my Eleven Plus examination in London in just 3 weeks' time. I was pretty 'brassed' off to hear this news because I had been hoping against hope that sometime in the past 3 months perhaps London would follow Hertfordshire's lead and abandon the exam. I discussed my concerns with Sister Lucy, and she agreed that this was a very unusual situation, but that she was sure that in spite of not having covered the curriculum, the exam would be no difficulty for me. All of my friends of the same age were happily going about their routines without the worry of sitting this exam. They all agreed that it was pretty tough luck that I still had to sit it, and in a strange school as well. I was not happy about sitting the exam without having covered the London syllabus, and I felt really hard done by. I also didn't share Sister Lucy's optimism about the possible outcome, and while I was flattered by her confidence, I felt that her confidence in me was somewhat misplaced.

Just two weeks later I heard by phone call that my Grandmother had died in Ireland, and that both of my parents would be flying over to attend the funeral. This meant that I would be staying with a friend of the family and that I would attend the exam from her house rather than from my own home. All of this was just a little unsettling and I was still waiting to find out which school in London would be host to my examination attendance.

At Ponsbourne Park, Sister Aloysius was still acting very much out of character and her previous change of attitude had continued to surprise everyone around her, including the other nuns. She called me out of line one evening on the way back from supper and asked me to take a walk with her, as she had something to show me. I was very nervous about this and wondered why she had singled me out, we hadn't spoken much since her return to the school long before Christmas. As we ventured out into that cold and dark January night, I thought it most unusual to be leaving the school grounds so late into the evening when I should have been doing Prep. Our walk took us a long way away from the school buildings along a muddy shingled drive, to what looked like a farmhouse. I was aware that prep would now be finished and most of my peers would be getting ready for the dormitory and 'lights out'. The journey had been a cold one and all of the roads were shrouded in a swirling damp mist that coated the surface of my blazer and school cap in droplets of water, very little had been said between us on that long walk, and I felt slightly uneasy being away from the school buildings on this long lonely road.

She knocked loudly on the door and we waited for what seemed like several minutes for the door to be open.

Standing there in the light from the interior was a tall giant of a man with greying hair and a neatly trimmed moustache who I had never seen before. He summoned us both in out of the cold and sat us in front of a welcoming and blazing log fire, I realised that he looked the 'spitting' image of the Hollywood actor David Niven and he spoke in that same refined way. He gave Sister Aloysius a large glass of wine, which surprised me a little for I always thought that nuns didn't drink, and without even asking, he placed a glass of Tizer and a plate of Battenberg cake in front of me, which I thanked him for.

It occurred to me that he had been expecting this visit and as he hung up Aloysius's long black cloak, he reached up to one of the shelves and took down a pipe full of tobacco. His house was sparsely furnished and the walls and ceilings were brown with what seemed years of cigarette, wood smoke and dust. On a few shelves were various models of cars, steam engines and locomotives. A radio in the background was playing Bob Dylan's 'Mr Tambourine Man' followed by several Beatles and Rolling Stones songs. He was clearly a fan of pop music, and I gleaned that, with the signal fading in and out, that he was either listening to Radio London, or Radio Caroline. He and Aloysius seemed very relaxed in each other's company and I sensed a familiarity that went further than the normal interaction of people in the early stages of getting to know one another.I wondered what their connection to one another would be, perhaps brother and sister, they seemed of a similar age. Of course my naïve 11 year old self had no conception of intimate relationships at this stage in my development, but I began to recognise an intimacy that seemed to be a little bit more than just formality. How had Aloysius come to know this man? He had never been seen in any of the activities surrounding the school, and I would have clearly remembered such an imposing person, had he been around the school at any time.

During the course of this visit, I was shown around the man's house and yard, and while I had previously thought this was probably a farmhouse, I was really surprised when we went into the main barn and found not straw bales or farm animals of any kind, but instead an array of carriages, wagons and even a wild west stagecoach, all in various states of repair. One of the coaches was a State coach as used by Queen Elizabeth 11, our monarch, and this was having work done to the leaf-spring suspension and a couple of the wheels.

Sister Aloysius informed me that Mr Whitton (as I later found out) was a wheelwright and coachbuilder by trade and all of his work was dedicated to maintaining and restoring carriages from not just England, but from all over the world. I was very impressed with the work that this man was producing and informed him of my growing passion for cars, especially the fast 'sporty' ones. He immediately smiled at my comments about the cars and I realised that I had hit a common interest with him. He took me into an adjoining barn and there parked in all its glory was a vintage turbocharged Bentley which he had spent the previous thirty years restoring. This car was festooned with badges for the London to Brighton annual run and as

I sat in the driver's seat, I realised that this guy really knew his way around the restoration of beautiful things. I stated that he must be very wealthy to own such a beautiful car but he intimated that he was always broke and in financial difficulties. He hoped that perhaps this car would one day solve all of his financial needs and problems - I did not disbelieve him. We returned to his house to enjoy further refreshments, and I felt comfortable and at ease sitting there listening to all of the hits on his radio.Aloysius seemed very, very relaxed in Mr Whitton's company,and I gleaned from their conversation that they had known each other for quite some time. She seemed very different from the 'ogre' that had chastised me so many times in the past, there was now no hint of the cruelty or malice that had existed back then.

That evening visit changed everything for me because on the way home Aloysius informed me that she was going to appoint me as acting Head boy and that this would be announced in about a fortnight from that day. I wondered whether I had been appointed on merit, or just because the incumbent head boy had been embroiled in the 'fracas' in the art room quite a few weeks earlier. I decided not to ask that question, just in case the answer would be in common with my own thoughts and beliefs. Aloysius seemed very calm on that walk home, and so out of character from the norm. She asked if I would like to accompany her on future visits to Mr Whittons house, and I replied that I would very much like that . I was already relishing the thought of a lot more cake and biscuits in the future, and a further chance to explore the many mechanical treasures that were being worked upon. As we walked slowly back to Ponsbourne Park, I intimated to Aloysius that I was not at all confident in being able to pass the upcoming Eleven Plus examination, and I was amazed by her subsequent comments. "It doesn't matter whether you do well in the exam or not" she stated, "you have already proved that you are capable of achieving a good standard of learning, but more importantly, you have survived all of these years here at St Dominics and overcome several drawbacks on the journey. No matter what you choose to do with your future life, you will find that you are one of life's survivors, and that is another reason that I am appointing you to head boy." Her words took me completely by surprise, here was this otherwise 'tyrant' nun going all 'soft' and 'mushy' in a manner that was completely out of character for her. This woman had certainly changed beyond all recognition, it was as if she had experienced some kind of 'Charisma' bypass during her absense from the school. Maybe she had experienced a sort of 'Road to Damascus' moment which had changed her whole personality, whatever the reason, I was pleased that she had changed for the better.

'It was well past 11.00 p.m. when I finally crawled in to my bed that night. All of the other kids had been asleep for hours, and here was I defying all the school rules with Aloysius's consent and participation. Things were certainly getting interesting in these latter days of my school life at Ponsbourne Park, I felt uplifted and much more confident in my thoughts after that strange and unusual evening. The thought of being made Head boy excited me a lot, and I realised that my last few terms, before leaving this place for good, may turn out to be quite exciting-in the meantime there were other challenges to fill up my remaining time.

A few days later, I was sitting in a strange school in Neasden, North West London, among a complete crowd of strangers, taking my Eleven plus exam. It seemed ironic that here was I back in Neasden after so many years, and that of all of the places I could have been sent to, this was the place appointed for me to sit an exam which would probably decide my future academic life. I had arrived early that morning in order to orientate myself with the layout of the school, and was greeted by a bunch of 'louts' who decided that my comparitively 'posh' accent and my formal school uniform merited a great deal of 'cat calls' and general 'piss-taking'. I was at that stage still wearing traditional short trousers, while these kids did not have a uniform code and presented themselves in all manner of brightly-coloured attire. I guess I must have looked and sounded pretty strange to these 'street-wise' inner city London kids, and any attempt at forming friendships were immediately rebutted with a tirade of abusive language and a great deal of insults and pushing and shoving. I held my ground by returning a few expletives of my own and even managed to surprise one of them with a well-aimed elbow in the stomach as he made a grab for me in the corridor leading to the exam room. Winston Churchill's funeral was taking place the following day, and there were pictures of him all over the school. Everything in this place seemed grey and gloomy, even the weather lacked any of the usual winter sunshine and for the first time in my life I became aware of the responsibility and dread of sitting an examination of this length. I knew just by glancing at some of the questions on that exam paper, that I was out of my depth, I was as nervous as a kitten, and lacked any inspiration even with the questions that I could answer. The limited amount of revision and study that I had previously put in was far to little and far too last minute.

The teacher adjudicating the exam class was distant and unfriendly and made no attempt to communicate with me or offer any hint of a friendly welcome. The other kids sitting the exam were foul-mouthed and confrontational, and I ran a gauntlet of abusive comments and gestures until the order to "open your papers" was boomed at us from the back of the exam room. Of course, these kids had all followed the London curriculum as part of their normal studies, and I had no doubt that there were probably, among this 'dross, quite a few bright ones sitting this exam. Here was my first experience of a non-private school, and it made me realise how fortunate I was to be receiving my education in an environment that was as alien from this place as chalk is from cheese. I also realised that a little bit of the discipline which we had experienced in our school life was greatly missing from this place. Notwithstanding all of this, most of the kids sitting around me were probably far more familiar with the questions on the exam paper having covered the syllabus for the past year. The silence that descended on that room was as opressive as the weather outside, and I could hear the slow tick of the clock that was counting away the minutes. The end of the exam came far too quickly for me, and I knew that I had not answered sufficient questions in the given time. "Put down your pens" was the closing statement that boomed around the room, and I remember thinking to myself that I wished I had never picked my pen up in the first place. This was an examination that I was not going to pass.

I later found out that my parents in collusion with Sister Lucy had decided that I was bright enough to go and take the exam in London - not a good decision on any of their parts. Where was my opinion, consultation and agreement in all of this? The exam had finally come to an end just before lunch and one of the teachers asked me if I would like to make my way to the dining hall to eat? I quickly declined his invitation on the basis that the food smelled awful, and more importantly, I had had enough abuse from this group of 'delinquents' to last me a couple of lifetimes. My short trousers and smart school uniform was almost sending out a message to these kids "here I am, come and kick the 'crap' out of me". There was no way in the world that I was going to expose myself to more threats from this shower of 'tossers' and so I made my way to the school gates like a 'bat out of hell'. I walked down to Neasden town in the cold January drizzle, my mood was as miserable as the weather and I threw a few verbal 'fucks' about which made me feel ever so slightly better. I then treated myself to a nice meal in the local Wimpy bar. Neasden town itself was very grey and dull, and I remember wondering if, by any remote chance, I

313

would run into Twiggy the famous model as this was her hometown. 'Dream on Ruthie'.

That evening I was staying with friends of my parents named Mc Craith who also lived in Neasden, and I intimated to them my grave concerns about the exam that I had just sat. My parents were still in Ireland in the aftermath of my Grandmother's funeral. And for the first time in my life, I felt very much alone and way out of my comfort zone. I sat that evening and thought for the first time about my future and what it might hold for someone, who at this moment, was looking down a dark tunnel, and not feeling very bright on the academic front.. It was that same evening that I heard the first 'Who' record on the radio called 'I Can't Explain' I almost immediately connected with the lyrics of this song and loved the sound of this exciting new band. It was repeated about four times that evening, and by the time that sleep had overcome me, I had learned the words by heart. The 'Who' were now added to my list of favourite bands joining 'The Beatles', 'Bob Dylan', 'Elvis Presley' and a host of other pop legends.

Two days later I boarded a train from Kings Cross station to Goffs Oak, followed by a local taxi back to the main gates of Ponsbourne Park. The long walk along the 'gravelled' drive gave me time to reflect on the happenings of the past few days, and looking at the school from this vantage point made me aware of what a beautiful building it really was. I thought about those kids I had met in Neasden just a few days earlier, and wondered what they would make of this place and its wonderful surroundings. It could almost be on another planet, as far as they were concerned, and I felt suddenly very grateful, in spite of the years of discipline and isolation, that my parents had chosen this place for our education. I was happy to be back here, for probably the first time in my life, enjoying the company of my friends and peers.

The boys brought me up to date with all of the latest news. In my absence Sister Aloysius had announced that I was to be appointed the new Head Boy, and that all of the people involved in the Art room riot would lose their ranks and privileges for good. I felt quite bad for some of the boys, as I knew that, had I been present in the class that day, I would certainly have been in the thick of it without any doubt. The 'luck of the Irish' would be a term often associated with my new situation, and I intended to get as much mileage out of it as I possibly could. John Mallory wasn't too upset with the outcome of the art - room affair "after all" he advised me "I didn't have that many priveleges to start with, and it was great to see Simson and some of his 'cronies' getting their comeuppance." I could always rely on John to put a smile on my face by his insistence in always seeing the bright and positive sides of all serious and negative situations.

I was thrilled to learn that Patrick's house was now top of the football results and were almost certain to get a finals place if they carried on in that vein. Things seemed to be going my way, and I was aware of a new respect from all around me which made me feel even better. There were, of course, a good few 'dissenters' around me as well, not least, the 'infamous' Vincent Simson who took every opportunity to criticise my forthcoming appointment to acting Head boy. He had made it known to most of the other kids that, in his opinion, he should have been appointed, and that he was positive that it was I that had destroyed the 'Simson' light. He was certainly right in one of these views, but I knew that as a possible future Head boy, he would be one of the most unpopular candidates possible, and would perform the role with a total indifference and a lack of empathy with anyone else;

I decided to ignore most of Simson's comments for the time being, and as he was no longer captain or vice captain of any of the houses, he didn't seem to pose much of a threat to my current situation. He did however, continue to put a lot of effort into destroyimg my reputation at every opportunity, and as all of the attempts filtered back to me on the school 'grapevine' they were becoming just a little bit tiresome. After a great deal of thought, and not a little bravity, I took him to one side in the dormitory one evening and advised him that I didn't give a 'flying fuck' about his opinions, and if he had any problem with that, he should take it up with Sister Aloysius. I also reminded him of his recent altercation with my friend John Mallory and the possibility that he had finally met his 'Nemesis' with that 'cocky' young Balham lad. He slinked away from me with all the prowess of a receding slug, but I knew that this would not be the last I would hear from the self - opinionated Mr Simson.

Sister Aloysius would be keeping a very close eye on my progress in the new role of acting head boy, I guess she must have figured that there would be a little 'flack' coming my way from, not only the disgraced previous incumbent, but more importantly the several other peers that had lost their titles and privileges. I was blissfully unaware of any problems or issues in that regard, but she approached me one afternoon to advise me that we would be visiting Mr Whitton's house that evening, and that she had a few concerns to discuss with me at that time. I was very excited at the prospect of visiting Mr Whitton's house once again, I had previously felt very comfortable in his company, and I admired his talent in restoring all those beautiful modes of transport. I did, however, have a few reservations about Sister Aloysius and her earlier comments, and wondered if I was in any sort of trouble....time would tell.

After supper I made my way to her study, and was surprised to find her in a very good mood indeed. Most of the other lads had already gone to prep, and some of them were making their way to the dormitories. Aloysius and myself made our way across the empty playground, and out on to the dark and lonely side lane that led to Mr Whitton's house. The lights of the school faded into the distance behind us and soon we were enveloped in total darkness. I took my torch from my pocket and shone it on the uneven surface of the gravelled lane and Aloysius took my arm which made me feel just a little uncomfortable. She asked about my new responsibilities as acting Head boy and how I was coping with all that it entailed, I replied that "everything was fine and I had experienced very little difficulty in adapting to my new responsibilities". She stated that she was surprised that I had not sent a single boy to her for punishment for any misdemeanours "this is a major part of your duties as Head boy" she stated. I explained that so far, there was no reason to send anyone to her, as there had been no major incidents requiring her intervention. For the first time in ages she raised her voice and stopped us both in our footsteps, "So what about the fight between John Mallory and Vincent Simson? Wasn't that a major incident?" I was quite taken aback by this sudden outburst and could feel my cheeks reddening up, I was quietly relieved that we were in complete darkness, as this would have been a dead giveaway. I realised in that moment that none of the two protagonists would ever have admitted to being involved in a fight, so I figured that I would feign ignorance of the whole affair and offer another story avoiding my own vivid memories of the day in question.

"I wasn't aware there was a fight between them Sister" I replied. "I was told that they had bumped into each other during a 'tackle' on the football pitch." Aloysius's previous scowl slowly turned to a knowing smile as she realised that whatever I knew about the incident would stay within my own domain. "I suppose you also know nothing about the damage to the Simson light last year?" This question took me completely by surprise, and I figured that Simson had obviously made some comments to her about the incident and his belief that I had purposely sabotaged the light. "Only what I have already told Sister Albertina" I replied. "The thing just exploded as I was walking underneath it". She stayed silent for what seemed an eternity, taking in my quick replies to her questions. As we approached Mr Whitton's front door she smilingly referred to my having acquired a new sense of diplomacy with my new Head boy's responsibilities. I was just pleased and releived that we had reached our destination, before many more questions could be asked.

Mr Whitton opened the door and a wide smile appeared on his face as he ushered us once more into his comfortable sitting room. I realised that we had been expected, as the customary glass of wine had been decanted and was awaiting Sister Aloysius, while on a neat little side table where I was previously seated was a tall glass of ginger beer and the usual plate of Battenburg cake. Aloysius removed her long black cloak, and I was quite taken aback by the observation that instead of the customary black bib apron which she normally wore as part of her daily attire, she was now dressed in an 'immaculately', well-ironed and pressed sparkling white habit, covered by a white woolen cardigan which was certainly a new fashion addition for her. I detected a slight smell of perfume as she brushed past me to hang her cloak on the back of the door, and her simple playground shoes were now being removed and replaced by a shiny pair of ladies fashion shoes...I was very impressed and certainly puzzled.

Mr Whitton apologised for having run out of Tizer and hoped that I would enjoy a ginger beer instead. I thanked him very much for the drink and cake and proceeded to imbibe these treats with relish. The ginger beer was delicious and certainly a luxury as far as I was concerned and Mr Whitton topped it up at regular intervals. I was becoming familiar with the layout of his sitting room and as I looked around, I realised that several additions including a record player and a rack of records had been added since our last visit. "Would you like to hear some music" he asked and both Aloysius and myself replied "yes please" almost simultaneously. After sorting through a bundle of long-playing records he very carefully removed one from it's cover and placed it on the turntable. The sound of Cliff Richard's 'Summer Holiday' filled the room, and while I wasn't a great Cliff fan, I enjoyed the warmth and relaxed atmosphere that had been created by the simple addition of the music.

After a little while Mr Whitton asked me if I would like to go and explore the barn and workshop once again to which I once again replied "yes please." I made my way across the darkened yard into the well-lit barn, and as I slid the large workshop door open I was thrilled to see the big green Bentley once again. It sparkled under the fluorescent lights of the barn, and I jumped in behind the steering wheel to see all of the amazing dashboard clocks and dials. Parked just behind the car, in the corner of the workshop was a vintage horse-drawn hearse which he was clearly restoring. 'Co-Op Funeral Services' was the legend written on the large glass side windows of this incredible vehicle. It's highly glossed black paintwork was enhanced by gold-leafed pinstripes which Mr Whitton was adding to both sides of the hearse, and it was clear that this vehicle was being restored very carefully and skillfully. I wandered around the workshop picking up various tools and looking into every nook and cranny of this amazing place. Neatness was the order of the day, with every tool and piece of equipment carefully hung on their own individual hook. Clearly Mr Whitton was a very organised worker, and from the variety of tools on display, it was clear that he was multi-skilled in several disciplines of engineering. I climbed inside the hearse and lay down in the back of it where the coffin would normally be placed. It was very surreal and reminded me of a song that my brother and I would sing very regularly together. I started to mouth the words as I continued to explore the interior of the hearse.

"Do not laugh when the coffin goes by, Ha Ha, Ha Ha.
Do not laugh when the coffin goes by, 'cos it may be your turn next to die, Ha Ha, Ha Ha.

They wrap you up in a big white sheet Ha Ha, Ha Ha.
They wrap you up in a big white sheet and throw you down six foot deep, Ha Ha, Ha Ha.

That's alright for the first six weeks, Ha Ha, Ha Ha,

That's alright for the first six weeks,
but then your coffin begins to leak, Ha
Ha, Ha Ha.

Rain seeps in and chills your bones,
Ha Ha, Ha Ha,
Rain seeps in and chills your bones,
wets your whistle and makes you
moan, Ha Ha, Ha Ha.

Worms crawl in and worms crawl out,
Ha Ha, Ha Ha.
Worms crawl in and worms crawl out,
worms make burrows up your snout,
Ha Ha, Ha Ha.

One little worm that's not so shy, Ha
Ha, Ha Ha.
One little worm that's not so shy,
crawls in one ear and out one eye, Ha
Ha, Ha Ha.

Then your brains turn sickly green, Ha
Ha, Ha Ha.

Then your brains turn sickly green,
come oozing out your ears like
Devonshire cream,
Ha Ha, Ha Ha.

So do not laugh when the coffin goes
by Ha Ha, Ha Ha.
Do not laugh when the coffin goes by,
'cos it may be your turn next to die,
Ha Ha, Ha Ha."

Somehow the words of the song, and the sudden realisation that I was sitting in this lonely spot within a big black hearse, put me into a mild panic. I was wondering how many dead people may have travelled inside this conveyance of death. Panic overtook me and I jumped out of the back of the hearse in a state of panic, and crashed out of the workshop doors as fast as my eleven-year old legs could carry me. As I ran through the front door of Mr Whitton's house and burst through the sitting room door, I was greeted with an image that I have never forgotten to this day.

Mr Whitton had Sister Aloysius pressed up against the mantel-piece and I could clearly see her bare leg and thigh held in a bent position against the side of his leg. A long white stocking had been pulled to just below the nun's knee, and I knew that I was witnessing something that neither I or my friends and peers could ever hope or dream of seeing. They were clearly embracing one another, and while I was still comparatively sexually unaware, I realised even in my naivety that this was a compromising situation that neither Sister Aloysius or Mr Whitton would ever wish to be caught in. Most of the boys at school, at one time or another, had conversations with each other around the mysterious under-clothing that nuns might wear beneath their habits, and here was I being given a very prolific answer to that mystery, which very few of us would ever be privy to. They were both so engrossed in their activity that it was some small time before they realised that I was back in the room.

I stood there shuffling from foot to foot, mesmerised by the sight of these two adults deep in intimacy. The thoughts that were running through my head were ones of making myself scarce and protecting their dignity, but unfortunately my presence was suddenly becoming very aware to both of them;

What followed was a lot of "Oh my Gods" acompanied by a lot of clothing adjustments on the part of Sister Aloysius, and, to a lesser extent, Mr Whitton. Sister Aloysius' face was now the colour of beetroot. Her breathing was, to say the least, heavy and was in another dimension when compared to any of the previous occasions when she had run herself out of breath, chasing us with a basket full of balls on the school playground. As he finished adjusting his clothing, and having ushered Sister Aloysius into an adjacent room, Mr Whitton tried to explain that what I had just witnessed was his vain attempt at sorting out a sudden leg 'cramp' that Sister had experienced while sitting in front of the fireplace, and that standing up was a more effective way of massaging the 'cramp' away;

Mr Whitton poured me another glass of ginger beer as I explained that I had rushed back from the workshop because I had become scared by the presence of the Co-Operative hearse. He smiled apologetically at me and then went off to find a very flustered Sister Aloysius. Looking back at the incident and with the benefit of hindsight, I realise that I was far too innocent and naïve to disbelieve Mr Whitton's explanation of what had occurred that evening, but I was also grateful to him for his concern in ensuring that I was not completely shocked by the whole incident. Notwithstanding any of that, perhaps his version of events was completely truthful and my retrospective memory has enhanced it to a sexual encounter. Whatever the truth of it, I prefer my version of the events, isn't it every schoolboy's dream to witness just a little adult intimacy?it is a night that will remain in my memory for ever, not just because of that event, but also, because of the event which followed on that very same evening;

When Sister Aloysius returned to the room she was very composed and the earlier 'blushing' and breathlessness had completely disappeared leaving a very composed and calm nun. She explained about the 'cramp' that had overtaken her earlier in the evening and she was grateful that Mr Whitton had flown to her rescue in relieving the pain. I was well aware of how painful a cramp could be, from my various trips to the infirmary after three hours of football on a Sunday. I always remember the football coach, Mr Best, applying 'White Horse Embrocation' to the calves of several boys who had succumbed to cramps on the pitch, and how effective he was at treating these injuries. Sister Aloysius sat down and finished her glass of wine, as I explained to her about being 'spooked' by the hearse in the workshop. As we got up to leave, Mr Whitton put on his overcoat, having insisted that he would drive us back to the school. Sister Aloysius, smelling distinctly of strong perfume, had donned her black cape once again in anticipation of a cold journey back to school.

His little blue Ford Anglia was parked outside the house, but Mr Whitton walked straight to the workshop, and to my delight slid back the large double doors which housed the Bentley. As the big car roared into life, I realised that this was going to be a very special trip for all of us. The large double headlights illuminated the front of the house as we climbed into the beautiful leather-clad seats that vibrated gently from the car's giant supercharged engine. Everything about this car exuded 'opulence' from the deep-piled carpets and mats to the shiny leather seats. In front of me was a display of several softly illuminated round dials on a 'highly-polished' wooden dashboard. As we 'cruised' gently down the gravelled drive to the school, I realised that we had passed the main school gates and were now speeding on empty roads away from Newgate Street village towards the town of Goffs Oak.

This was a journey that I never wanted to end, the beautiful car rode smoothly on the undulating roads that were so typical of this area of Hertfordshire. The wind was tossing my hair around as the big car gathered speed, and the trees and fields rushed by in a blur that indicated we were travelling very swiftly. Sister Aloysius held on to her veil as the wind buffeted it like a great sail, and Mr Whitton gently steered the giant car with a calm confidence that all experienced drivers exude. All too quickly our adventure was finishing, and it was some half hour later that we pulled back in through the school gates and along the gravelled driveway that led to the school. We pulled sedately into the school playground, and I secretly wished that all of my pals could witness me alighting from this beautiful car. Unfortunately the dormitory windows were in complete darkness, and not a single, solitary figure was evident in the reflected light of the car's headlights. As I stepped out of the car, I thanked Mr Whitton for a lovely evening, "a pleasure my boy" he replied. He walked round to the passenger side of the car and released the door to allow Sister Aloysius to exit the vehicle, there followed an akward moment, and slight hesitation as Mr Whitton appeared to kiss her on the cheek, but most of this was hidden from my view and under the shadow of Aloysius' veil.

As we both walked back in silence to the school dormitories, I could hear the gentle roar of the Bentley's engine disappearing into the distance and then there was total silence with neither one of us attempting conversation. There was definetely an awkwardness between us which had not existed in our earlier exchanges, and as I reached the dormitory door she kissed me on the forehead for the first time ever, and I closed the door silently behind her. The smell of her perfume combined with just a slight hint of wine from her breath hung around my forehead for quite a time, and before falling into a deep sleep, I puzzled at the thought that this gentle kiss was probably the first sign of affection that this nun had shown to me in nearly six years. A picture of her naked thigh, with the long white stocking stayed in my head for a long time, and I pictured some of the other more attractive nuns in a similar stance. With these happy thoughts racing around my mind, I finally closed my tired eyes to embrace the darkness of the night.

Chapter 18
Some Midnight Rambling. Ambrose Departs. A Final Reckoning, and Goodbye to all that

The term year had rapidly evaporated in a frenzy of activity, and we had reached the Easter break. Many of us in our last year at Ponsbourne Park were unable to believe how quickly the years had disappeared, and how much we had advanced from those early days when we were comparative babies. I, for my part, was relieved to have survived all of that time, and to have come through the whole experience with a great part of my sanity still in tact. I pondered the time that the complete journey had taken, and as an exercise in mathematics, I calculated the amount of days that had elapsed since my arrival at the school back in September 1959.

Altogether some 2500 days had flown by in a flurry of fear, misunderstanding, discipline, learning, religion, sports, elocution, eating, sleeping, praying and travelling to and from this place from my home in North London. The most shocking aspect of this calculation was the comparitively few days that I had actually spent with my parents in all of that time. Just 434 of those days were spent in their company at our home in Kingsbury and the previous 'digs' in which we lived. Nearly seven years had elapsed since my first arrival at boarding school. I pondered the reality that I had basically become institutionalised as a result of all that time spent at Ponsbourne Park, I realised that settling into a new life with my parents and other siblings was now going to be as great a challenge to me as my previous school life.

In those years I had matured from a very naïve five year old Irish immigrant into a confident, well-educated and assertive eleven year old English schoolboy. Of course, I had plenty of weaknesses lurking in my psyche as well, but these were very well hidden from everyone's view by my ability to exude confidence and feign innocence and detachment when required. The sometimes 'harrowing' journey had transformed me into a product of the English boarding school system, and all hints of my previous Irish accent and heritage had all but disappeared. One or two words of vocabulary managed to escape this transformation especially words with rolling 'R' s. This tended to give me a hint of a north country accent or a Bristol sounding dialect on certain words and pronunciations. Apart from that, there was now no hint of the strong Irish accent that had accompanied me to this place.

All fear had now disappeared from my life, and this had been replaced by a strong sense of right and wrong and an intolerance of deceipt, 'bullying' and coercion of any kind. I also possessed a healthy and stoic mistrust of those in positions of authority or leadership who would abuse those who were weaker and more vulnerable.

These people would, in the future, have to prove themselves worthy of my trust. I would, of course, treat them with respect, if I felt that this respect was being reciprocated. I realised that a few people such as these had put the fear of God into us over the past seven years, and had lost a great deal of respect from us in the execution of what they thought was their 'sacred' calling and duty.

I almost felt sorry for them, knowing that their years would be filled with a lot more of the same tiresome tedium and disciplne, while our lives would now change in a very drastic way, and, hopefully, for the better.

Things were becoming a lot easier for the new arrivals to the school, and a lot of the old rules, traditions and customs were being replaced by more liberal approaches to the education of children in the 1960's. A lot of the old 'disciplinarians' were being replaced by younger, smarter and better educated nuns, and some of the older ones were even relaxing their strict, unyielding practices as in the case of Sister Aloysius. My school blazer was emblazoned with three impressive badges of rank, all of them, in my opinion, evidence of some hard work and commmitment.

My short period as head boy had been a very rewarding time, and there were quite a few challenges and accomplishments that were unique and very much a part of my own planning and execution. In my role as games captain I had influenced a much greater interest in football and cricket, and was proud to see Patrick's house winning the end of year football cup. The overall standard of football had improved greatly due to the extra coaching that we all received, and the cricket team was now travelling to other schools to compete in various competitions and even win a few of them. Our inventory of kit and equipment had been totally modernised, and as this year was leading up to the World Cup competition, football had become the 'buzzword' on everyone's lips, especially as England would be hosting all of the competing nations in 1966.

Even the Marx Brothers barbers were showing some 'levity' in allowing some of us to sport Beatle haircuts. Although these did not take the form of the real 'moptops that the Beatles wore, there was a distinct hint of Beatles appearance turning up in the playground, and the nuns had kind of resigned themselves to the fact that even if the boarders were restricted in their choice of haircuts, the day pupils would still turn up like Beatle 'clones'. There was no doubt that things were becoming much more relaxed.

Playground life still consisted of the many games that had become a tradition over the preceding years, but many new games and trends were making their way into the playtimes including boomerang flying and rocket launching. In the dormitories and common rooms there was a new fad in car racing called Scaletrix, and Lego and Meccano sets were becoming far more sophisticated. James Bond was becoming the most popular film franchise and, naturally, kids were now purchasing anything connected with 007 including the latest Corgi model of the Aston Martin car from the films. This car had a pop-up bulletproof shield at the rear, machine guns that popped out of the front bumpers, and an ejection seat that fired the front seat passenger out of the top of the car. Clothes were getting brighter and more body-hugging, while skirts were getting shorter, much to the delight of lads like myself who were experiencing our first sexual 'stirrings'. The swinging sixties were gathering momentum with most of the trends being created and focused in London. Beatles records were now being played by a few of the nuns, and that really knocked our socks off, as prior to this the only sounds that could be heard from the convent gramophone were either orchestral marches, the occasional 'Oratorio' or 'The Singing Nun' delivering a french-worded version of a song called 'Dominique'.

The one big disappointment for me at that time came in the shape of a large brown envelope, from the London Examination board, which proclaimed that I had failed my Eleven Plus examination. While this was an expected result, the reality of finally reading it in black and white raised all of the old questions about my future school and education choices. Since nobody at the school had enquired about these results, including peers and teachers alike, I decided not to announce them to anyone and the sad brown envelope was placed uncerimoniously among my other paperwork to be forgotten for the moment. If noone was going to query my results with me, that was absolutely fine by me, I could do without the embarrasment. I did, however, write a letter to my parents giving them the bad news, so at least they were aware of the situation and would be able to search for a suitable secondary school before I finally arrived home for the Summer.

This felt like a good moment to be moving on, and there was an optimism everywhere one looked, driven by the music, the culture ,the fashion and 'ambience' of the times. My peers and myself were now in class 6 the final part of our journey through Ponsbourne Park. The 'swinging' sixties were instilling a great sense of confidence in our daily lives as we counted down the days until our final one on the 21st July 1965 when we would all receive our freedom. The journey we had made as little boys now becoming bigger ones, brought with it a confidence and maturity that seemed to be unique to all of us at that time. We found ourselves comparing not just our academic achievemets with children of our own age from other schools, but also our seemingly unlimited confidence in everything that we did outside of the classroom as well. In arts and crafts, we had all acquired skills that would certainly be useful in our futures, and our abilities in English and Mathematics were of a very high standard as well. Our final year had included several debates in the classroom, and there were a few budding 'orators' growing out of this confidence building subject. The Eleven Plus results continued to haunt me, especially as I had only failed on the General knowledge questions, while my English and Mathematics were above average. Another 20 points or so would have ensured me a Grammar school place, so I felt pretty cheated at the time.

Aloysius was still in 'buoyant' good humour and we continued to visit Mr Whitton on a fortnightly basis, although there appeared to be no more visible close contact between the two adults. I guess her cramps were now fully cured and required no further intervention on the part of Mr Whittle! I wondered if these were the only visits that occurred between them these days, or were there times when they met up when I wasn't present myself. I still had vivid memories of that fateful night, when the mystery of what nuns wore under their habits was finally revealed to me in such a 'prolific' way. I had experienced some of my first naïve sexual thoughts as a direct result of that encounter, and I felt pretty good about it; There were many times that I had failed to understand what I was doing on these excursions away from the school, but I was also very grateful to have experienced a little of life outside of the classroom and dormitory environment. On some of these visits I felt a little intrusive at times, but then Mr Whitton would introduce me to one of his new projects and everything fell into a 'comfortable' place once again. Maybe it was a reward for achieving the head boy's badge or perhaps it was a privelege reserved for the 'acting' head boy. Whatever the reason, I was just going to enjoy the experience while it lasted.

It was about this time that Sister Ambrose disappeared from Ponsbourne Park, there were no goodbyes, she was just missing one day much to my sadness and consternation. She had been one of my more caring 'mentors' for so many years, and her sudden absence from the school made me glad that I was also leaving.

Under other circumstances the only other way that a nun left the convent was in a horizontal mode, having succumbed to old age or illness. These unfortunates would make the short journey along the gravelled paths and through the woods to the nun's cemetery, and I and several of my peers had certainly experienced our fair share of these funerals in our role as alter servers. Sister Ambrose, however, was in very good health and still had plenty of useful years in front of her. She was a 'lay' nun devoted to looking after her youngsters in the cottage and doing various laborious tasks within the laundry and convent. I was saddened to think that she could leave without saying goodbye to myself and a few other lads that were her special 'charges'. I was later heartened by the news that she was just too emotional at having to leave so many of her young 'charges' and goodbyes would have been far too painful for her. She had been transferred to another Dominican convent in Edgware, Middlesex, and as this was close to my home address. I realised that their would be plenty of opportunities to visit her once I had left Ponsbourne. This made me feel a lot happier about her sudden disappearance, and had also spared me the embarrasment of having to tell her of my poor exam results.

With just a few more weeks left until the end of term, life in the classrooms, the playground and the dormitories took on a very different aspect. We were now collecting up our belongings not just for the usual Summer break but for our final leaving. Trunks and cases were being packed with all of our clothes and books, while in the dormitories a general cleanout was organised in which all of the boys were allocated various chores. Floors were being polished, windows cleaned, bathrooms scrubbed and all of these activities were carried out with the usual fun that accompanied such happenings. The whole place was buzzing with excitement as we counted down the days until the Summer Holidays.

We were effectively closing the whole dormitory down and preparing our spaces for a new influx of lads who would replace us in the following September. In my case, there were very few items that I wanted to take home with me, save a few good books and some personal effects that may be required in the future. Most of us were passing possessions on to kids in the classes and dormitories below us. These included toiletries, items of unwanted clothing, toys, stationary and writing materials which we would no longer have any use for. I dug my old catapult out of it's hiding place and placed it in the bottom of my suitcase together with the brown envelope containing my exam results. I felt a little relieved in the knowledge that both of these items were well concealed from prying eyes. I also pulled out my old monkey Mickey that had been given to me so many years before by the kindly Sister Ambrose. Mickey had resided in recent years at the back of my school locker, and as I was now supposed to be well beyond the need for a cuddly toy to take to bed with me, I could never quite let go of him. I walked across the playground to the Cottage building and found a young lad of just five years old to make a gift of the monkey. I remember thinking how small and vulnerable these young lads were, and hoped that their future schooldays would hold less fright and drama than ours had.

Our last weeks at the school were filled with a mixture of fun and regret, we were all very conscious of the massive separation that would soon take place. Like a band of brothers, we had all shared some amazing adventures on our journey through the school. Friendships were about to be tragically broken as we went on our separate journeys to so many separate destinations in this country and abroad. We exchanged contact adresses with our friends, promising to stay in touch and maybe get together at some time in the future. Many of the boys already knew which new schools they were going to in September, but I didn't have a clue where I would end up. My knowledge of the schools in our area was very limited, although I knew that both my brother and sister were already installed in a Catholic Secondary modern school in Kenton Middlesex. All I knew at this stage was that it would certainly be another Roman Catholic school somewhere in North West London.

There was just one final dramatic happening that showed up in these last few days before the end of term. It was to mark my final mischevious action before finally quitting this place for ever. Unbeknown to me, Vincent Simpson had somehow come across my hidden Eleven plus exam envelope and was now broadcasting my poor results to all of my friends and classmates. What followed was a lot of gossip and general piss-taking from every direction. For the first time in a very long time I was feeling embarrassed and humiliated and within a few days this had turned to outrage and anger. It didn't take me long to find out where the 'snitch' had found my exam results, as I was only taking one suitcase home with me on my final journey. One of the boys in my class had spotted Simpson going through my belongings in the dormitory one lunchtime, but didn't think much about it until the news of my exam results started circulating.

The fact that Simpson had rifled through all of my belongings in my suitcase was totally outrageous and certainly unacceptable by any standards, because trust was a very big part of the unwritten code that we all shared together. Clearly, Simpson had no scruples, and he more than demonstrated what a fucking 'cad' he really was by that one action alone. He now knew that I had a contraband catapult hidden among my possessions, and I was sure that he would use this knowledge against me in some way. I decided there and then that I had no choice but to get back at this horrible 'snake in the grass' in the best possible way that I knew. I could quite easily have informed Aloysius and let her deal with him in whatever way she felt appropriate but this would have served no real purpose, and Simpson would probably have informed her of the illicit object hidden in my case.

The old dictum, 'dont get mad, get even' took on a whole new significance for me and I was now working on a little bit of revenge that would teach Simpson a final lesson. I knew that I had to be utterly discreet in whatever action I was to take, as I was now supposed to be a good example and 'role model' to all of the other kids. Once again, complete secrecy was the order of the day and I would need a cast iron alibi should there be any repercussions about my proposed actions. Noone was going to have the slightest hint that I was involved in any way in a pre-emptive revenge attack on the person of the 'sly' Mr Simpson. There was now a great urgency to come up with a plan, as the final days were counting down to the end of term, I needed to act quickly and decisively.

I plotted like Cassius and Brutus to come up with a fool-proof plan to get back at Simpson, it needed to be simple, effective, and most-importantly discreet in it's planning and execution. I realised that there was no way that I could involve anyone else, but at the same time, I needed to have a perfect alibi to cover the exact time of the incident, so that there would not be the slightest hint of my involvement. I was still running the gauntlet of sneers and 'snide' comments from the now several people that had been informed of my exam results. Fortunately there were also a lot of old friends who were more loyal and sympathetic to my situation. One or two of them had already intimated that they would like to get back at Simpson for me, but I convinced them that this would not be a good idea as we would all be in trouble for it. I made a point of staying away from Simpson, for fear of losing my rag, and confronting him, in the words of John Mallory, 'with the aid of a good kick in the bollocks'.

One evening after prep, I was relaxing with an Airfix model kit when a mischevious plan started to race around in my head. The basic idea would inspire the revenge that I would inflict on Simpson, ensuring that he would attract a lot more ridicule than the small amount that he had visited on me. It would require a lot of careful planning on my part, and needed to take place under the cover of darkness while Simpson was very much asleep.

Providence must have been smiling on me, because an incident which occurred just after tea one afternoon would provide the perfect cover for my plan to succeed, and ensure that I was nowhere near the senior dormitory when Simpson received his 'comeuppance'. A young lad named Stevie Sullen had reported to Sister Albertina with the most tremendous stomach ache and vomiting symptons, and she promptly put him in the infirmary with a diagnosis of possible food poisoning. Stevie had received a parcel from home that morning which contained among other 'goodies' a jar of Shippams crab paste which he promptly buttered on to his bread. He had given myself and a few other lads a knifeful of the paste, which we all imbibed, and it was delicious. Whatever was giving Stevie his 'dodgy' stomach was not the crab paste as I was feeling as right as ninepence, and no other boy had come down with the same symptons. I realised that here was a golden opportunity, which would allow me to be away from the senior dorm for a night or so, and provide me with the perfect alibi in my action against Simpson. That evening after supper I made my way to see Sister Albertina with the most tremendous stomach ache. She promptly sent me to the infirmary where Stevie was already in residence, "It must have been the 'bloody' crab paste" I lied, but Stevie was convinced that I had indeed contracted the same bad stomach ache that he was experiencing, and apologised profusely for my bad fortune. Stevie didn't have the slightest clue that I had contrived this whole scenario, but he was pleased that he had some company with him in the infirmary, which, even at the best of times, can be a very lonely place. Stevie's stomach was still giving him a lot of discomfort and I felt a little guilty at faking my illness at his expense, but needs must.

Later that night, long after lights out, I put my plan into action. I silently made my way down the fire escape from the infirmary, checking first to make sure that Stevie was asleep. I crept carefully across the darkened quadrangle into the senior dormitory block and waited in the toilets until I was sure that all of the dormitories were silent. In my pockets were the tools of my proposed action - a tube of Macleans toothpaste, a bottle of black ink, and a full tube of polystyrene model cement which we used to build our 'Airfix' kits. I sneaked very quietly into the senior dorm and made my way to the dressing gown cupboard which was adjacent to Simpson's bed. In this cupboard was kept the daywear for all of the boys, and every morning these would be replaced with their dressing gowns. I found my way to Simpson's locker and quietly removed his clothing. A little dab of glue was applied to the zipper on his trousers, the buttons on his blazer and all of the buttons on his shirt. Of course, I made sure that all of these items of clothing were buttoned up, so that the glue would effectively stick them together forever. I then made up his tie with a nice 'Windsor' knot and applied yet more glue to the now made up tie. There was no way that he would ever be able to undo these items without ripping them to pieces. Turning my attention to his shoes, I carefully knotted them up with an impressive double bow and then glued the laces, the eyelets and the knots, ensuring that these would be impossible to undo. Even the tongues of the shoes were glued to the uppers, effectively turning them into a set of useless footwear. I then applied copious amounts of black ink to the various clothes in his locker.

The smell of the polysyrene glue filled the cupboard with its pungent aroma, and I realised that this might be noticed by the sleeping lads if the fumes were to escape in to the dorm. I needed to very careful, very quiet and very focused. I silently opened the door of the cupboard and crawled on all fours along the shiny wooden floor boards towards Simpson's bed. It seemed an eternity in getting there, as I was stopping every so often when someone would cough or turn over in their sleep. Simpson was as still and rigid as a 'tailor's' dummy and lying on his back. A soft snore attested to the fact that he was in a deep sleep, and his slow breathing was interrupted with the occasional whistle as he exhaled slowly. I carefully unscrewed the cap of the tooth paste and started to write very neatly across his forehead with the tube, in very large block capitals. Simpson gave an occasional whimper while I was carrying out this delicate operation and I would stop writing momentarily, but there was not the slightest hint of him stirring, so deeply was he sleeping. If all went to plan, the toothpaste would harden overnight on Simpson's forehead. When this was eventually washed off there would be a nice bright red imprint of the writing on his lily-white skin which would, hopefully, last for days. I could hardly contain my laughter at the thought of what might happen in the morning, and what kind of reaction would ensue from both Simpson and the rest of the dormitory boys as these various acts of sabotage were discovered.

I then turned my attention to the polystyrene model cement, and gently squeezed copious amounts of this into his hair just at the scalp line. I was terrified that Simpson would wake up at any moment, as my heart was beating like a bass drum, and the smell of the polysyrene cement was so strong that it was actually stinging my eyes. Simpson just lay there motionless with both his hands outside of the covers and neatly placed by his sides. I used the whole tube of polystyrene cement across the visible part of his hair, it was just unfortunate that the back of his head was firmly buried in the pillow, as this prevented me gluing up his complete scalp from back to front. When all of these operations were completed, I carefully placed the half empty tube of toothpaste in his right hand and the exhausted tube of glue in his left one, ensuring that they were firmly glued to his individual hands. I finally poured the remaining black ink across his scalp and onto his chest ensuring a shocking sight when he awoke in the morning. I was now imagining his reaction, when he would be waking up to all of this 'carnage,' and I had real problems in trying to stifle a fit of the giggles.

As I crawled away from Simpson's bed, I could no longer contain my laughter and I had to quickly slide away to the dormitory door for fear of waking him and the rest of the boys up. It was a very strange experience for me, that one minute I was laughing profusely and the next I would be experiencing a great fear of getting caught. My heart was beating ten to the dozen and I realised that a lot of time had elapsed since arriving in the dormitory, it was time to get out of here. The thought of getting caught, or being seen by anyone really worried me, as I could lose all credibility, not to mention putting myself in a heap of aggravation for the sake of a practical joke. I had pictures in my mind of Aloysius ripping my badges from my blazer lapel and consigning me to the ranks of the great 'unwanted'. I was supposed to be a 'role model; for all of the boys around me, and here I was sprawling around on all fours in this darkened dormitory, in the middle of the night. The floor boards creaked as I slid quietly away from the scene of the crime with just an empty ink bottle to be disposed of.

As I was climbing back down the dormitory stairs in the darkness, It occurred to me that maybe I was a little light-headed from breathing too many glue fumes at close proximity. This may be fuelling my sudden changes of mood from extreme fun to extreme fear. I reflected on the happenings of the past, and my various tangles and battles with Simpson over the months and years that I had known him. I realised that of all of the people who I had interacted with or 'fallen out' with on my long journey through school, he was the only one that I truly disliked during all of that time. I pictured him lying there with the toothpaste and glue still neatly placed in his hands, or rather glued to his hands, and felt not the slightest regret or remorse for the evening's activities. The strong smell of glue seemed to permeate almost to the bottom of the stairs, and I guessed that the whole dormitory must seem the same. I hoped that there were no light sleepers who might be disturbed by the smell of it, because it was now really pungent and still stinging the tears out of my eyes. I slowly and deliberately opened the outside door to the darkened quadrangle, leaving the boys of the senior dorm silent and, hopefully, undisturbed in their sleep.

Back in the infirmary Stevie Sullen was still sleeping soundly, and as I crept back to my bed in the darkness he let out a small whimper which indicated to me that his stomach pain must still be bothering him a little. My heart was still pounding from the night's activities, and as I slipped under the blankets, I refelected on the events that would follow when the senior dormitory were awakened in the morning. My head had hardly hit the pillow when I was awakened by Stevie who was now screaming in pain and rolling around on the infirmary floor. Sister Albertina rushed in to the room just as I was lifting Steve back on to his bed, and she didn't take long to realise that Steve's stomach ache was now far more serious. The poor lad was rolled up like a ball in the foetal position and vomiting profusely in between gasps of what was now agonising pain.

Within 30 minutes an emergency ambulance was driving on to the playground, it's flashing blue lights lit up the whole of the junior and senior buildings, and Stevie was stretchered away with an oxygen mask around his face and wrapped securely in a bright red blanket. I didn't

346

sleep for the rest of that night, as Sister Albertina was running in and out every half an hour checking my temperature in case I suddenly developed the same symptons that Stevie had fallen foul of. I felt really guilty about having feigned the illness, but I was also aware that I now possessed the perfect alibi for any investigations that may ensue around Simpson's late night visitor. I realised that had Stevie's deterioration occurred any earlier in the evening, I would have been discovered missing by Sister Albertina, and all of my activities would, by now, be out in the open. I breathed a huge sigh of relief, when an hour later Albertina informed me that Steve was going into an operation for suspected appendicitis, and that he was fortunate that his appendix hadn't perforated. I told Albertina that I was feeling much better and my stomach ache was now completely gone. She insisted however that I remained in the infirmary for at least another day just to be sure that there were no other problems. This news really dampend my spirits as it was just three days before the end of term, and I badly wanted to see the results of my final prank.

That morning Simpson woke up as normal, he immediately discovered that a tube of toothpaste had been glued to his hand, and that his hair felt stiff and matted. Like a greyhound leaving the 'slips' he leaped out of bed and made his way to the dormitory sinks. All around him, lads were quietly pointing and laughing, and it wasn't until he looked in the mirror for the first time that the full horror of my night's activities became obvious to him. His hair stood up in spikes, he looked like like a

347

'bedraggled' porcupine, and for the first time he realised that both of his hands were covered with a 'stiff' skin of glue. Across the front of his forehead, in large capital letters, the words 'NIL VERITAS' were now permanently emblazoned in white toothpaste. Scrubbing away the toothpaste with copius amounts of soap produced beautiful red lettering which would remain on his skin for a quite a few days. Below his neckline the black ink had done its work, and his pyjamas and bedding were permanently stained, not to mention his own skin. No amount of shampoo would clean away the glue and ink that covered his hair and scalp and the only solution offered by Sister Aloysius was a drastic and immediate haircut. Previously, Simpson had thrown an enormous temper tantrum, and rampaged around the senior dormitory like a wild man. John Mallory was the main target for Simpson's accusations, but John just smiled and reminded Simpson that there were several lads around the 'dorm' who would love to take the opportunity of showing him up.

The narratives of the mornings happenings went around the school like 'wildfire' there were even more raptures when Simpson discovered that all of his clothes and shoes had suffered a similar fate. I wished that I had been present to witness all of these discoveries first hand, but I was pleased that most of my pals had turned up in the infirmary to give me a full 'run-down' on the happenings of that morning. Simpson's hair had to be cut all along the front and top into an almost 'crew' cut, but the back of his head retained normal length hair giving his head a distorted and 'skeletal' appearance. Parts of his eyebrows had to be shaved off, giving him the most bizarre facial distortion. His embarrasment was compounded by his having to appear at breakfast in his pyjamas, dressing gown and slippers until suitable replacements for his clothes could be found. The legend 'Nil Veritas' stood out in angry red letters against the pale white of his forehead, and even a few nuns were seen to snigger and turn away as they read the latin translation of "No Truth".

John Mallory told me that he had been summoned by Sister Aloysius and questioned about the attack on Simpson. John, of course, was the main suspect because his previous altercation with Simpson had been well noted by everyone. John stood his ground and vehemently denied any connection to the incident, which Aloysius was forced to accept in the absense of any evidence. She promised to get to the bottom of it, but there was just one more day before the end of term, and in the end she had to accept that there was just no time for a full investigation. I have no doubt that when she had seen the 'legend' neatly printed on Simpson's forehead, she probably had a good idea why Simpson had been singled out for such attention.

The following morning I was released from the infirmary having demonstrated no further deterioration of the symptons that had put me there. Stevie Sullen had undergone emergency surgery at the hospital in Hatfield and would be there for some time. I regretted that I did not have time to say goodbye to him, but was glad that he was in good hands.Tomorrow we would be breaking up for the Summer, and I busied myself with the completion of packing and making my goodbyes with various teachers and pupils that had been such a big part of my life for several years. I had never imagined a time when I would be sad at leaving this place, but looking around at all the beautiful grounds and buildings brought me to the realisation that here was a wonderful environment in which to exist. The good times that I had experienced here had certainly eclipsed the bad ones, and, unlike my brother and sister who held the place in complete contempt, I felt a real sense of sadness at the prospect of leaving here for the final time. Our last supper in the refectory was full of animated chatter and laughter, and the usual 'eating in silence; rule was always relaxed during the last few days of term. The one exception to this was Simpson who sat silently 'fuming', while others around him poked fun and ridicule at him, to add to his embarrasment and humiliation. On this occasion I didn't feel the slightest pang of guilt for Simpson's predicament, knowing well that he spent most of his waking hours over the previous few months and days in attempts to ridicule me. As I walked past his place at table that evening, I quietly whispered in his ear "not so funny now, is it Simpson".

July the 21st dawned bright and sunny, and we all woke with a sense of euphoria that this was our very last day at Ponsbourne Park. Our race was run and, in my opinion, we were all winners. I felt a little like Robinson Crusoe about to escape my island prison after so many days, months and years in this beautiful but challenging environment. Aloysius caught up with me just after breakfast and we walked along the gravelled driveway leading to the schoool buildings for the very last time. There was an awkward silence between us as we exchanged small talk. She asked briefly if I had any idea who might be responsible for Simpson's dishevelled and ungainly appearance, and I replied that "he was probably the subject of an outstanding 'grudge' attack or even the brunt of some end of term high spirits." She could tell from my swift reply that I didn't give a damn about Simpson's present condition, I was, however, somewhat taken aback when she commiserated with me over my 'Eleven Plus' exam results. I wondered where she may have got that information from, but then, I realised that the school 'grapevine' was probably still carrying that bit of news. I couldn't help thinking that, just perhaps, she may have suspiscions about my involvement in the Simpson affair.

Our conversation was stinted and she seemed concerned that I was taking a good opinion of the school with me into the next chapter of my life. "Don't forget that a lot of sacrifices have been made by your parents and teachers alike to provide you with a good grounding and a sound education to carry you into your future life." I had to smile at these comments while considering how different that future life might be. I wondered how many years it would take to erase some of the bad memories that I would also be carrying with me into that future life. We parted on that note, and I'm sure I detected a slight glistening in her eyes as she turned away from me for the very last time. Was that a handkerchief that she was pulling from her habit pocket to perhaps dab away a small tear, or was that just a figment of my own distorted and wishful imagination?

Ponsbourne Park glistened like a jewel in the warm July sunshine as I loaded my suitcase on to the bus for the very last time. The boy had now become father to the man, and while I still had a lot of growing up to do, I realised that the biggest part of my growing had probably already occurred in this time and place. Looking back at my experiences of these surroundings over the previous six years gave me a strange feeling of love and hate, these feelings also applied to the people who had been part of that journey. I accepted these anomolies without question, because the alternatives were too deep to ponder.

The school coach rolled into Kings Cross station at two o clock that afternoon. The journey had been filled with a euphoric mix of singing, shouting, joke-telling and animated farewell conversations. The radio on board the bus was playing all of the latest hits of the 'sixties' and even the bus driver, tapping his fingers on the edge of the steering wheel, seemed in more than just a good mood. Guys were throwing their school caps at one another as the bus made it's way through the crowded streets of London. The afternoon sunshine cascaded through the windows adding further warmth and well-being to this happy band of brothers. Outside the paper-sellers were promoting the pre-World Cup football headlines in their latest editions, and World Cup Willy cartoons festooned every shop – front and street corner in a blaze of colour.

London was 'swinging' to a new age of youth culture and felt, to me, like the centre of the Universe.

There in the midst of the crowded bus terminal was my Dad quietly puffing on a cigarette and waiting patiently for our arrival. I climbed down from the coach for the very last time, Petula Clarke's song 'Downtown' was playing on the radio, and amid the chaos of claiming our suitcases and greeting our various parents, it suddenly struck me that this really was the end of a massively long journey. Here I was in the middle of the noisiest and busiest streets in London, while less than two hours earlier I had been standing in the quiet beauty and serenity of the Hertfordshire countryside. It brought to mind the complete opposites that these two places represented for me in my childhhood, and reminded me of some words that I had once read in my long educational journey to this very time and place.

"They were the best of times, they were the worst of times".

The End

Lightning Source UK Ltd.
Milton Keynes UK
UKOW01f1123160817
307408UK00002B/320/P